MARINE CORPS MUSTANG

ROY MORRIS

Copyright © 2017, Roy Morris
First Edition

Without limiting the rights under copyright reserved above, no part of this publication may be reproduced, stored in or introduced into a retrieval system, or transmitted, in any form or by any means (electronic, mechanical, photocopying, recording, or otherwise), without the prior written permission of the copyright owner of this book.

Published by Aventine Press
55 East Emerson St.
Chula Vista CA 91911
www.aventinepress.com

ISBN: 978-1-59330-930-5

Library of Congress Control Number: 2017911368
Library of Congress Cataloging-in-Publication Data
Marine Corps Mustang / Roy Morris
Printed in the United States of America

ALL RIGHTS RESERVED

Acknowledgements

As with my first book, *Thicker than Water,* this second attempt would simply not have been possible without the help, support, encouragement and love of my family and friends. Family is all-important. And good friends, like the Burnett family, the Duvall family, the Ennis family and the Johnston family (in alphabetical order) are truly priceless treasures and I thank God for allowing me to grow up around such wonderful folks. But there are also others who have been there for me when I really needed help. First, there is Emily Bailey, of the Russellville Library, who arranged for me to be a guest speaker at the first seven events of a Summer Reading Program for children, which strengthened my resolve to write this second book. Then, there is Janna Brinkley-Long, of the Atkins Library, who provided invaluable computer assistance and instruction. Also, there is Christine Hamby, who designed and produced the cover of this book. She and her husband, Jim, are computer geniuses but, more importantly, they are my friends. Thanks to Gerald and Charlotte Johnston, who not only financed both books but who have allowed me to live for years in one of the houses on their farm in the Economy community northeast of Atkins. Finally, thanks to Van and Ginnie Tyson, who have published my articles and poems in the Atkins *Chronicle* and the Dover *Times* over a period of many years. They have consistently treated me with kindness, always stressing my few strengths and talents while graciously overlooking my many mistakes and inadequacies.

Like my first book, this one will also be considered a biography of at least part of my life but, while the first book centered on family and friends, the characters and personalities in this book are folks that I met, worked with and fought with while in the Marine Corps and since people in the Corps are representative of American society, at large, there will be good guys and villains, heroes and heels. In some ways, I seemed to bring out the very best in many of these people. In other ways, I brought out the worst in a few of them. As the author, I am solely responsible for the contents of this book. The facts presented here are self-evident and can stand alone on their own merit but the observations, opinions and conclusions are mine and are based on those facts. And since this is in a biography format, I hereby certify that all of these stories are true and I have the background data and original source documents in my files to support this. For any of you who might wish to go into detail with me, I invite you to contact me at 1145 Hurricane Road, Atkins, Arkansas 72823 or at email roymorris0302@gmail.com or at 479-747-1528.

I was proud to serve. I was especially proud to serve in the United States Marine Corps. I have written about some of my successes and triumphs but, to be fair and honest, I have also chronicled some of my failures, too. In some ways, I have been superhuman. In some other ways, I have been subhuman. Hopefully, the superhuman ways will outnumber the subhuman ways but after all, I have to admit that I am not the Great American Hero - except in my own mind, of course. But, hey, don't we all feel that way, sometimes?

So, giving thanks to my family and friends is a 'must-do' because they endured my bragging AND my complaining about the events that occurred during my time in the Corps. Patience and understanding were the two things I needed most. I always received what I needed.

Preparation

I always wanted to be a Marine...a Jarhead...a Leatherneck...a Devil Dog. I can't remember a time when that wasn't part of my master plan, even when I was too young to know the meaning of a master plan. My childhood was spent preparing for the test that would earn for me the emblem worn by U S Marines, the Eagle, Globe and Anchor. I was willing to work for that emblem in the same spirit in which the ancient Olympic athletes competed for the champion's wreath.

Even though I didn't know what that test would actually consist of, I knew that I would have to be in really good physical condition. I was lucky enough to be blessed, at birth, with all of my regular body parts and reasonably good health so I figured all I had to do was to carefully guard what I had been given and not do anything that would lessen my chances of passing the test.

So I decided, at an extremely early age, that I would not use any form of alcohol, tobacco or drugs. There was nothing about my decision that involved any sort of religious conviction and I didn't consider myself to be morally superior to any of my acquaintances who did partake of any of those substances. For me, it was simply nothing more than a health issue.

How lucky I felt! I reveled in the good health that seemed to be my birthright and I wasn't going to do anything to squander it. I knew plenty of kids who simply did not have the strength, stamina or speed that I had. I could break an apple in half with my bare hands. I could bend a coin between my thumb and forefinger. I was the school champion arm wrestler - even football players who outweighed me by 80 pounds could not defeat me. But I readily accepted the responsibilities that came with my abilities. I became the universal protector of weaker students. None of the school bullies tried to run roughshod over anybody while I was anywhere around because I would not hesitate to "correct" their behavior.

As time went on, I progressed from wanting to be a Marine to wanting to be a GOOD Marine. And from there, I went on to wanting to be one of the best Marines. I knew, of course, that I could never be THE best, simply because I was not big enough. My height never exceeded 5'7" and my maximum weight was 179, so I would never be a towering hulk of masculinity.

But I was able to accept that fact with a reasonable amount of stoicism because my body was totally 'ripped'. Even though I wasn't a BIG man, my physique compared favorably with Steve Reeves and Gordon Scott (popular actors of that era who portrayed Hercules and Tarzan in the movies). With my rippling muscles, V-shaped torso and "six-pack" abs, I was the perfect picture of health. The proverbial physical fitness statement was true - There wasn't an ounce of fat anywhere on me.

I was always attempting new physical feats. If two cars were parked at the right distance from each other, I would put one hand on the bumper of each car and do pushups between the cars, going all the way down until my chest and chin touched the ground. I quickly added a touch of difficulty by starting to do one-arm pushups (with either arm) off the bumpers of cars, still touching the ground with my chest. Then I started using folding chairs from school. I would put both my feet on the seat of a chair and place my palms on the seats of two other chairs that were facing each other. Then I would do pushups between the chairs, all the way to the floor, as usual. A final degree of difficulty with pushups involved doing a handstand against a wall. With my feet straight up against the wall, I would do pushups, going all the way to the floor with my nose while my feet slid up and down along the wall.

And I didn't neglect the development of my lower body, either. Standing on my left foot, I would stick my right leg straight out in front of me while holding my foot with my right hand. Then I would do a dozen one-legged squats on my left leg. After that, I would do a dozen one-legged squats on my right leg in the same manner. I supplemented this training with a great many other unique exercises which I simply made up as I went along.

I did a lot of jogging, wind sprints and marathon-style running but I also worked out with weights. I had a really beautiful set of weights, with 2 barbells, 2 dumbbells and a wide variety of weight plates. All of this self-imposed physical training, combined with my daily routine of performing hard manual labor on farms and at sawmills in the area, turned me into one of the toughest kids in the state of Arkansas.

Obviously, I expected to be welcomed with open arms when I decided to grace the Marine Corps with my presence. After all, how could I miss? I was a superb specimen of young manhood. However, when I contacted the Marine Corps recruiter, I was considerably surprised to learn that the Marine Corps was interested not only in my physical abilities but also in my mental abilities. During that era (because of the Viet-Nam War), they were reluctantly willing to accept recruits who had not finished high school but they really PREFERRED graduates. Even though I had been blessed with a high IQ (when tested, it was 132), my school work did not reflect that. Intelligence is one thing while education is quite another matter.

So it would greatly improve my chances of winning the Marine Corps emblem if I finished high school. At best, I was barely average as a student. In fact, it took me 13 years to complete a 12th grade education. My first problem was one that was never recognized or acknowledged. I had dyslexia. Basically, that meant that I saw letters and numbers in reverse, although it's really more complicated than that. When I tried to write, the letters came out backward and I wrote from right to left because I was left handed. A page full of my written words could be read by normal people only by holding the page in front of a mirror and reading the mirror image. I don't really think the education system of the late '40's and early '50's realized what dyslexia was. They just called me "Stupid". Granted, I didn't study as long or as hard as I should have, but the grading system worked against me, too, because attendance in class was one of the factors that determined overall grades - and my attendance was spotty. Missing a certain number of days during any single semester would automatically lower my grade in each class by one percentage point. For instance, a B minus would become a C plus or a D would become a D minus. Missing another few days in the same semester would automatically lower my grade in each class yet another percentage point so, even if I got caught up on the missing homework from the days missed, my grades would continue spiraling down. But if Dad had a lot of hay bales to haul or chicken houses/barns to clean out, I would skip school to work with him. In my opinion, education was all well and good, but helping to put food on the table was of paramount importance in our daily struggle to survive. Education was important for the future but first, we had to get through the present without starving to death.

Anyway, I graduated, almost in spite of myself. I deserve very little actual credit for that accomplishment because it was the sacrifices that were made by my older brother, E. Ray, and by my sister, Shirley, that made it possible for me to continue attending school long enough to complete my education. They took up my slack at helping to earn a living for the family so that I could wear the cap and gown. They deserve partial credit for my Marine Corps emblem.

Some of my exercises were so unique that I am the only person who could perform them. In my entire life, I have never found anybody else who could do one-arm chin-ups without grabbing his wrist with his free hand. Nobody else has ever been able to place his hands on two folding chairs two feet apart with his feet on a third folding chair and do pushups between the chairs, taking his chest all the way to the floor. Nobody else has ever been able to do a one-arm pushup (with either arm) by placing his hand on a single folding chair, lowering his chest all the way to the floor and raising all the way back up. During my many years in the Corps, I met a lot of very tough men. There were Army Rangers and Special Forces (Green Berets), Navy SEALs, and Recon Marines. Those are the toughest individuals on earth. Most of them were a lot bigger, a lot tougher and a lot stronger than I was and most of them could have beaten me to a pulp. But NONE of them could duplicate my feats. They could not do my exercises. In almost seventy years, I have never found anybody like me. Not bragging – just stating a simple fact.

Incidentally, just so that you, the reader, will understand something regarding the intensity of my self-imposed physical training regimen and the value of a good health and fitness program which is started early and maintained throughout life, I want you to know that I was able to do those weird push-ups between two chairs until the day I turned sixty years old. On that day, I was helping to herd some cows into a series of corrals. One cow decided she didn't want to go into one of the pens, so she charged at me and head-butted me, right in the sternum. A couple of days later, my sister took me to the hospital because I was still having trouble drawing a deep breath. Ever since, I have not been able to go all the way to the floor between chairs because my rib cage won't allow my arms to fully extend backward. But you know, when that 1,000 pound cow hit me, I was glad. I was glad she didn't have horns.

Boot Camp

That is what recruit training is called. That was where I would go through the process of transforming from a simple civilian to a fledgling member of the greatest fighting force in the history of the United States.

In the Marine Corps, there are only two places where recruits are trained. All those who join west of the Mississippi River are sent to Marine Corps Recruit Depot, San Diego, California. Those who join east of the Mississippi go to Marine Corps Recruit Depot, Parris Island, South Carolina.

There were some aspects of boot camp that were very pleasant, even enjoyable. For example, successfully navigating the obstacle course was viewed by every other recruit as a rather daunting challenge and they all dreaded it. However, I considered it to be a really wonderful gigantic playground. At that point in my life, I had never been to Disneyland but I couldn't imagine that to be any more fun than being allowed to play on the obstacle course.

Another great thing about boot camp was fighting with pugil sticks (just think of a broomstick with padding on each end). That exercise was intended to simulate personal combat against an enemy soldier using a rifle with a bayonet attached. That was very cool stuff. I entered into those sessions with enthusiasm and with a ferocity that surprised and intimidated my opponents. I was undefeatable. I was having a great time in boot camp.

And I would amuse myself by applying my own interpretation to orders received from the Drill Instructors. For example, a DI might order me to do 10 pushups for some transgression (either real or imagined). He might say, "Get down and give me ten, maggot". I would reply, "Sir, with which hand, Sir?" Regardless of which hand he designated, I would immediately drop to the ground and execute ten perfect pushups. No matter how excited he acted or how much he screamed at me, I was displaying complete willingness to instantly obey my orders but I simply requested clarification regarding the manner in which I was expected to comply. He was unable to fault me for that, no matter how badly he wanted to.

However, as a young, very naïve, brand new Marine recruit, my introduction to life in the Corps was quite disappointing. This was where I first found out that life isn't fair. Being the best at any given endeavor is not automatically going to guarantee that I will be officially recognized and acknowledged as the best. Excellence, in itself, is not a guarantee of receiving the rewards reserved for excellence.

For example, consider our final physical fitness test near the end of recruit training. My arms and shoulders were incredibly strong because of the physical training regimen I had imposed on myself during the first 17 years of my life and because of my country/farm life upbringing.

When we all lined up at the chin-up bars for that portion of the test, the Drill Instructor made me tell the scorekeeper a name other than my own. After I did ten chin-ups for that recruit who I was impersonating, then the DI put me back in line again and had me do ten chin-ups for a second recruit with a different scorekeeper. Finally, I was allowed to give my own name and I did twenty chin-ups (that's the maximum number, for scoring purposes) for myself.

You see, the Drill Instructor wanted to have the Honor Platoon of our Recruit Company but he couldn't have that unless everybody in the platoon passed the physical fitness test portion of our training. Those two recruits that I took the place of would have failed the test because they could not do three chin-ups (that's the absolute lowest allowable number required to obtain a minimum passing score) so the DI made me take up their slack.

Furthermore, during rifle qualification when we were firing for final record near the end of training, the Drill Instructor placed me on the firing line right between two recruits who had been having trouble all along on the rifle range. They were not going to qualify. That means they weren't going to attain the minimum number of points required to be classified as Marksmen. The highest rating is Expert, the second highest is Sharpshooter, the third (and lowest) rating is Marksman. If a shooter fails to accumulate enough points to qualify as at least a Marksman, he is listed as Unqualified. If these two spastic idiots didn't qualify, then the Drill Instructor would still be knocked out of having the Honor Platoon. He had a solution for that. The solution was named Recruit Morris.

There are several different types of ranges which Marines fire on but at that time, the one that was used for rifle qualification for recruit training was called the "Known Distance" range. On this range, we fired from 200 yards, from 300 yards and from 500 yards.

At the 500 yard line, we were allowed to take up to ten minutes to fire ten rounds, loaded into the rifle one round at a time. The DI ordered me to fire my ten rounds as quickly as possible so I would have time to fire the final three rounds at their targets for each of the men on either side of me. Both of them were doing so poorly that I had to put those six rounds in the bull's eye on their targets. (A hit in the bull's eye was worth five points. A hit anywhere else on the target scored a lower value, depending on how far away from the bull's eye the round hit.)

I don't know what the Drill Instructor would have done to me if I had missed the bull's eye, even once. But I didn't miss so I didn't have to find out what the penalty might have been. After all, when I was a kid, I could knock the head off of a match with a .22 rifle at forty paces, so hitting a bull's eye at 500 yards with a high powered rifle was not the most difficult thing I had ever attempted. Well, okay, it wasn't necessarily guaranteed, either, but I did it.

However, those were not the only times I was used and abused by "the system" in boot camp. All during recruit training, I had been either a squad leader or the platoon guide. That's the five recruits who march in formation in front of the platoon. The guide carries the guidon - the staff with the platoon flag - and the squad leaders head up the separate files (squads) of the platoon. The rest of the recruits are simply lined up in ranks behind the squad leaders, according to their individual height.

There are several reasons why I was usually either a squad leader or guide. I could march better than most. I was better than most on the rifle range and the pistol range. I scored higher than most on the physical fitness test. I scored higher than most on the various written tests that were given on various military subjects. On every day and in every way that was subject to review, I was clearly superior to the other recruits. Anyway, the bottom line is that I had EARNED the right to be either a squad leader or guide.

Now, here's the important thing about being a squad leader or guide during recruit training: There were five meritorious promotions from Private to Private First Class at the completion of the training cycle. Those five promotions would go to the squad leaders and the platoon guide because they were presumably the best leaders. That's a bit of knowledge that I was not even aware of until after boot camp was over. Furthermore, with the meritorious promotion came a free issue of a Dress Blue uniform, with PFC chevrons already sewed on.

So, during the last three or four days of recruit training, I was replaced as squad leader by another recruit simply because he was married and the Drill Instructors for our platoon (all of whom were married, presumably) wanted him to get the promotion simply because of the few extra bucks that would go with the promotion. You see, back in the mid-sixties, it was extremely difficult for poor people to make ends meet - and this guy would wait a long time for a regular promotion if he didn't get it on graduation from boot camp because he wasn't much of a "hard charger". But he was married and the DI's figured he needed all the help he could get.

They chose to bump me instead of one of the other squad leaders because I was already so good at everything that they just knew I would be getting promoted faster than most other people, anyway, later on, after getting out into the regular Marine Corps. That's the way the situation was explained to me by the Senior Drill Instructor after boot camp was over and we were all being given our transfer orders to our next command. From their perspective, I suppose it was the logical thing to do to help out a new fellow Marine who had a family to support and, besides, I didn't have a wife and child depending on me

It took me a long time to figure out that I might have won back my promotion if I had taken the situation up through the chain of command but, at the time, I was still operating on the single most important rule that had been stressed during every waking moment of every single day in boot camp: Marine recruits absolutely, positively do not EVER argue with Drill Instructors.

But it was my destiny to be an Honor Graduate out of recruit training, thereby receiving that all-important first promotion which would have served as a springboard for all of my future endeavors in my new chosen profession and I was cheated out of it. My rightful destiny was stolen from me to benefit somebody who was totally undeserving of the promotion that was handed to him, practically on a silver platter.

And I must point out that this was done to me after I had successfully accomplished every task the Drill Instructors had given me. My performance during all of recruit training - and especially during the final physical fitness test, when I was ordered to do chin-ups for those two recruits who would have failed the test AND my performance on the rifle range when I fired for those two other recruits who would have failed to qualify - proved that I had earned the right to have those PFC chevrons.

In this day and age, you might argue that I had willingly participated in two illegal (and immoral) acts when I obeyed the order to do chin-ups and fire rounds for those other recruits.

I can only tell you that, in Marine Corps Recruit Training (especially in that era), there was no right or wrong. There was only the will of the Drill Instructors whose ultimate responsibility was to instill in recruits the kind of mind-set that fosters instant obedience to orders, regardless of the possible circumstances, and my obedience of their orders was a result of the kind of training that inspires Marines to advance across no-man's land in battle, or attack a tank armed only with a rocket launcher, or attack an enemy stronghold by fire and maneuver, or fix bayonets and jump out of a foxhole to meet and repel an enemy attack, and to do so without any hesitation or reservations. In combat, if the Sergeant gives an order, there is only one thing that will prevent a real Marine from accomplishing his assigned mission: Death.

So, in the final analysis, I had worked hard and I DESERVED that promotion, not to mention the distinction of having an entry in my service record indicating that I was one of the Honor Graduates from Marine Corps Recruit Training. But that was not awarded to me. That was September 1966 - over fifty years ago - and Yes, I still hold a grudge.

Advanced Infantry Training

After completing boot camp, we were shipped to Camp Pendleton, California for Advanced Infantry Training. When we were raw recruits, we had become quite accustomed to having the Drill Instructors address us as 'maggots', 'worms', 'pukes', 'slimes' and a great many other highly imaginative and colorfully descriptive epithets. (Yes, back in the '60's, they got away with that - and a whole lot more that modern day folks would find appalling). However, in AIT, we were called "Privates" or "Marines" by our trainers because we had earned the Marine Corps Emblem, thus qualifying for membership in this great "Band of Brothers".

In boot camp, we had learned the theories of "The Rifle Platoon in Offense and Defense"; escape and evasion from POW camps; suppression of enemy activity by requesting and directing fire support from artillery units, from naval warships and from fighter aircraft; detection and elimination of enemy ambush sites; fire and maneuver; land navigation and a great many other skills that would improve our chances of survival in a hostile environment.

In AIT, we experienced the practical application of those theories in the field, thus enhancing the military skills that would complete our metamorphosis from regular, ordinary civilians into real Marines. Being allowed to fire the rifle on the rifle range in boot camp was fun but it was actually rather routine and tame and it simply could not compare with AIT, where carrying a loaded weapon through a combat course, firing at pop-up targets and executing maneuvers that simulated combat patrols through enemy territory was an exhilarating daily event. In AIT, we were introduced to (and allowed to fire) other weapons, also. Hand grenades were entertaining, rocket launchers (bazookas) were fun, flame throwers were frightening (and hot), rifle propelled grenades were exciting but machine guns were totally awesome. I really loved the 7.62mm, air cooled, compression-gas-operated, belt fed, full automatic M60 machine gun. I was determined that I would someday carry a machine gun in Viet-Nam. (I would eventually get my wish).

Training and Expertise

On 1 November 1966, three months and two weeks after enlisting, I was promoted to PFC (Private First Class). It was an early promotion by regular standards but it was two months late, in my personal opinion - I was still sore over being cheated out of my boot camp promotion.

And of course, I had already received my biggest shock. The Corps was more interested in utilizing my mental abilities than in taking advantage of my very extensive physical abilities. They assigned me to the supply field rather than to the infantry. I was truly shocked and amazed. I didn't understand and I did not believe it. How could they not want me, desperately want me, as a "Grunt"? How could they so casually waste what I had to offer?

But I had neglected to consider the basic philosophy of the Marine Corps: Every Marine is a Rifleman First. This fundamental truth has been in existence since Day One of Marine history. No matter what military occupational specialty (MOS) is assigned to any given individual, he is still personally responsible for continually maintaining his knowledge and expertise in the infantry/combat field. Regardless of his regular daily duties, he absolutely MUST be qualified to pick up his rifle and go into combat at a moment's notice.

Even though he may be an admin clerk, truck driver, warehouseman, typewriter repairman, or whatever, his ability to function as an infantryman is of paramount importance when he is being considered for promotions or awards. Although he must certainly be able to perform his regular assigned duties in his MOS with a high degree of efficiency to even be considered for promotion, he will also be judged by his scores on the general military subjects test, on the rifle range and on the physical fitness test when being considered for awards or advancement. After he spends a full-duty day performing tasks in his assigned specialty, he is obliged to spend what might otherwise be considered his personal time developing his expertise as an infantryman.

Of course, this is blatantly not fair. A Marine assigned as a basic infantryman is not required to exhibit any significant expertise in any military occupational specialty other than infantry. He doesn't have to know how to be an admin clerk, or truck driver, or warehouseman or whatever. He spends all of his on-duty time concentrating on the skills required to serve efficiently and effectively as an infantryman, so he is deeply immersed in general military subjects and physical fitness training on a daily basis and has the opportunity to practice on the rifle range - and with other weapons - very often. Like any other Marine, his opportunities for advancement depend on his proficiency and expertise in his assigned specialty (infantry), but also by his scores on the GMS test, the PFT and the rifle range. However, for an infantryman, high scores in those areas should be a "given" because they are all part of his average day.

The army and the navy have specialist rates for enlisted personnel but I don't think I would want to have our system set up any other way. The Marine Corps has always been designated as a "Force in Readiness". We fulfill that credo because, as I said, every Marine is a rifleman first.

When I learned that I was going to be sent to Camp Lejeune, North Carolina to attend supply school, I tried not to feel slighted or unfairly taken advantage of. We had been given a great many tests during boot camp, such as intelligence tests, psychological evaluations, aptitude tests, manual dexterity tests, etc., and the Corps was going to assign us wherever it thought we could be best utilized. The Corps had decided that I had the intelligence and aptitude to be a supply man. Okay, I would try to be a good supply man but I wasn't going to accept the fact that I might never be anything other than that.

I graduated from supply school on 29 December 1966 and was sent to the Marine Corps Supply Center, Albany, Georgia for duty, where I was subsequently chosen to attend Industrial Technical Training School. Albany was a major storage and repair facility for heavy equipment, such as tanks, bulldozers, forklifts and trucks and they needed people who could figure out how to order, store and issue, on a timely basis, the proper amounts of repair parts, components and raw materials needed to keep the operation in full swing. I could do that.

It was amazing. All through school, as a kid, I had been a poor, haphazard, not-very-serious student but after I started attending various schools in the Marine Corps, I was always at or near the academic top of my class. Go figure. But I had not forgotten my original promise to myself. I was going to keep my chances alive for a future in the infantry/combat arms field.

General Military Subjects School

I was chosen to attend the General Military Subjects School at Albany, Georgia. This was basically a "Super-Grunt" school and I was determined to be the #1 super-grunt. The emphasis was on infantry fire team and squad tactics (both offensive and defensive) but also included firing the rifle and pistol for qualification record purposes, the physical fitness test, conducting drill and tactical maneuvers, land navigation/map reading, unarmed (hand to hand) combat, clothing/equipment inspections, classroom testing and, finally, leadership evaluations by the instructors. Both the training and the leadership evaluations were conducted by Sergeants and Corporals, with two Staff Sergeants and a Captain providing overall guidance.

I was treated unfairly by the instructors in this school. As was evidenced by my graduation certificate, I graduated with special honor, ranked 2nd out of 44 students. So you may wonder how it is that I claim to have been treated unfairly. Well, the point is, I should have been 1st in the class but I was cheated out of that honor.

You see, the man who came out in first position was a near and dear cousin of the senior Sergeant Instructor and the Sergeant wanted his cousin to be the honor graduate. There was nothing he could do about our rifle and pistol scores because there were too many individuals involved in verifying the accuracy of the scorecards. The same situation applied to the various written tests, the physical fitness tests, the land navigation tests, the unarmed (hand to hand) combat competitions and the drill and tactical maneuvering competitions. In all of those areas, excellence of performance was clear-cut and obvious to all observers. And in every category, I was the better Marine. My scores were indisputable. My nearest competitor was the Sergeant's favorite cousin. He was good - I freely admit that - but he just wasn't good enough to beat me.

However, I could not control the leadership evaluation scores, which were assigned by the instructors. That's where they were able to shave off a few points from my score while adding a few points to the score of my nearest competitor, simply because the leadership evaluations were based ONLY on the opinions of the instructors. That Sergeant was able to influence the other instructors (his subordinates) so that their opinions reflected that the other student exhibited leadership skills which were supposedly superior to mine.

The two Staff Sergeants (and the Captain) apparently did not consider the fact that favoritism (or nepotism) might be a factor in the leadership evaluation scores assigned by the Corporals and Sergeants who served as instructors. Were they really that ignorant? Would it have been better for my peace of mind if they were? At that point in my career, it was painful for me to consider that they might have been willing accomplices in regard to the injustice that had been perpetrated against me. That's a hard judgment call for a PFC to make regarding the professionalism of his seniors. But the fact remains - they were either incompetent or they were collaborators in the art of backstabbing.

The other students told me, pointblank, that I was very clearly a better leader than our Honor Graduate was but their opinions didn't count because they didn't get to vote. Leadership is more than a skill, much more. Leadership is something intangible. It's not just an ability that a person might possess. It's an attitude, a character trait. Leadership is something that almost defies description. But that is the very quality of leadership that made it possible for the instructors to pretend that my opponent had more of it than I had. So I lost.

A normal person might think that I should be quite proud of the fact that I was 2nd out of 44. Granted, it is nice to have that "Special Honor" placard affixed to my graduation certificate. But it doesn't make up for the fact that I should have been recognized and acknowledged as the # 1 Honor Graduate. Once again, I was cheated out of my rightful destiny. Actually BEING the best is worth nothing if I am not officially RECOGNIZED as the best. If a fact isn't part of the official record, it isn't really a fact, at all. It is a non-fact.

My overall performance clearly earned me the distinction of being the Honor Graduate but the official record, as of 4 March 1967, indicates that I was only second best. That simple fact has grated on my sensibilities for more than fifty years, and yes, I still hold a grudge.

Moving On

Being assigned to Albany, Georgia as my first regular duty station was really nice. It was a beautiful base with all the various amenities, such as a post exchange, gymnasium, bowling alley, movie theater and enlisted club. I hardly ever left the base, although the city of Albany was a wonderful place to visit.

My duties were simple, working in a warehouse, stocking shelves, receiving and issuing various repair parts for heavy equipment. I had operated tractors and other farm equipment on the many various farms where I worked while growing up, so learning to drive a forklift was a snap. I quickly became a master operator of all types of forklifts, from 5,000 lb warehouse forklifts to 10-ton rough terrain forklifts that could pick up almost anything. In spite of my low rank as a junior enlisted Marine, I was frequently assigned to teach new arrivals the intricacies of forklift operation and I gave numerous demonstrations to visiting dignitaries.

And of course, we were Marines right down to our core, so we performed the usual military activities. For example, there was a monthly awards and retirement parade and I was ALWAYS selected to march in that. The base didn't have a large paved parade ground so, while ceremonies were conducted, we did our marching and standing in ranks on a large grassy area in front of the headquarters building. So naturally, this being Georgia, we were assaulted constantly by bugs. Any grassy area was home to chiggers, gnats and fire ants. It took a great deal of discipline and self-control to refrain from swatting the gnats or from scratching the bites but we were Marines, still human beings admittedly, but just a little bit more than the regular, average, run-of-the-mill humans. So we marched or stood in ranks frozen at the position of attention while our bodies served as a feast for the critters.

We also practiced weapons training and tactical maneuvers in the wooded areas of the base, which broke up the tedium of our supply oriented routine. It helped us to maintain our image of ourselves as Leathernecks, as Devil Dogs, as honest-to-goodness Marines, still worthy of the Marine Corps Emblem (the Eagle, Globe and Anchor).

I spent almost all of my free time continuing my personal training regimen. Jogging on base was interesting because it was a large, sprawling place with thousands of acres and miles upon miles of roads, lanes and trails. The gymnasium had a very well-equipped weight room and there were several outdoor exercise areas where I could do chin-ups and assorted outdoor type exercises. The only drawback was that the base did not have a regulation obstacle course so I really missed what I considered to be my playground.

However, I had not forgotten my reason for joining the Corps. Whenever the time limit expired on my last application, I would submit a new application requesting transfer to overseas duty. I wanted to go to Viet-Nam and nothing was going to keep me from my destiny.

I eventually got my wish for overseas assignment but it didn't quite turn out as I hoped. My transfer orders sent me to Okinawa. Hey, at least it was the western pacific, so I was a little closer to my objective.

I was not assigned to a warehouse operation, this time. I was put into a section which had only four other Marines and was titled the Technical and Research Unit. Our library was stocked with every technical and repair manual for every piece of equipment used by the Marine Corps, whether it was vehicles, weapons, or whatever. We advised the various local repair facilities, motor pools and armories regarding the use, application and availability of any repair part or component, from an entire engine block (for example) right down to the tiniest piece that was part of that engine.

This was interesting and challenging work but it never ceased to amaze me that the Marine Corps seemed so intent on utilizing me in areas which were so completely opposite from the life I had lived as a country boy/farm laborer, especially considering that I had been such a miserable excuse as a high school student.

I did have one small problem at the mess hall. Excuse me, they are called dining facilities, now. I felt that I was being discriminated against because I like scrambled eggs. To be more to the point, I DON'T like runny egg yolks. However, every person who asked for sunny side up eggs was receiving fresh eggs, cracked and cooked on demand, while those of us who asked for scrambled eggs would receive a portion of egg batter from a vat in which powdered eggs had been mixed with water and reconstituted.

The conversation went something like this: I said, "Hey, I want scrambled eggs but I don't want powdered eggs. Take a couple of real eggs and crack them for me". To which the cook replied, "You don't get fresh eggs if you want scrambled". So I said, "Fine, give me a couple of eggs sunny side up but just break the yolk while they are cooking. I don't like runny yolks." The cook said, "I can't do that. That would be scrambled". I insisted, "No, it wouldn't. I'm not asking you to scramble the yolk. I'm just asking you to break the yolk so it won't be runny".

I was, in effect, holding up the chow line and other people were starting to pile up behind me so, at this point, the Mess Sergeant (a Staff Sergeant) came over and asked, "What's the problem, here?" The cook said, "This guy is making trouble about the eggs". I said, "Staff Sergeant, I'm not trying to make trouble. I just want fresh eggs". The cook said, "No, he wants scrambled eggs". To which I responded, "Well, that's partially true. I want fresh eggs but I just want the yolk broken so it can properly cook. Why does that seem like too much to ask?"

The Mess Sergeant was getting upset and said, "We have a policy and if you don't like it, you can go see The Old Man". (Among the ranks, the Commanding Officer was referred to as The Old Man). I asked, "What's the matter with you people? The cook broke both yolks of the eggs he fixed for the guy in line ahead of me, so why can't he break the yolks of my eggs?" The cook responded, heatedly, "That was an accident. I didn't break them on purpose". But he HAD done it on purpose. I had seen him. Maybe the other guy was a friend of the cook.

At this point, the Mess Sergeant ordered me to get out of line and to give him my ID card. He said, "I'm writing you up for disrespect and disorderly conduct". By then, I was mad, too, so I told him, "You do whatever you want, Staff Sergeant, but if you refuse to serve me what I want for breakfast, when you send me in front of the CO, I'll tell him about it and if he doesn't file charges against you for dereliction of duty, I'll go see the Battalion Commander and, if he doesn't fix this problem, I'll go see the Regimental Commander and, if I'm still not happy, I'll go see the Base Commander. We both know I have the right to do that. And, by the way, I want back in line right where I was because I'm not going all the way to the end of the chow line just because of you".

This was incredible behavior, on my part. At the time, I was only a Lance Corporal so I was seriously outranked. However, I firmly believed that I was within my rights and I was not going to be intimidated. If I had to take this matter all the way to the Commandant, I was going to eat what I wanted to eat for breakfast. This was garrison duty, not combat, and I firmly believed that I was not being unreasonable.

The Mess Sergeant put me back in line where I had been and told the cook to serve me whatever I wanted and I was never called in front of the CO to answer any charges against me. After that, all of the cooks thought of me as a troublemaker but I always got what I wanted and it was cooked the way I wanted it.

My personal records are incomplete. I don't have a copy of my promotion warrant for the rank of Lance Corporal but I was promoted to Corporal and became a squad leader on 1 October 1967, just one year, three months and two weeks after I joined the Marines as a Private, so I was obviously moving up the ranks quite fast. That's a pretty good promotion record, considering the fact that I was cheated out of being an Honor Graduate twice, once in boot camp and again in General Military Subjects School.

Okinawa is the birthplace of the Shorin-Ryu style of Karate, so I started taking classes right away. It was great fun. It was a full-contact sport and we used no padding.

I took advantage of the fact that I was on an island by learning how to snorkel in the ocean. That was really great fun, but it took a while to remember that I was supposed to blow OUT through the snorkel BEFORE trying to breathe IN upon returning to the surface after making a dive to check out some coral or to try to catch an octopus. Most octopi are quite small, by the way. You know, when you catch one of those things, you can't throw it away. It has all those suction cups on its arms. After you grab hold of it, it grabs hold of you. Dang!

At the base pool, I took advantage of a free training opportunity to become certified as a SCUBA diver, on my own time. SCUBA means self-contained underwater breathing apparatus. I figured that would help me in my future plans to become qualified as a 0324 (reconnaissance man, combatant diver qualified).

I also took part in a program that was run by the Army Special Forces (Green Berets) on an ad hoc basis, in which they provided instruction in the technical aspects and tower-training portions of parachute training, so I could eventually qualify for Jump School, which would help me to become qualified as a 0326 (reconnaissance man, parachute and combatant diver qualified).

This particular part of my plan was put on indefinite hold because I finally received orders to Viet-Nam. I was assigned to First Bridge Company, Seventh Engineer Battalion, First Marine Division (Reinforced), Viet-Nam. My dream of going to war was finally coming true. Little did I know that achieving my dream would result in my having nightmares for the rest of my life.

The Viet-Nam War

This is the first time I have ever written anything about the Viet-Nam War. I have, on occasion, briefly discussed a couple of situations or episodes of the war with some family members or with trusted friends. My reasoning for not putting anything into print was that I didn't want to give it a life, an existence of its own.

I was involved with a program called "Every Hero Has a Story". This was part of a summer reading program for children, sponsored by the Pope County Library System. They had representatives from the police department, the fire department and emergency medical services. I was their token "veteran of foreign wars", partially because I am a published author (my first book was titled *Thicker Than Water)* and partially because I am known to the various local library employees (and especially to Ms. Emily Bailey of the Russellville library. She organized the summer reading program and she recruited me as a volunteer). Over a period of five days, I gave a series of seven presentations, combining demonstrations and lectures, to the kids - and to their parents. The children ranged in age from 4 years old to 12 years old.

Thanks to Ms. Emily. Her character and personality were perfectly suited to the task of bringing together the parents, the children and the guest speaker into a meaningful and organized unit. She truly created order out of chaos. Thanks to the other Library workers, and especially to the many volunteers, who gave freely of their time and efforts to make each event successful.

Thanks to Staff Sergeant Ryan Butler and Sergeant Wesley Kelly of the Marine Corps Recruiting Station in Russellville. They really went out of their way to collect Marine artifacts and memorabilia that I could use as training aids and displays at the events.

Thanks to my sister, Shirley, who videotaped several of the events and provided many of the materials which I used as displays depicting the way we lived in the 1940's and 1950's. Thanks to my brother, E. Ray and his wife, Jannie, who designed and printed a huge stack of calling cards, which I distributed among the parents who attended the events. The cards highlighted my first published book, *Thicker Than Water.*

Thanks to the parents, who enrolled their children in the Summer Reading Program in order to reinforce the premise that the ability to read well is the first building block of a good education. Thanks to the families who approached me after each event to thank me and to share their thoughts, their stories and photos of their own service members. They really touched me.

Thanks to the children, who made wonderful audiences. A gesture of friendship and gratitude from a child is a very special and precious gift for any adult to receive, so thanks to all of the young ladies who gave me hugs and to all the young gentlemen who very solemnly and formally shook my hand and said, "Thank you for your service".

Finally, special thanks to Miss Josephine Schroeder, a young lady who used her time at the craft table to make (and beautifully decorate) a "Hero" mask, which she presented to me as a special gift. It has an honored place on my living room wall among my other treasures. The way I was treated at each of those events helped to heal some of my bitterness. I drove away from each event with tears in my eyes. But they were happy tears. Thanks, Kids!

Other guest speakers included policemen, firemen and emergency medical technicians. I was quite willing to let the kids know that I think of all those people as heroes because of the jobs they do. But there was one aspect of their jobs that I did not mention. For instance, policemen generally work an 8-hour shift over a 40-hour week. Granted, that work is dangerous but when the shift is over, they go home to their families and they are relatively safe while they are off duty. It's a different situation for a member of the military while he or she is in a war zone. We might get killed at any hour of the day or night. The enemy might drop rockets or mortars on our tents while we sleep or a sniper might shoot us while we eat our c-rations, so we aren't safe even then. So, the bottom line is this: While at war, we are in jeopardy every minute of every day. Basically, that means we are on duty from the minute we arrive in a war zone until we leave the war zone. In Viet-Nam, the typical tour of duty was 13 months. At an average of 30 days per month, that is 390 days. Since we could be killed at any minute during any of those days, then we did the same as three 8-hour shifts per day, every day. That's 9,360 continuous hours on duty. If a policeman worked a regular 40-hour week, it would take 4 ½ years of police work to equal just one tour of duty in Viet-Nam.

The above example deals ONLY with the periods of time when the policeman is actually on duty during his 8-hour shift. At the end of each 8-hour work shift, he is allowed to spend 16 hours embracing his wife, enjoying the company of his children and living a normal life. On the other hand, a Marine in a war zone serves 1,170 consecutive 8-hour shifts on duty without even one minute to spend embracing his wife or spending time with his family. How precious would one embrace be to that Marine? How much would he be willing to pay for one hug, one kiss or one moment of ecstasy with his beloved? What would he give to spend a few minutes playing catch in the backyard with his son or having a tea party on the veranda with his daughter? Those moments are lost forever to a man in a war zone, moments that can never be restored. Combat pay in Viet-Nam was a mere 30 extra dollars per month, over and above the regular pay scale.

There wasn't much about Viet-Nam that I was comfortable telling the kids but I did tell them about being a Marine, what Marines do, what it takes to become a Marine and about the kind of childhood I had which led me to a successful transition from being a civilian to being a Marine.

In this treatise, I have written about some of the things I could not discuss with the children.

Duties and Responsibilities

I served as a combat engineer, machine gun operator, patrol leader, squad leader and supply clerk during two consecutive assignments in the Republic of South Viet-Nam. I helped build permanent and temporary bridges in support of tactical operations. I helped build and operate pontoon barges capable of transporting multiple trucks and/or tanks across various water-covered areas and rivers. I conducted road sweeps in advance of vehicle convoys to detect possible booby traps or buried explosive devices. I operated a machine gun in offensive and defensive tactical operations to overcome and eliminate assaults and ambushes by insurgent enemy forces and to provide security during the assembly and operation of bridges and barges. I explored caves and tunnels to determine whether or not they might contain supplies, equipment and/or food which could be used by insurgent enemy forces. I led a 4-man fire team in patrolling the terrain in advance of our main force during the movement phases of tactical operations. I manned observation and/or listening posts from 100 meters to 300 meters outside the defensive perimeter of our main camp area during hours of darkness in order to detect and give advance warning of approaching insurgent enemy forces prior to possible attacks. I led a 13-man squad (composed of three 4-man fire teams) in conducting various offensive and defensive tactical operations (patrols) in the terrain surrounding work sites and camp areas in order to detect and neutralize possible ambushes and/or insurgent enemy infiltrations or assaults. I provided map grid coordinates to various fire control centers to initiate and/or adjust artillery fire support and close air support for ongoing operations. While in our reasonably secure base camps, I prepared requisitions to replenish supplies, bridge components and motor transport repair parts to support the unit's mission. I drafted all forecasts for fiscal obligations for all of First Bridge Company. I controlled all financial transactions between First Bridge Company and higher headquarters for supplies, components and repair parts.

South Viet-Nam was smelly

When I got off the plane, it was obvious that this was a world in which I would never be comfortable. I was a country boy, raised in rural Arkansas and I had worked with animals all the time. But horses, cows, chickens, even hogs could never produce the smells that assailed my senses when I arrived in South Viet-Nam.

Water buffaloes were used as beasts of burden everywhere over there. Even in the cities, where they pulled carts filled with produce or merchandise. They were used by Vietnamese farmers in the same manner that tractors are used in the United States. And they smelled terrible.

The Vietnamese people used one particular sauce on EVERY food item. It was called nuoc-mam sauce. It smelled really bad. Not only did it stain the teeth and foul the breath of every person who ate it, but the smell of it permeated the atmosphere at incredible distances and it was one of the many smells which indicated that we were approaching a village, even while we were still deep in the woods. One other food item that stained the teeth was betel nut. Almost all of them chewed it. It was ugly but it didn't make their breath smell QUITE as bad as nuoc-mam.

Except in cities, sanitary facilities were virtually non-existent. "Using the bathroom" was a phrase which would be totally meaningless in rural South Viet-Nam, simply because there were no bathrooms. Even on military bases (except for various high-level headquarters areas) things were generally quite primitive. There were "outhouses", similar to those used in rural America during the first half of the 20th century. However, the military outhouses were equipped with a container which was placed underneath the "commode" hole. The container was one-half of a 55-gallon drum which had been filled with diesel fuel. At various intervals, this half-drum would be pulled from underneath the outhouse. Then the diesel fuel would be set on fire, which would effectively dispose of all waste which had been deposited. Predictably, the smoke from the burning fuel had a particularly repugnant smell but, even so, it was a definite improvement over the outhouses of the native population.

South Viet-Nam was dirty

Walking through the countryside and through remote rural areas of South Viet-Nam was nothing like hiking through a forest in the United States. And wading through a rice paddy was not like wading through a normal muddy area back home because the Vietnamese fertilized their rice paddies with virtually every type of waste, including human excrement. And Heaven only knows how many acres of South Viet-Nam were devoted to growing rice.

When we departed from our base camp on any given "project", we really had no idea how many hours or days it might be before we could return to our relatively comfortable tents. Even though we would be briefed by our commanders beforehand, changes to our schedule were so numerous, nothing was considered routine.

Even the most basic personal amenities could not be taken for granted. For instance, a normal person can't possibly comprehend how comforting it can be to put on a pair of clean socks after several days of wearing the same pair, even though we might not be able to clean our feet during the process. Obviously, bathing or showering was not in the realm of possibilities. In fact, we might feel lucky if we could wash our hands before eating our c-rations or if we could rinse our mouths after eating. Having the opportunity and time to brush our teeth was pure ecstasy.

Sleeping on the ground might be alright if you are in Yellowstone National Park at a regular campsite with a comforting campfire and a down-filled sleeping bag and, perhaps, even a tent. Such was not the case in South Viet-Nam. When spending a night away from base camp, it was generally necessary to sleep fully clothed (in clothing which I may have already been wearing for at least a couple of days). And instead of a nice sleeping bag, I would probably have only a blanket or a poncho with which to cover myself. In case of rain, I was guaranteed to get wet and muddy because a shelter half would have taken up too much room in my pack. (A shelter half is exactly described by its name. Two shelter halves are combined to make a simple two-man tent).

Furthermore, sleeping on the ground in South Viet-Nam was not a simple process. Not only would it be not prudent to simply lie down and wrap up, it might even prove to be hazardous to health, even deadly. I had to dig in. I didn't usually dig holes that were deep enough to stand up in. That is mostly done just in the movies. I would dig out a slight depression long enough and wide enough to lie down in and only deep enough so that most of my body would be below the level of the surrounding area. If the enemy threw a grenade or if a rocket or mortar landed nearby, most of the shrapnel would go over me instead of through me. At the base camp, our bunkers and line positions were deep and heavily sandbagged but while on the move or out on a project, we tried to keep things simple.

South Viet-Nam was exhausting

When I went to South Viet-Nam the first time, I weighed 179 pounds and had only a 29-inch waist. I was the absolute perfect picture of excellent health. That changed. Our days were filled with activities, projects, patrols and the occasional clash with people who didn't seem to like us very much at all (in fact, they got downright confrontational, even hostile, from time to time). Our nights were filled with guard duty, perimeter security duty, listening posts, night patrols, ambushes and those occasional clashes with some very belligerent members of the indigenous population. For months at a time, we might get no more than three or four hours of sleep at any one given time. That had a tendency to just sort of slowly wear me down. And it affected my health in ways that would come back to haunt me in later years, impacting my overall strength and stamina.

South Viet-Nam was confusing

Picture this scenario: Three or four Marines are manning a defensive position, perhaps on the edge of a village or town or along a road. A lone Vietnamese approaches the position, carrying a weapon and pointing it at the Marines. The Marines respond to this obvious threat by ordering the Vietnamese to stop and to put the weapon down. He keeps advancing, making it clear that he is intent on doing serious bodily harm to the Marines. They have the right to fire at that person.

Now picture this second scenario: Three or four Marines are manning a defensive position. A lone Vietnamese CHILD, wearing a backpack, approaches the position, carrying several cans or bottles of coca-cola and offering to sell the sodas to the Marines. The child is presumably an innocent civilian. However, the Marines have orders to allow absolutely no one to approach their defensive position. They shout at the child, telling him to stop, to go away, but he continues to approach. The Marines don't have the heart to fire at an unarmed child so they allow him to approach. Unknown to the Marines, the child is carrying an explosive device in the backpack, placed there by a Viet Cong soldier who lied to the child and told him the Marines would pay him very well for the sodas. When the child gets close enough to the Marines, the hidden Viet Cong soldier turns a switch on a detonator, which causes the backpack to explode, killing the child AND the Marines who made the mistake of allowing him to approach.

That was the confusing part. We Marines of that era truly loved children, probably just as Marines do to this very day. Kids are special and all decent young Americans automatically see themselves as natural protectors of children. We would simply be incapable of opening fire on a child. But the Viet Cong and the communist North Vietnamese had absolutely no regard for the life and well-being of a South Vietnamese child. If a child could be used as a tool against the enemy (us), they would take particular delight in doing so. Their sense of values was so utterly different from ours, there was no way we could ever comprehend or understand their thought processes. It was the worst possible clash of cultures.

South Viet-Nam was disgusting

I suffered from culture shock. I didn't think about it before I went over there but if I had, I would have been unconcerned about the possibility of it because I was a country boy. To be specific, I was a poor country boy who had grown up without electricity or running water. And, of course, I knew that creature comforts were in short supply for the majority of the Vietnamese populace so I assumed that I would consider them to be kindred souls. That was not the case.

The alien smells of South Viet-Nam were just the tip of the iceberg. They were not just different smells. They were bad smells. They were really bad.

The people also disgusted me. I expected them to be uncultured and unrefined but I didn't expect them to be totally revolting. Women would urinate in public at the side of the road in plain view. Fathers would offer their daughters for rent for sex. Small children - very small children - would beg for candy and c-rations...and even cigarettes. And every one of them would try to pick our pockets.

However, the atrocities that were committed against these same people disgusted me even more. The people who were committing these atrocities were people just like the victims. They were the same race, spoke the same language, and had the same heritage. The only difference was that the evildoers were communists.

The communists treated the South Vietnamese like animals. If a village did not collaborate with them, the headman and his entire family would be tortured, raped and killed. Communists would occupy a village and shoot at an approaching American patrol from inside the village. Then they would sneak away while the Americans called in air strikes against the village because we thought it was an enemy stronghold. But the only ones who got hurt were the villagers, innocent pawns of a war they did not start, did not want and did not understand.

The communists would force the local villagers to fight as Viet Cong. Even the children. Especially the children. My heart cried for them, then. Whenever I spend time thinking about the children of South Viet-Nam, my heart cries again. 49 years later. Still.

South Viet-Nam was educational

Before I begin this section, let me explain that I was only a Corporal while I was in South Viet-Nam. Senior NCOs (noncommissioned officers) are Master Gunnery Sergeant or Sergeant Major, Master Sergeant or First Sergeant, Gunnery Sergeant and Staff Sergeant. Junior NCOs are Sergeant and corporal. Junior enlisted Marines are Lance Corporal, Private First Class and Private.

Generally, the only commissioned officers I dealt with personally were Second Lieutenants, First Lieutenants and Captains. My education consisted mostly of learning to dislike those officers, along with some of the senior NCOs. And even some of the junior NCOs when they used the power of their assignments to influence the decision making processes within the infrastructure of the Company or Battalion administrative sections.

My main reason for disliking officers was because 90% of those with whom I came in contact were self-serving, inconsiderate, sycophant jerks who were interested only in making themselves look good in front of other, more senior officers. They were very reluctant to give recognition and praise to the men under their control and, whenever possible, they took credit for things that were accomplished by their subordinates. Some of them even wrote up recommendations for themselves so they would receive awards, commendations and medals which they did not deserve. They also wrote up recommendations for any of the senior NCOs who aided and abetted them in their efforts to enhance their self-image. But for some reason, they generally neglected to write recommendations for any Marine below the rank of Sergeant, probably because the junior enlisted men didn't have enough seniority to reciprocate with comparable return favors. It was basically as if the officers were saying, "Sure, I'm willing to recommend a medal for you, but what's in it for me?"

I believe I earned more than what I got while I was in Viet-Nam... and there were other men in my platoon who earned more than they received, too. But our leaders didn't take care of us the way they should have. They were generally too busy taking care of themselves. For example, I saw our Lieutenant (the Platoon Commander) and our Staff Sergeant (the Platoon Sergeant) photographing each other while they took turns firing their pistols into the water off the end of one of the bridges we were building. After they both went back to the States, there was a rumor that the Platoon Commander had been awarded a Bronze Star Medal for bravery in combat and the Platoon Sergeant had received a Navy Commendation Medal for leadership under fire. But I knew that Staff Sergeant well and, in my humble opinion, if he hadn't been a Staff Sergeant in the Marine Corps, he would have been a drunken bum on the streets of some large city. And I'm not saying I did anything that would have earned me the Medal of Honor but there were several instances when my actions were significantly worthy of honorable mention if only the officers and senior Staff NCOs had been conscientious enough to write the citations documenting my efforts (or the efforts of various other members of the platoon) instead of spending their time trying to make themselves look good. In regard to my disliking some junior NCOs, I bring to mind the Corporal who was our company administrative clerk. Both of us had been recommended for an award called "Marine of the Month" of our battalion. I won the award but he got his revenge by using the power of his assignment to secretly sabotage my service record book. A lot of things were purposely left out that should have been in there. Things like favorable comments, recommendations for various awards and decorations and entries regarding my proficiency and conduct. Things that I really deserved to have listed - things that were hard-earned, considering that I had such a low rank. And some other things were inserted that did not belong in my record and should not have been there.

You see, the thing about a service record is this: If something happened but it wasn't written into the record, then it is the same as if it never happened. And if something is written into the record, it becomes a fact, even if it never actually happened. His actions against me sabotaged my early career in ways that I wasn't even aware of until years later because, as odd as it may seem these days, enlisted Marines were not allowed to routinely peruse their own service record book. Even so, he might not have succeeded at his secret sabotage of my service record if my Platoon Commander had done his job by periodically reviewing the service records of his platoon members – he might have noticed the entries that did not belong there and the other entries that belonged in there but had been left out or deleted but he was too busy making sure his own commendations and awards were being processed to worry about a junior Marine.

However, being bumped out of being named as "Marine of the Month" wouldn't have been so bad for the admin clerk if there was an award of that type every month. He could simply have been re-nominated the next month. But, illogical though it may seem, Marine units of that era didn't designate a "Marine of the Month" every month. Commanders might wait two or three months before deciding that one of their Marines had been exceptional enough to earn the award.

South Viet-Nam was lonely

Today, we live in an era of instant communication. We don't have to get up from a chair and walk over to a desk or to a wall unit to answer a phone. Our phones are in our pockets, now.

With a device small enough to fit in our shirt pocket, we can talk to people thousands of miles away without even a pause between sentences. On these tiny phones, we can even send personal photos and informational texts anywhere in the world.

With a small laptop computer, we can have face-to-face real-time conversations with people on the other side of the planet. Nowadays, a soldier in Afghanistan can sit in front of a computer and chat with his or her spouse and children in the middle of Arkansas.

This was not the case in the mid 1960's. There was no such thing as a cellular phone. Even most televisions still received only black and white images. A small computer was the size of a living room. A large computer could take up as much as a city block. In the computer age we live in now, all of the information that was on that block-sized computer will fit in a microchip the size of a button.

From South Viet-Nam in 1967, instant communication was an absolute impossibility. It was something that we hadn't yet even dreamed of. The only contact we had with the "real" world was through the postal service. One of my friends or family members could write a letter and mail it. Seven to ten days later, I would receive it. That was considered quite fast.

A letter from home would brighten my day, regardless of my circumstances. No matter what else was happening at the time, having a letter in my pocket from a family member or a loved one enabled me to perform superhuman feats. If my sister wrote of ordinary daily events or if my sweetie was telling me how much she missed me, it lifted my spirits to unbelievable heights.

To write me a letter, Shirley (my sister) or Juanita (my sweetie) had to actually take at least half an hour out of her life to sit down, take pen in hand and concentrate on me, and only me. Today, we can talk or send texts on our cell phones while we are doing all kinds of other things. Some people even talk or text while driving. Face it, they do. But the act of writing a letter in the old days required a singleness of purpose. It was extremely important to me to know that they regarded me so highly that they were willing to commit themselves to that task.

In South Viet-Nam, a day without a letter was a dismal day. Going four or five days without a letter was pure torture. I would start to not care if I lived or died. That kind of attitude was not a good thing, considering my location and situation. But it helped to have the last couple of letters still readily available. I always kept the last couple of letters with me, at all times. Some letters were read and re-read dozens, even hundreds, of times. You can't really do that with a text or an email. A handwritten letter from home was solid evidence of another existence, proof positive that somebody out there cared enough about me to send me their thoughts.

Smelly, dirty, confusing, disgusting, exhausting, lonely, scary..... these factors made South Viet-Nam a bad place to spend time. Loneliness helped to get people killed over there. While sitting with twelve other men in a squad tent or with a platoon or a squad on patrol or working on a project, I still felt alone, empty, without a letter from home in my pocket. My woodcraft, higher-than-average intelligence and country-living-enhanced powers of observation (not to mention pure dumb luck) helped to put me in the right places at the right times to avoid nearly all of the booby traps and at least some of the places where most of the enemy rockets and bullets were impacting. Having my fellow Marines watch my back while I watched theirs helped to keep me from harm, generally. But the truth is, with their letters and with their love, my sister Shirley and my sweetheart Juanita, well, you see, they saved my life.

South Viet-Nam was scary

Our base camp was really nice. We had semi-permanent squad tents that we could stand up in. I had a fold-out canvas cot to sleep on. My main worry was that the sentries on the perimeter might not be as alert as they should be and that one of the Viet Cong might sneak through the line and cut my throat while I slept, or simply throw a grenade into our tent.

While on patrol or while working on a project, I was afraid that an enemy sniper might single me out as a target of opportunity and there was nothing I could do about that.

I wasn't really very afraid of booby traps. Well, I should say that I wasn't very afraid that I, personally, would encounter a booby trap. After all, I was a country boy and had played in the woods all the time as a youngster so I knew where to put my feet and I was intelligent enough to know that a booby trap could be set off even by the simple act of brushing aside a limb or a bush while walking past if a trip wire was tied to that limb or bush. At any given moment, what I WAS afraid of was that one of the people walking along close to me might set off a booby trap and the resulting explosion might injure or kill both of us. Some of my fellow Marines were city boys and I didn't think they might have known how to be as careful in the woods as I. And I have to say, with all possible candor, that most of my fellow Marines were not nearly as intelligent as I was.

I was afraid while on listening post. A listening post was a position that might be as far as two hundred yards out in front of the platoon or company defensive perimeter while the unit was spending a night out anywhere away from base camp. With one other man, I would sneak out during the twilight hour and pick a hiding spot to listen for sounds of approaching enemy. We had our weapons, of course, but we weren't supposed to use them except in case of an absolute emergency. Instead, we had a two-way radio with which we could inform our platoon or company commander of the size and direction of any enemy that might try to sneak up on our front lines. We had to stay out all night. We had to be utterly quiet. We had to be alert. We took turns sleeping. I was afraid that someone might sneak up on us and it might be someone who was better in the woods than I. I was afraid that my fellow Marine might fall asleep while he was supposed to be awake. I was afraid that we might get surrounded if the enemy decided to hit our unit in force. Getting captured would be an infinitely worse fate than getting killed.

I was afraid whenever I went into a tunnel, armed with a flashlight, a knife and a pistol, to check for enemy soldiers or supplies. We were working as combat engineers, not full-fledged infantry, so it was not all that often that we had to sweep through a village or clear a tunnel but when it was necessary, I was my unit's first choice for checking out an old bunker, a sinkhole or a tunnel. My platoon sergeant usually had me carrying a machine gun because I was extremely strong for my size but I was also very skinny, so I could fit into those small places. I never encountered an enemy soldier inside any of those places but I did once have an encounter with a rat who did not appreciate my invasion of his space. When the tunnel caved in behind me and my flashlight blinked out, I was more afraid than I had ever been in my life, up to that point. The rat attacked me several times but I managed to kill it with my knife and, when my platoon pulled me out of the tunnel using ropes that had been tied to my ankles, I dragged the rat out with me so it could be tested for rabies. Luckily, it tested negative so I didn't have to take shots. That was not my first tunnel and it would not be my last but it was the most memorable.

I was afraid whenever we exchanged gunfire with the enemy. Most of the time, they were not even clearly visible. We might receive fire from a tree line, or across a rice paddy, or from the edge of a village. We would shoot at figures moving around in the distance or at muzzle flashes in the woods at night.

I was afraid whenever our leader would call in an air strike because the pilot might drop the bombs or napalm in the wrong place. If I thought our leader was an idiot, I would offer to determine the map coordinates of our position for him, simply to ensure my own safety.

Generally speaking, I was afraid the whole time I was in South Viet-Nam, both times. I was even afraid while boarding the airplane and while flying away from South Viet-Nam until I was absolutely sure we were out of range of a surface-to-air missile. My active imagination left absolutely nothing to chance and there was no way I could even begin to relax until I was back in my own neighborhood.

South Viet-Nam is forever

When I came home from South Viet-Nam the first time, naively traveling in uniform, American citizens were spitting on me at the airport in Los Angeles. They called me 'baby killer' and 'warmonger'. The memory of that episode has stayed with me and still affects my attitude toward certain types of people and toward certain events, right up to this very day.

For example, I had more respect for the "Hell's Angels" biker gangs than I had for hippies, yuppies and flower children because when my wife, Juanita, and I encountered a group of "Hell's Angels" at a rest stop area along the coastal highway in California, every one of those bikers treated me with deference, with respect and even with admiration, simply because they saw a Marine Corps decal on the back window of our Volkswagen Bus. That particular encounter could have been infinitely different under almost any other circumstances.

I will always feel envy toward all of the returning veterans of other conflicts. Veterans of World War I, World War II, the Korean War, the Cuban Crisis, Desert Storm, the Gulf War, Iran, Iraq, Afghanistan - and even Grenada - got ticker tape parades with marching bands and crowds of cheering citizens. Collectively, they are all acknowledged as 'heroes', even though, individually, many of them may have done nothing that was actually heroic. Each and every one of them gets handshakes and smiles. All I got were epithets. And spit.

The Viet-Nam War was the only war the United States ever lost. I was ashamed of my own participation in that failure and for some reason I always felt personally responsible and thought I should apologize to the American people.

I am extremely claustrophobic, partially because of being in that tunnel when it caved in. I have trouble sleeping in a bedroom with the door closed. In fact, I don't like to have any of the interior doors closed in my house when I am at home.

For thirty years or so after I came home, my feet would develop jungle rot every summer. The skin would get all scaly and red. Blotches and blisters would appear all over, especially between the toes. It wouldn't get as bad as it did in South Viet-Nam, with patches of skin coming off when I removed my socks but it was still painful. Over time, it gradually happened less frequently. In fact, it hasn't happened in the last 3 years.

It is extremely rare that I ever sleep continuously for more than three hours at a time.

I spent so many months sleeping and working (or standing watch) in three or four hour shifts that the habit became practically second nature. It's almost as if it is now part of my basic DNA. I can sleep longer, of course, and I sometimes do but that's usually only if I am really exhausted, or sick. That is not really conducive to a proper good night's sleep.

My left ear doesn't work.

My right knee (and hip) gets stiff and sore if I sit too long or drive too far, although it usually loosens up after just a few steps.

During cold weather, my hands and feet suffer considerably. I have had a lot of injuries to my extremities so I have poor circulation in those areas. This situation is particularly annoying to me because, during my youth, I rarely needed more than a thin blue jean jacket as protection against the cold, even in the middle of winter. That wasn't a case of a country boy just trying to be macho. The weather was just not much of a factor and I generally ignored it, in those days.

I have a very strong gag reflex. I can't work with fresh, raw meat so cutting up a chicken or stuffing a turkey in the kitchen is an impossibility and even carving a turkey at the head of the table would not be a pleasant chore. I can manage putting a hamburger patty on to cook but it has taken years to manage that simple task. For years, I worked for Tyson Foods but I was in the sanitation department, washing machines on the production line and cleaning loading dock areas.

I have a persistent, hacking cough, even though I have never used tobacco, alcohol or drugs.

I have had this cough since 1967. But I am an incredibly lucky man, even so. A lot of people who went to South Viet-Nam and got exposed to Agent Orange contracted diseases like leukemia and various cancers and they died. All I got was a chronic cough.

Sometimes, perhaps when I'm shaving, I might notice some particular scar or mark and I will stand there for long minutes, remembering, or perhaps in a daze, not thinking of anything at all.

Even to this very day, I don't like to have open spaces at my back and am distrustful of anybody behind me while I am out in public. For example, in restaurants, I prefer to sit with something solid at my back. In the aisles of stores, I keep looking over my shoulder.

I don't care much for fireworks displays on Independence Day. I appreciate the meaning of the celebration. But I always know that I will have a few restless nights, afterward.

I can't sleep without a night light. It isn't that I'm afraid of the dark. That isn't the problem. I can go out into the woods at night. I can go into dark barns, chicken houses, sheds and spooky old deserted houses at night. I can walk along deserted roads through the countryside at night. I can load hay bales onto my truck out in a lonely hay field and then stack them in a remote barn or shed at night. It doesn't bother me to simply do things in the dark. It's just that I don't like to AWAKEN in the dark. I need to be able to immediately focus my eyes on something as soon as I am awake. Otherwise, I sometimes think I am waking up in a hostile situation or in that tunnel after being unconscious.

I have nightmares. Yes, still, 50 years later.

In one of my nightmares, I am surrounded by people who are dead. They are all skinny and ugly with pasty looking faces and they are all trying to get close to me and surround me. But I actually made peace with these people just a few years ago. One ugly old woman stood right in front of me and said, in slow and halting English, "Not to hurt you, only to help you". Then she smiled and turned away. And they all disappeared.

In another nightmare, I am lying in bed while a black-shrouded, hooded figure-Death-is sitting on my legs. (Imagine the Ghost of Christmas-Yet-to-Come who haunted Ebenezer Scrooge - that is what Death looks like). He has a "death grip" on my right wrist. I can't move. When I open my mouth and scream, no sound comes out. The figure slowly turns toward me. Just before I see his face, I awaken. I know that if he ever completely turns toward me, if I ever actually see his face, that's the moment I will die.

In yet another nightmare, I am sitting up, cowering in bed while a giant rat runs back and forth, around and around the bed. From both sides of the bed, he rears up and reaches toward me, clawing and scratching. He is so big, he could easily jump completely over the bed but, for some reason, he can't quite reach me.

After I'm dead, depending on the circumstances of my death, people might say, "Well, at least, he died peacefully in his sleep". They will be wrong. Either that rat finally reached me or I will have finally seen..... the face of Death.

I often wonder why I lived to come home at all. Call it Survivor's Guilt. On several occasions, in South Viet-Nam, if I had been walking four positions toward the rear, or perhaps five positions toward the front, I would have been sent home in a body bag. Why me? Why did I get the privilege of walking away? Was there some sort of Master Plan? Or was it simply nothing more than pure dumb luck?

These are just a token few of my thoughts and impressions about the experiences I had while serving as a Marine in South Viet-Nam. These are only a cross-section. There are many writers who are much better, more talented, more prolific than I am, who have written hundreds of books on this subject. All I can do is to assure you that all of the written materials only scratch the surface.

As for me....I will be fighting the Viet-Nam War until the day I die.

Hopefully, that will be the end of it.

The following two documents are samples of many such communications we received as a unit during the time I spent in Viet-Nam. As a junior Marine, I did not really have access to copies of these letters and citations. A few of them were placed on the bulletin board outside the Company office for very short periods of time. Most of them were simply read aloud to us while we were in formation. I simply stole copies of these two citations from the bulletin board.

Note: In the citation from the Secretary of the Navy, Song Thu Bon refers to the Thu Bon River and, in the letter from Lieutenant Colonel Ray Funderburk, the Commanding Officer of the 7th Engineer Battalion, Song Cau Lau refers to the Cau Lau River.

DEPARTMENT OF THE NAVY
Headquarters United States Marine Corps
Washington, D. C. 20380

The Secretary of the Navy takes pleasure in presenting the MERITORIOUS UNIT COMMENDATION to the

FIRST BRIDGE COMPANY (REINFORCED)
SEVENTH ENGINEER BATTALION
FIRST MARINE DIVISION (REINFORCED)

For service as set forth in the following
CITATION:

For meritorious achievement against insurgent (Viet Cong) forces in Viet-Nam from 1 January to 28 February 1968. During this period the First Bridge Company (Reinforced) constructed, removed and repaired over 80 tactical bridges in general support of the Southern I Corps Tactical Zone. The company's efforts were instrumental in keeping open the main north-south routes, critical to the tactical traffic between Danang and Hue. Throughout this period, centered on the communist Tet Offensive, the company was constantly called upon to erect and repair bridging directly under fire. In at least one instance, enemy fire was so sustained that work during safe periods was impossible. Disregarding their individual safety, resisting two ambushes and intermittent mortar and sniper fire, the men erected two fixed span bridges in the Phu Bai area from 9 January to 12 January. Called upon on several occasions to open the Hai Von Pass, the company was forced to resist ambushes, sniper and mortar fire to repair individual bridges as many as eight times. Forced to move into the pass area without mine sweep teams or adequate security, the company assumed both responsibilities and continued the mission. Unable to procure heavy equipment because of their extended area operation, ingenuity and manpower was often used to overcome difficult missions, otherwise impossible to accomplish. On 4 January, the company erected two bridges by hand in three hours, freeing a trapped 100 vehicle convoy before nightfall. Exemplary of the individual initiative inspired by the company's professional enthusiasm, a First Bridge Company ferry detachment operating on the Song Thu Bon went to the rescue of an Army riverine patrol under Viet Cong ambush, saving four of the six men. By their effective teamwork, aggressive professional attitude and individual acts of heroism and daring, the men of First Bridge Company and supporting Marine Engineer and security detachments not only achieved significant results but demonstrated outstanding qualities of courage and skill which were in keeping with the highest traditions of the Marine Corps and the United States Naval Service.

All personnel attached to and serving with First Bridge Company (Reinforced) during the above period, or any part thereof, are hereby authorized to wear the Meritorious Unit Commendation ribbon.

For the Secretary of the Navy

HEADQUARTERS
7th Engineer Battalion (Reinforced), FMF
FPO, San Francisco 96602

1/EAH/wjs
1650.2
11 May 1968

From: Commanding Officer
To: Commanding Officer, 1st Bridge Company,
7th Engineer Battalion (Rein), FMF

Subj: Letter of Commendation

Ref: (a) Commanding General,
1st Marine Division message 081049Z May 68

Reference (a) is quoted, in part, as follows:

"The officers and men of the Seventh Engineer Battalion and First Bridge Company who participated in planning and execution of the installation of about 180 feet of M-6 bridging over the Song Cau Lau on 4 and 5 May can be justly proud of their accomplishment.

Although receiving extremely short notice, working during hours of darkness and being taken under fire by insurgents, the bridge was completed and in good order. Well done to all concerned."

Comments such as these are a source of great pleasure to me. Please convey my appreciation to your men for a job "well done".

Ray Funderburk

Back to Real Life

After returning from overseas, I was reassigned to Albany, Georgia, where I was promptly promoted to the rank of Sergeant on 1 April 1969, with only 2 years, 8 months and 2 weeks in the Corps. But this time, I had arrived in Albany as a married man. I had come home from Viet-Nam in July of 1968 to marry Juanita Mae Davis, my childhood sweetheart, in Oregon, where we had stayed until my vacation was over and I had returned to Viet-Nam.

In Albany this time, I returned to the supply field, working with a civilian woman named Margaret Barrett in a two-person section, receiving, storing and issuing perishable and non-perishable subsistence to the dining facilities and commissaries on the base. So I was back to operating forklifts and keeping up with paperwork.

I had the privilege of serving simultaneously as a Platoon Sergeant, teaching individual and unit tactics and maneuvers, land navigation/map reading, rifle and pistol marksmanship, unarmed (hand to hand) combat, traits and principles of leadership and various other military skills.

Other Sergeants were eligible for assignment as Platoon Sergeant but the Platoon Commander and the Company Commander were authorized to designate whoever they wanted for this particular leadership billet. They both chose me. I was able to justify their faith in me because my platoon was always the Honor Platoon in every type of competition. I trained my platoon hard and I trained them well.

Back in those days, there was an award called Proficiency Pay for Superior Performance. It consisted of an additional $30.00 per month for six months. It wasn't offered every six months but whenever it was added to the budget and was offered, I won it, every time.

Besides the proficiency pay, there was one other reward I received for my performance of duty. The following document is a copy of a Meritorious Mast I received from Lieutenant Colonel Boles, my battalion commander.

Meritorious Mast

The Commanding Officer, Headquarters Battalion, Marine Corps Supply Center, Albany, Georgia, takes pleasure in awarding to:

Sergeant Roy Lee Morris
United States Marine Corps

a MERITORIOUS MAST for performance of duties as follows:

While serving as a Supply Administrative Clerk, Storage Section, Direct Support Stock Control Branch, Materiel Division, Marine Corps Supply Center, Albany, Georgia, during the period from 25 March 1969 to 28 April 1970, you performed your duties in a noteworthy manner.

Your professional knowledge, initiative and leadership directly contributed to the training of active duty and Reserve personnel who were either temporarily or permanently assigned to this Section. These personnel had little or no experience but, after training, were able to replace experienced personnel without any loss of effectiveness to the Section. In addition, you were highly responsible for the efficient transfer of an Issue Point from DSSC to the Center Mess Officer.

Your neatness, bearing, personal appearance and high degree of military proficiency are a credit to yourself and the United States Marine Corps. Your devotion to duty and performance of that duty, coupled with a desire for self-improvement, are highly commendable for a job 'well done'.

Jack F. Boles
Lieutenant Colonel
United States Marine Corps

In 1971, I went to Camp Lejeune on temporary additional duty orders to attend Supply Administration Course 5-71. The school lasted from 25 Feb until 30 April. This is a school that is normally attended only by Staff NCO's (Staff Sergeants and Gunnery Sergeants) but this year, the Marine Corps included quite a few Sergeants. My fellow Sergeants and I were quite pleased to have been chosen to attend because only the most highly qualified Sergeants were selected.

The class started out with 50 students but, during the course of instruction, 20 students were dropped from the class and returned to their parent commands, mostly for failure to maintain the minimum academic standards. And just think, many of those who were dropped were Staff NCO's. My class standing was 9th out of 30. That means the 30 students who actually finished the course. But considering the fact that the class started out with 50 bona fide legitimate students, I prefer to think that my class standing was 9th out of 50.

Anyway, we top ten students were separated by only three points on our grade point average. The # 1 student had a grade average of 93.55. My grade average was 91.64. A difference of 1.91 points and there were 7 students between us. You can imagine how highly competitive we were. All of the students in the top ten were Staff Sergeants and Gunnery Sergeants, except for me, the only Sergeant. I was very proud for three reasons: 1-The only people who ranked higher, academically, than I were Staff NCO's. 2-There were many Staff NCO's who ranked lower than I. 3-None of my fellow Sergeants ranked close to me. As a mere Sergeant, it was very gratifying to be able to academically compete so successfully with Staff NCO's. And they didn't like that, at all, although several of them had come to me for tutoring. Actually, I might have finished higher than 9th place, if I hadn't spent valuable study time helping them. Maybe that is just my ego talking....then again, maybe it isn't.

In the Marine Corps, enlisted personnel below the rank of Sergeant are assigned proficiency and conduct marks to reflect the quality of their service. Sergeants and above are given written performance appraisals for every six months of duty. These appraisals are called fitness reports. They all have a standardized format with blocks that can be checked off reflecting a reporting officer's opinions regarding an individual's leadership abilities, followed by a written narrative summary by the reporting officer. I was not able to obtain copies of every fitness report I ever received but I will provide a copy of every one that I do have as I work my way through this autobiography. You will also note that, although I usually had access to the reporting officer's narrative comments, I have not always had access to the reviewing officer's comments. Those are generally available only from Headquarters Marine Corps.

Fitness report for 1 March 1971 through 30 September 1971

Section C: Performance of Duty:
Regular duties:	Outstanding
Administrative duties	Excellent
Handling enlisted personnel	Excellent
Training personnel	Excellent

To what degree has he exhibited the following:
Personal appearance	Excellent
Military presence	Outstanding
Attention to duty	Outstanding
Cooperation	Outstanding
Initiative	Outstanding
Judgment	Excellent
Force	Outstanding
Leadership	Excellent
Loyalty	Outstanding
Personal relations	Outstanding
Economy of management	Excellent

Considering the possible requirements of service in war, indicate your attitude toward having this noncommissioned officer under your command:
Particularly desire to have

Indicate your estimate of this noncommissioned officer's general value to the service:
Excellent to Outstanding

Narrative comments:
 Sergeant Morris is an industrious, competent NCO who displays qualities one would expect to find in NCO's with much more time and experience in the Marine Corps. His duties require that he be fully qualified in the storage and issue of both perishable and non-perishable food products. During the recent inspection of these areas by Colonel W. H. Watson, Jr., Medical Inspector, U. S. Air Force, Command Veterinarian,

Col Watson commented highly on the meticulous care and management Sgt Morris was showing toward his area of responsibility. In view of his outstanding effectiveness, Sgt Morris was recommended for, and has been awarded, Proficiency Pay for his outstanding performance of duty. Sgt Morris' growth potential is considered to be outstanding and he does possess the prerequisites in his military occupational specialty (MOS) for advancement to the rank of Staff Sergeant.

Reporting Officer
Marvin H. Fey
Captain USMC
Head, Warehousing Unit

Fitness Report for 1 October 1971 through 11 February 1972

Section C: Performance of Duty:
Regular duties   Excellent
Administrative duties   Excellent
Handling enlisted personnel Excellent
Training personnel   Excellent

To what degree has he exhibited the following:
Personal appearance   Outstanding
Military presence   Outstanding
Attention to duty   Outstanding
Cooperation   Excellent
Initiative   Outstanding
Judgment   Excellent
Force   Excellent
Leadership   Excellent
Loyalty   Outstanding
Personal relations   Outstanding
Economy of management   Excellent

Considering the possible requirements of service in war, indicate your attitude toward having this noncommissioned officer under your command:
Particularly desire to have

Indicate your estimate of this noncommissioned officer's general value to the service:
Excellent to Outstanding

Narrative comments:
    Sergeant Morris assumes all his tasks in a highly competent and professional manner. Furthermore, he accepts responsibilities with a "can do" attitude. During this marking period, his performance of duty was of such an excellent quality that he was again recommended for, and was awarded, Proficiency Pay for a second six month period. Sgt Morris' sincere devotion to duty has not only set an example for his fellow

Marines, but also for his civilian counterparts. His growth potential is considered to be excellent and he does possess the prerequisites and skills in his MOS for advancement to the rank of Staff Sergeant.

Reporting Officer
Marvin H. Fey
Captain USMC
Head, Warehousing Unit

My fitness reports provided positive reinforcement to make me believe that I might actually be starting to get the recognition that my performance deserved. I know that sounds terribly egotistical but I am the only person who really knows how hard I worked. It takes time to do the things I did to hone the skills required by my chosen profession. There was a lot of dedication and self-discipline involved. Reading the *Guidebook for Marines* and other military literature like *The Rifle Platoon in Offense* and *Functions of the Infantry Noncommissioned Officer* was not as exciting as reading a good mystery or science fiction novel. Spending time working out in the backyard or jogging around the base took time away from quiet moments with my wife, even if we were only sitting on the couch watching television. Saying no to an extra soda pop at the movies or restraining the urge to have a second bowl of ice cream for dessert was no easy matter. But I really believed that the end result would be worth the self-sacrifice, eventually. Mentally, I wanted all the knowledge I could attain that applied to the Marine Corps lifestyle. Physically, I wanted the ability to utilize and apply that knowledge. I simply wanted to be good at my job.

I had three really great years at Albany. Supply Clerk, Platoon Sergeant, Married Man. Life was wonderful. Juanita and I didn't do a great deal of socializing - we weren't party people - but we did participate in bowling leagues. In fact, in the Albany citywide tournament, we became the mixed doubles bowling champions. Yep, we beat everybody in the tournament. Juanita bowled her first 200-plus game in that tournament.

Then I received orders transferring me to Okinawa. The duty status of my orders did not allow my wife to accompany me so she decided to remain in our mobile home where we had been living in a trailer park just a mile or so out the back gate of the base.

When I got to Okinawa, I was assigned to the Base Supply Department as a supply clerk, controlling blank forms and data processing supplies, so that part of my assignment was routine and non-challenging because there was nothing about the supply field that I didn't know. My supervisor was Captain Richard Abraham, the stock control officer in the Direct Support Stock Control (DSSC) Section. The Officer in Charge of DSSC was Major Bobby D. Chambless.

However, I also had extensive knowledge of the infantry field and my reputation as a leader had apparently preceded me so I was again assigned as a Platoon Sergeant. I really enjoyed doing that sort of thing. In my opinion, that was how a Marine Corps Sergeant was supposed to be spending his time.

In this assignment, I received my first recommendation for promotion to Warrant Officer. The recommendation was drafted by Major Chambless and signed by Lieutenant Colonel Beard, the Base Supply Officer, and it would be forwarded through the chain of command to the Warrant Officer Selection Board. The following document is a copy of that recommendation:

UNITED STATES MARINE CORPS
Marine Corps Base
Camp Smedley D. Butler, Okinawa
FPO Seattle, Washington 98773

21/BDC/we
1040
29 March 1972

From: Base Supply Officer
To: Commanding Officer, Company A,
Headquarters and Service Battalion

Subj: FY73 Warrant Officer Program; case of Sergeant Roy L. Morris USMC

Ref: (a) MCO 1040.14C
(b) MCBul 1040 of 18 Feb 72

In accordance with references (a) and (b), the following recommendation is submitted for your use in preparing the endorsement on the subject case.

Sgt Morris joined this command on 8 March 1972 and has already made a most favorable impression as a sincere hardworking NCO. He was assigned as the commodity manager for blank forms for all USMC units in WESTPAC. On his own initiative, he devoted many hours of work after normal hours and has gained a significant level of understanding of his specific tasks as they relate to the overall supply operation. He has displayed a keen awareness of the exacting details necessary to make an automated system function as designed. He tackled his job with enthusiasm and has impressed all members of his section with his ability to grasp the intricacies of a new assignment. He has displayed a high level of sincerity and devotion to duty. In view of his progress to date, based on one month's observation, it is believed that Sgt Morris will produce effectively in any assigned task and that he has sufficient growth potential to merit consideration in the Warrant Officer selection program.

Accordingly, Sgt Morris is recommended with enthusiasm for selection as Warrant Officer, MOS 3202.

DAVID J. BEARD

Roy Morris

Fitness Report for 12 February 1972 through 31 March 1972

Section C: Performance of Duty:
Regular duties	Outstanding
Handling enlisted personnel	Excellent
Training personnel	Outstanding

To what degree has he exhibited the following:
Personal appearance	Outstanding
Military presence	Outstanding
Attention to duty	Outstanding
Cooperation	Outstanding
Initiative	Outstanding
Judgment	Excellent
Force	Excellent
Leadership	Excellent
Loyalty	Outstanding
Personal relations	Excellent
Economy of management	Excellent

Considering the possible requirements of service in war, indicate your attitude toward having this noncommissioned officer under your command:
Particularly desire to have

Indicate your estimate of this noncommissioned officer's general value to the service:
Excellent to Outstanding

Narrative comments:
 Immediately upon joining the Direct Support Stock Control office, Sgt Morris was given a brief orientation into DSSC procedures at Camp Foster and assigned as a commodity group manager. Personnel shortages at the time dictated that he replace a commodity manager who was departing that same week. The group, FSNs 00-09, includes all blank forms for which DSSC has a mission to support all Marine units in WestPac. This group was recognized, at the time, to be in an extremely

poor state. Sgt Morris has made an extraordinary effort to improve the situation. To date, he has demonstrated an uncommon initiative and willingness to sacrifice personal time for supply matters. On occasion, he has even been directed not to spend as much time as he does in the office. The commodity group itself reflects his efforts. Excesses have been largely disposed of and items 'not in stock' has been cut by fifty percent. Through continued research and reading, Sgt Morris has become an expert in the area of blank forms. Customer satisfaction has dramatically increased and numerous favorable comments made concerning Sgt Morris' work. Sgt Morris' personal conduct and appearance are impeccable and he has provided an excellent model to his contemporaries, especially the new Marines on their first assignment in the Marine Corps and those considering reenlistment. He is the most impressive NCO of his age and experience I have met to date. The delay in submitting this fitness report was an administrative error on my part.

Reporting Officer
Richard L. Abraham
Captain USMC
Stock Control Officer
Direct Support Stock Control

Giving freely of my spare time to improve the condition of the stock accounts I had inherited and to fulfill my responsibilities at the office did not really constitute self-sacrifice and was not a burden, even though Captain Abraham couldn't understand why I didn't mind putting in the overtime. Even so, none of my (otherwise) free time was spent at the enlisted club or at the base movie theater and I didn't waste my time playing cards or wandering around off-base in the towns and villages of Okinawa.

When I had been on Okinawa as a PFC and Lance Corporal, I had taken up martial arts training in my off-duty hours so, since I was back on Okinawa as a Sergeant, I got back into a karate class. My style was Shorin-Ryu Karate. While competing as a Brown Belt, I won my division of a Karate Tournament which was staged at the Kadena Air Force Base. Later, during the same tournament, I tested for and won my Black Belt.

I did a lot of jogging, weight training and working out at the gym. And of course, I trained with my platoon. We distinguished ourselves quite often, winning competitions in platoon drill, tactical maneuvers and physical training. I read a lot and wrote a lot of letters to my sweet wife, Juanita. I stayed busy. That helped me keep my loneliness under control. I didn't allow myself to have slack time. Time spent doing nothing was time wasted, in my opinion.

But at least, my efforts were not in vain. My hard work in all areas resulted in a letter of commendation, which is reproduced as follows:

UNITED STATES MARINE CORPS
Marine Corps Base
Camp Smedley D. Butler, Okinawa
FPO Seattle, Washington 98773

21/BDC/jt
1400
10 October 1972

From: Officer in Charge, Direct Support Stock Control Branch
To: Commanding Officer, Headquarters and Service Battalion, Camp Smedley D. Butler

Subj: Letter of Commendation; case of Sergeant Roy L. Morris

During the period 8 March 1972 to present, Sergeant Morris performed his duties as Non-Commissioned Officer in Charge (NCOIC) of the Receipts Section and additionally as the Commodity Manager of approximately 1300 line items of supply in a highly professional and commendable manner. His responsibilities include management of Blank Forms and DPI (Data Processing) Consumables and providing these commodities for all Marine units in WESTPAC.

Sergeant Morris has continually displayed exceptional ability and dedication in ensuring the accomplishment of his tasks. His technical knowledge and tireless effort enabled him to identify and correct numerous accounting errors. In addition, his responsible supervision of civilian and military subordinates assisted in reorganizing and perfecting many procedures within the Stock Management Section. Such significant improvements could not have been accomplished without his willing and ceaseless effort.

His appearance, at all times, is impeccable. His physical inventory rating of Class V is the highest rating attainable. At marksmanship requalification during this period, he attained a score of 232 out of a possible 250, which qualifies him as High Expert.

His overall performance is representative of the professionalism the Marine Corps seeks in its Noncommissioned Officers and has served to bring credit upon himself and has upheld the highest traditions of the Marine Corps and the United States Naval Service.

B. D. Chambless
Major USMC

Christmas 1972

This unaccompanied tour of duty on Okinawa had begun in February 1972 and would not end until March 1973. To combat loneliness, I had thrown myself into my work so wholeheartedly I earned my first recommendation for promotion to Warrant Officer, an outstanding fitness report and a Letter of Commendation. While off-duty, I did a lot of weight training, jogged at least thirty miles a week (regardless of the weather), did some snorkeling, went a few rounds in the boxing ring and practiced karate with the local instructors. And through it all, through every moment of it, I missed my beloved wife, Juanita, so terribly much. Of course, we corresponded often but by December, I was desperate to hear her voice so I had made extensive plans to make a phone call to her on Christmas Day.

First of all, you have to understand that it was over 44 years ago. There were no personal computers, no internet and no email. We could not just turn on a laptop and converse through cyberspace while staring into each others' eyes on the screen. There were no communications satellites to support a worldwide cellular phone network. Actually, there were no cell phones.

What I had to do was get special permission from my OIC (Officer in Charge) to spend at least a 24-hour period, during the holiday, in the office where we worked in order to make the call. First, I had to place a call to the MARS station on Okinawa to get on the waiting list. MARS stood for Military Affiliated Radio Stations. When my turn came up, the MARS operator would establish shortwave communication with a ham radio operator on the west coast of the United States, who would place a landline collect call to Juanita in Albany, Georgia. Then we would be able to talk via this linkup. Of course, after each sentence, we would have to say "over" so the various operators would know when to flip the appropriate switches from incoming voice communication to outgoing voice communication. It wasn't going to be easy but it would be well worth the effort. At least, it would be for ME. I had written to Juanita and had explained the entire process, in detail, so she would know what to expect and how to respond when our turn came up.

Christmas Day was on a Monday in 1972. Because of the many various time zones and the International Date Line, there was a 15-hour time difference between Georgia and Okinawa. For example, 8:00 am in Georgia on Christmas morning (Monday) would already be 11:00 pm on Christmas night (Monday) on Okinawa. I was told that there could be as much as a 24-hour waiting period for me from the time of my first call to the MARS station.

I was determined to make that call. I HAD to make that call. I was totally committed. After so many months of being alone, just hearing her voice would be almost as good as touching her. I went to the office at 11:00 am on the morning of Christmas Eve (Sunday). I took a few snacks and sandwiches with me. There was a soda machine just down the hall from the office. I was prepared. I called the MARS station and got on the waiting list. There was nothing left to do except wait.

Once my vigil began, there was no way I was going to leave that office. I couldn't take the chance of going back to the barracks or to the mess hall. Even when I went to the bathroom, I propped the door open so I could hear the phone. I stayed in the office from 11:00 am on Sunday and on through Sunday night. Monday morning came and went. Christmas Day had arrived on Okinawa. I waited all Christmas day in that office. Every two or three hours, I checked in with the MARS operator to make sure I was still on the list. I waited some more.

It was just a couple of minutes before midnight when the phone rang. From the phone in my work office to the MARS station operator on Okinawa to a ham radio operator on Hawaii to a ham radio operator in California to the phone at home in Georgia, the call was going through. Our turn had finally arrived.

For Juanita, it would be about 9:00 am on Christmas morning (Monday). The phone at home was answered by a friend of ours, Linda Paul, the mother of our honorary godson. Juanita was not there. She had gone to a convenience store that was open so she could pick up something that Linda wanted for our godson.

I knew that Juanita had stocked up on household items for the Christmas period so there should not have been any regular items lacking in her pantry or refrigerator. I don't know what Linda might have wanted but Juanita should have said, "No, I don't want to leave the house today. I'm expecting a call from Roy. He's been gone since

February and we just want to hear each other's voice". But she didn't say that. She put someone else ahead of me. True, she was gone for only a few minutes but cruel fate chose those few minutes for my call to go through.

Do you understand? There was no fire, or earthquake, or tornado or any kind of emergency that made it necessary for her to leave the house. But she CHOSE to leave even though it would have been obvious that the timing for my call could be coming up at any moment.

We were only going to be allowed 3 minutes for our conversation so there was no point in trying to stay on the line until she might return. There was nothing I could do so I hung up the phone. I had been awake for two days. I would have to be at work in just a few hours on Tuesday morning. I had spent 37 hours in that office, waiting to hear the voice of the woman I loved, even though it would be for just a couple of minutes. And she had chosen that specific few minutes to be unavailable. I was exhausted. I was heartsick. I sank into the very depths of despair. I had never felt so terribly alone.

Juanita has always been the sweetest, kindest and most caring person I have ever known. Nobody could ask for a better friend. That has always been - and will always be - my opinion. But it truly broke my heart to know that she didn't wait for that call with the same eager anticipation and determination that I had so when I think of that particular Christmas, the same sense of utter desolation comes over me so intensely that I cry. How could the most wonderful woman in the world have done something that seemed to be so callous?

Fitness Report for 31 September 1972 through 2 March 1973

Section C: Performance of duty:
Regular duties   Outstanding
Additional duties   Excellent
Administrative duties   Excellent
Handling enlisted personnel Excellent
Training personnel   Outstanding

To what degree has he exhibited the following:
Personal appearance   Excellent
Military presence   Excellent
Attention to duty   Outstanding
Cooperation   Excellent
Initiative   Outstanding
Judgment   Outstanding
Force   Excellent
Leadership   Excellent
Loyalty   Outstanding
Personal relations   Outstanding
Economy of management Excellent
Growth potential   Outstanding

Your estimate of this Marine's general value to the service:
Outstanding

Considering the requirements of service in war, indicate your attitude toward having this Marine under your command:
Particularly desire to have

Narrative comments:
    Sgt Morris completes his tour with Direct Support Stock Control, having served in a variety of duties, all of which he accomplished in an outstanding manner. His prime responsibility within the Stock Control Section has been the management of blank forms and data processing consumables, and the support of all Marine units in the Western Pacific area with these commodities. In the accomplishment of this mission, Sgt Morris has continually displayed exceptional ability and dedication. His technical knowledge is excellent and his application

of this knowledge is superior. He has tirelessly strived to increase his own effectiveness as an item manager and the records he maintains are consistently superior to those maintained by his peers. Sgt Morris, at all times, presents a highly professional image. His excellence extends to all areas of NCO leadership. His appearance, as well as his military bearing, is impeccable. He is extremely well-spoken and able to converse on any subject with ease, especially events that most affect the individual Marine. He enjoys excellent relationships, at the office and on liberty, with all Marines. He especially prides himself on his military skills and, in my opinion could, at any time, successfully serve in an infantry billet and perform as well as any individual already holding that MOS. I have marked Sgt Morris outstanding in 13A (Regular Duties) and 15 A (Estimate of this Marine's general value to the service) for the reasons stated above and because he is the finest NCO of his rank I have observed during my tour of duty at DSSC.

Reporting Officer
Richard L. Abraham
Captain USMC
Stock Control Officer
Direct Support Stock Control

Statement of Reviewing Officer:
Although dated on 29 March 1973, the reporting officer did not make this report available for my review until my return from leave on 5 April 1973; accordingly, the review has been delayed. This report was prepared several times before I found it administratively acceptable for submission. Sgt Morris is a fine example of dedication, loyalty and concern for his job and toward the basics and technicalities of the Marine Corps. There is no doubt that Sgt Morris would be a success in any MOS field because he works hard at learning all details of his job. The outstanding marks in performance of duties and general value to the service are concurred with.

Reviewing Officer
Bobby D. Chambless
Major USMC
Officer in Charge
Direct Support Stock Control

The preceding fitness report was very gratifying but, in all honesty, it could not have been otherwise. As usual, I had committed myself so completely to accomplishing my assigned duties that the successful completion of those duties was a foregone conclusion. My motivation, my drive, my NEED to excel is an inherited trait (sort of). My older brother, E. Ray, and my sister, Shirley had always been utterly successful in every one of their endeavors, regardless of the difficulty of their chosen tasks. Little brother Roy was just trying to keep up. Plus, I had the added incentive of a wonderful wife to provide for. Juanita had quickly and easily become the light of my life and the reason for my continued existence. Each and every success in my chosen field would translate to a better and more secure future for us as a couple, as a team.

So, I came home from Okinawa. After getting reacquainted as husband and wife, we spent a little time visiting with our families. Then we proceeded to Marine Corps Recruit Depot, Parris Island, South Carolina, which was my newly assigned post.

Immediately on arrival, I was assigned as an item manager in the Direct Support Stock Control Branch. Then, on 1 May 1973, I was promoted to Staff Sergeant. I had spent four years as a Sergeant but, even so, my promotion came through faster than did most of the promotions for my contemporaries. Military commitments in Viet-Nam had been winding down and the ranks had been glutted with NCO's and it took a little time for the Corps to separate the "chaff" from the "wheat".

My return from overseas assignment re-qualified me for an award of Proficiency Pay for Superior Performance. As I had at my previous commands, I easily won that award, naturally. Sure, I know that sounds like my ego talking but the fact remains that my performance WAS superior. I had been blessed, at birth, with a reasonably sound mind and a fairly healthy body and I put forth a lot of effort at developing both to the utmost of my ability. Being born lucky is one thing. Staying lucky is another thing, altogether, and it takes a lot of hard work.

My first fitness report as a Staff Sergeant was a typical one for a newly-arrived and newly-promoted Marine and it covered only two months and two weeks, so there were a lot of grade categories that were pronounced "not observed" simply because my reporting senior did not have daily contact with me. But I am willing to present it, as it was prepared.

Fitness Report for 16 May 1973 through 31 July 1973

Section C: Performance of duty:
Regular duties   Excellent
Administrative duties   Excellent

To what degree has he exhibited the following:
Personal appearance   Above Average
Military presence   Excellent
Attention to duty   Excellent
Cooperation   Excellent
Initiative   Excellent
Judgment   Excellent
Force   Excellent
Loyalty   Excellent
Personal relations   Excellent
Economy of management   Excellent
Growth potential   Excellent

Your estimate of this Marine's general value to the service:
Excellent

Considering the requirements of service in war, indicate your attitude toward having this Marine under your command:
Particularly desire to have

Narrative comments:
    S/Sgt Morris is a newly promoted Staff NCO but is already demonstrating excellent supply knowledge and versatility. He adapts quickly to changing requirements and thinks clearly. His judgment to arrive at sound conclusions forced by changing support situations is always reliable. He is a graduate of Human Relations School and applies the principles in his daily endeavors. He possesses a high degree of initiative and requires a minimum of supervision to get a job done.

Reporting Officer
James M. Reardon
Major USMC
Assistant Depot Supply Officer

Statement of Reviewing Officer

S/Sgt Morris has been both a subsistence and general supply item manager in the DSSC. He is highly qualified in mechanized supply accounting procedures and is an asset to this department. His promotion was well deserved and he shows much promise in assignments of increased responsibility.

Reviewing Officer
J. L. Altman
Lieutenant Colonel USMC
Depot Supply Officer
Marine Corps Recruit Depot
Parris Island, South Carolina

Women Marines' Clothing Outlet

The promotion from Sergeant to Staff Sergeant was like the difference between light and dark. No longer a junior NCO, I had suddenly become a Staff NCO so it was decided that I would be the perfect replacement for a Staff Sergeant who was being "relieved for cause". The female Staff Sergeant who had been serving as Noncommissioned Officer in Charge of the Women's Clothing Outlet had been performing very poorly in her assigned duties and she was being transferred out.

All Women Marine enlisted recruits take their version of recruit training at Parris Island and, upon successful completion of boot camp, receive their initial issue of military clothing from the Women's Clothing Outlet. Additionally, all Women Marine officers, upon successful completion of Officer Candidate School at Quantico, Virginia, buy their initial issue from the Women's Clothing Outlet. Finally, Women Marines at posts and stations all over the world buy their replacement military clothing through mail order service from the Women's Clothing Outlet at Parris Island.

Obviously, I was inheriting a high-profile assignment and a lot of high-ranking people would be observing the results of my efforts. And this was my first job as a Staff NCO, so success or failure would determine the nature of my future in the Corps. I was determined that this would be a solid stepping stone upward and, in my opinion, success was guaranteed.

The Officer in Charge of the Women's Clothing Outlet was 2nd Lieutenant Jo Anne Johnson, new to the Corps and serving in her first job assignment. She definitely needed a good, knowledgeable, highly capable Staff NCO as her second-in-command. Luckily, she got me.

I was forced to endure the presence of the outgoing Staff NCOIC for three days and she gave me many pages of notes she had compiled on the performance and qualifications of all of the Marines who worked at the Outlet. Finally, to the relief of everyone concerned, she shipped out.

My first day as NCOIC of the Women's Clothing Outlet was a notable occasion, a memorable event, a "Famous First". All of the

Marines assigned to the Outlet were women. I was the very first male assigned as the NCOIC. Not even Lt Johnson knew what they might expect of me and everybody was quite apprehensive. They all knew that the former NCOIC had been filling me in on the faults and mistakes of all assigned personnel. She had been "bad-mouthing" everybody.

I picked an hour when we didn't have recruits in the warehouse/fitting/sizing area and called everyone together. I even asked the Lieutenant to sit in. My speech went something like this.

I said, "Ladies, I am now officially the NCOIC of this unit. I have spent the last three days being briefed on my new duties by your former boss. She has also described, in detail, the many problems she has had in her dealings with each and every one of you. In fact, she has given me an entire pamphlet of notes describing all of the difficulties you have all caused".

At this point, all of their faces reflected sadness and despair because they figured I was going to be nothing more than a continuation of the situation that had existed under their former NCOIC. The tension in the room was so thick you could have cut it with a knife. I held up the notes she had left with me and said, "These are her opinions of all of you". Then I said, "This is my opinion of her opinions", while tearing the pages into small pieces and dropping them into a wastebasket. The looks on their faces turned to surprise, to shock, and then to relief and delight. I would not normally do or say anything to belittle a fellow Staff NCO in front of junior Marines but there were obviously major problems at the Women's Clothing Outlet and the situation called for drastic action. I did what had to be done.

I told them, "Each and every one of you starts fresh, today. I will form my own opinion of you based only on your performance and your conduct from this moment forward. You and I will have different ideas and opinions regarding procedures and policies but we will try to settle our differences in a calm and professional manner. If you convince me that I am wrong in any regard, then I will make the appropriate correction. But even if you can't convince me, I will not hold a grudge against you for having tried. Now, if there are no questions, let's get to work".

There is absolutely nothing else I could have done that would have better ensured that I would be starting off on the right foot with my new work crew. From that moment on, there was a new and better attitude evident at the Outlet. It was like a completely different bunch of people had come in and started working there. Even Lt Johnson was visibly relieved - and pleased. As this was her first position of authority in the Marine Corps (and she had not been at the Outlet very long before I arrived), she didn't really have a clue as to how to lead and motivate the Marines under her authority, and she had apparently been unable to rein in the former NCOIC, who was a forceful but ultimately ineffectual Staff NCO who tried to lead by the authoritarian method rather than by example.

I worried about the first fitness report that I would eventually receive from Lt Johnson because she obviously would not really know how to write one, even if she tried to make it a favorable one. But I knew that, with Major Reardon as the reviewing officer, he could offset any inadvertent damage she might do as a result of her inexperience.

One problem with the day-to-day operation of the Outlet was that there was no formal training for incoming replacement personnel. When a new Woman Marine was assigned to the Outlet, a decision was made regarding who she would be the eventual replacement for and she worked with that person until it was decided she had learned enough. I wanted to abolish that method of assignment. I knew that different people have different skills and those skills may not necessarily coincide with their newly-assigned jobs. I decided to work personally with each regular worker until I had fully learned every aspect of her job, even the parts of her job that she did not know. Then I would write up a job description for that particular job. When I got done, there would be a complete set of written instructions covering every contingency for each and every assignment at the Outlet. If a brand new replacement could read, she could easily step into any job. Cross-training would be much easier. I wanted everyone to know how to do everyone else's job. The final result: A workplace that would be a marvel of modern efficiency.

But it would take time. And it was a "hands on" process, even though that may not be a good descriptive phrase to use to describe how a male Staff NCO would be working with junior female enlisted Marines. Be that as it may, there were times when I had to do a task myself rather than allow it to be done by someone who was not yet trained sufficiently to handle it. In my opinion, the most important thing was that the mission of the Women's Clothing Outlet would be accomplished and I would eventually be able to relax and concentrate on the responsibilities that were actually part of my assignment as NCOIC. Because after all, the best boss is a boss who has his or her team trained so thoroughly that it can function quite well whether he or she is there or not.

The problems of being the male NCOIC of an all female section were interesting and unique. I was obviously unable to assist them in the process of fitting and sizing the female recruits, although I was required, from time to time, to enter the warehouse area while some of the recruits were rather scantily dressed. But I conducted myself in such a manner that none of them ever had any reason to complain and nobody ever filed charges against me for inappropriate speech or actions. That, alone, was a major military coup, in my opinion, because some of those recruits were absolutely gorgeous and had fantastic bodies.

One of the first tests of my leadership skills regarding the Women Marines assigned to the Outlet involved PFC Debra S. Ten Hagen. One of her many duties was serving as the Primary Cash Collection Agent. She was responsible for all cash, checks and money orders for clothing sold locally and through mail orders. The daily totals could run into hundreds of dollars and she was required to be exactly correct, to the penny. But, seriously, nobody can be that perfect.

One of my duties was to verify the on-hand value of accountable funds, as compared to the register record. For several days, she was absolutely correct but one day, her total was short by several dollars and she was terrified of what I might do about it because of the way she had been treated by the former NCOIC. But we went over her records together, trying to figure out where she could have gone wrong. There were no mistakes in the actual paperwork, so I decided that she may have made a mistake while making change for one (or more) of the customers. Maybe she mixed a five in with the ones, or some such thing.

She looked heartbroken and was apparently prepared for the worst but I took pity on her. I took money out of my own pocket and made up the difference. She was totally shocked. Then I said, "Now, look, we can't do this every time but this is your first discrepancy since I started here and there's no reason to make a disciplinary case out of it.

I believe you sincerely did your best and sometimes a person's best is good enough and sometimes it isn't, so let's just get over it and move on, okay?"

I made her promise not to discuss the situation with her fellow Marines because we both might get into trouble for falsifying a financial report but it was obvious, by the look on her face, that I had become her hero.

Luckily, she turned out to be well worth the effort. Her professionalism, her performance and her conduct were absolutely top notch. She was recommended for meritorious promotion to Lance Corporal and was later recommended for meritorious promotion to Corporal. I personally drafted both letters of recommendation for Lt Johnson's signature.

Another notable worker at the Outlet was PFC D. L. Strausbaugh, who was assigned as the alterations clerk, document clerk and alternate cash collection agent. She was an exceptional Woman Marine who was recommended for meritorious promotion to Lance Corporal before she got transferred. I drafted the letter of recommendation for her, too.

Ten Hagen and Strausbaugh were both also recommended to receive Proficiency Pay for Superior Performance. I drafted those letters of recommendation, also.

But there were other exceptional Women Marines working at the Outlet, too, and their efforts were starting to be recognized and rewarded. All any of them needed was a supervisor who was willing to give them a chance to learn and to develop their individual skills. And I never had a disciplinary problem with any of them during my entire time at the Women's Clothing Outlet. They were good people but they had been poorly led before I arrived.

The following document is my first fitness report from Lt Johnson. Since Major Reardon had taken care of the fitness report for the departing 'relieved for cause' former NCOIC, mine was the first actual fitness report Lt Johnson had ever written. Scary thought.

Fitness Report for 1 August 1973 through 31 January 1974

Section C: Performance of Duty:
Regular duties   Excellent
Administrative duties   Excellent
Handling enlisted personnel Outstanding
Training personnel   Excellent

To what degree has he exhibited the following:
Personal appearance   Excellent
Military presence   Excellent
Attention to duty   Excellent
Cooperation   Outstanding
Initiative   Excellent
Judgment   Excellent
Force   Excellent
Leadership   Excellent
Loyalty   Outstanding
Personal relations   Excellent
Economy of management   Excellent
Growth potential   Excellent

Your estimate of this Marine's general value to the service:
Excellent

Considering the requirements of service in war, indicate your attitude toward having this Marine under your command:
Particularly desire to have

Narrative Comments:
    S/Sgt Morris is conscientious, devoted and very hard working. As NCOIC of the Women's Clothing Outlet, he is serving in the capacity of a Gunnery Sergeant. He perhaps devotes too much attention to detail and carries too much of the load himself when it could be delegated to someone else but he gets the job done by willingly working long hours. His loyalty, concern and understanding manner toward his subordinates has captured their complete loyalty and willingness to exert their highest

efforts. His personality and personal characteristics are highly desirable and he maintains this personable manner even under adverse conditions. His work provides results, if not always quickly, at least correctly. S/Sgt Morris, by example and persuasion, is an excellent asset to his work section.

Reporting Officer
Jo Anne Johnson
Second Lieutenant USMCR
Officer in Charge
Women's Clothing Outlet

Statement of Reviewing Officer
I do not consider any of the remarks in section C as derogatory. However, I have shown the report to S/Sgt Morris to discuss his supervisory shortcoming. His main problem at the Women's Clothing Outlet was that it was staffed with all NEW low-ranking personnel (including the Officer in Charge) so he performed many duties himself, rather than delegate the jobs (which would require several extensive training sessions). This Staff NCO is highly competent and conscientious. The branch which he is NCOIC of has made strong progress since his assignment there. He is a "hard charger" and can be depended on to get a job done with minimum supervision. He should be considered for Drill Instructor duty upon completion of his current tour of duty.

Reviewing Officer
James M. Reardon
Major USMC
Assistant Depot Supply Officer
Marine Corps Recruit Depot
Parris Island, South Carolina

Working conditions at the Women's Clothing Outlet improved steadily during 1974. A lot of Women Marines came and went. For many, their assignment at the Outlet was their first tour of duty following recruit training. They all agreed that it looked like a very different place than it had appeared to be when they were going through being fitted for uniforms. It was amazing how easily and how quickly the new arrivals blended in with the "old hands". And they were all extremely pleased to be able to start working at jobs that had written instructions covering every aspect of their new assignment. So my original plan of preparing "job descriptions" was starting to pay off and was proving to be well worth the effort I had put into it.

Throughout my assignment, my wife, Juanita, had always been a welcome visitor in the office at the Outlet and she had quickly got a job working for the civilian company that had the contract for doing the alterations of the uniforms issued to the recruits. Juanita had always been a very good seamstress and was a 'natural' as an alterations worker.

All of the girls who worked at the Outlet were welcomed into our home, too. We lived in a mobile home at Argonne Trailer Park on Parris Island, only about two miles from the Outlet. Under other circumstances, this would have been frowned upon by higher authority, who might have considered it to be fraternization. But it was Juanita who invited them out for week-end cookouts and marathon monopoly games. Any of them who could not go home for the holidays crashed at our place on Thanksgiving and Christmas. But they were very understanding and they never took advantage of the situation. Visiting was one thing and work was something else.

Roy Morris

Fitness Report for 1 February 1974 through 31 July 1974

Section C: Performance of Duty:
Regular duties	Outstanding
Administrative duties	Excellent
Training personnel	Excellent

To what degree has he exhibited the following:
Personal appearance	Excellent
Military presence	Outstanding
Attention to duty	Outstanding
Cooperation	Outstanding
Initiative	Outstanding
Judgment	Excellent
Force	Excellent
Leadership	Outstanding
Loyalty	Outstanding
Personal relations	Outstanding
Economy of management	Excellent
Growth potential	Excellent

Your estimate of this Marine's general value to the service:
Excellent to Outstanding

Considering the requirements of service in war, indicate your attitude toward having this Marine under your command:
Particularly desire to have

Narrative comments:
    S/Sgt Morris has been assigned to the Women's Clothing Outlet for one year. During this time, his devotion, initiative and ingenuity have combined to produce an effective administration. As a male Staff NCO, S/Sgt Morris has been placed in a rather unique leadership situation. His entire work section consists of Women Marines. This often presents unusual leadership problems, all of which are handled diplomatically and professionally by S/Sgt Morris. He is an excellent influence by example and persuasion. S/Sgt Morris presents a neat, military appearance and

is cognizant of regulations pertaining to his troops, and ensures their enforcement. S/Sgt Morris is an asset to the human relations program.

Reporting Officer
Jo Anne Johnson
Second Lieutenant USMCR
Officer in Charge
Women's Clothing Outlet

2nd Lt Johnson had become much better at her job as OIC. She was starting to get the hang of survival in the Corps. Another change she made during the last half of 1974 was getting married to Chief Warrant Officer Murdock (a really good guy) so she was now 2nd Lt Murdock. I think he had been teaching her some of the finer points of how officers and Staff NCO's could work together for the betterment of their work sections.

I started feeling much better about my working relationship with the Lieutenant. We had long since evolved into a solid team that could effectively and efficiently handle any leadership problem that might arise. Situations that involved our unit were handled by whichever one of us was best fitted to bring the problem to a proper and successful conclusion.

It was interesting to watch her develop into an officer who would be properly equipped with the knowledge, expertise and experience that would help her succeed in any future assignment. It was also gratifying to watch because I knew that I had been instrumental in her development.

I knew that every other male Staff NCO she would ever meet would be compared to me and that at least some of them might not measure up to what she would think they should be. I hoped there would not be so many of that type that her faith in Staff NCO's would be shaken.

My time at Parris Island was unique, not only because it was there that I had been promoted to the Staff NCO ranks, but also because I was not automatically selected to shoulder the additional responsibilities of a Platoon Sergeant. Major Reardon may have had a hand in that decision. I was already in a key position of authority, in a high profile assignment in which I would quickly come to the attention of the entire chain of command aboard the base in the event of a problem between myself and any of the Women Marines and he didn't want anything to distract me from the successful accomplishment of my duties and responsibilities at the Women's Clothing Outlet. Especially since the former (female) NCOIC had failed so miserably in that assignment. All things considered, it was probably an act of kindness.

However, I knew several of the male Drill Instructors and one of the Close Combat Instructors assigned to the male Recruit Training Regiment so, from time to time, I assisted in a few martial arts demonstrations where I served as an evil enemy soldier so the instructor could teach the recruits the preferred methods of neutralizing an opponent in the quickest, most efficient manner, regardless of his armament. In other words, I was a sacrificial 'crash dummy'.

Finally, the time came for me to leave the Women's Clothing Outlet. The main reason for this was that the buildings that housed the Women Recruit Training Regiment were being fully renovated. Many were being totally rebuilt. The Women's Clothing Outlet would no longer be a separate building and the setup of the warehouse/fitting/sizing area would be drastically changed. The office area would be situated in such a manner that it would be impossible for a male to be anywhere in the area without compromising the dignity and decorum of the female recruits.

During all of my dealings with the various administrative sections in the chain of command, I had always listed Albany, Georgia as my first preference as my next duty station. So I was not surprised to learn that I was being transferred to the Marine Corps Supply Activity, Philadelphia, Pennsylvania. (The Marine Corps often sends an individual in the opposite direction from where he would prefer to go-the needs of the Corps always hold top priority)

During January 1975, Juanita and I got an apartment in Blackwood, New Jersey from which I would carpool to work in downtown Philadelphia. Juanita got a job with the David Stevens Manufacturing Company as a seamstress in Blackwood.

The Supply Activity covered most of a city block on South Broad Street just a few blocks from the city center (also just a few blocks from where the Liberty Bell was positioned). I was assigned as a combat readiness evaluator for motor transport vehicles and equipment on a worldwide basis. I arranged for the transfer of major components and repair parts as necessary to remove vehicles from deadline status. I interpreted reports from all commands and reviewed available assets to determine their distribution.

In other words, I spent most of my time on the phone talking to motor transport maintenance officers all over the world, trying to figure out how I could help them get the machinery, raw materials, technical support and repair parts they needed to fix their broken vehicles.

New Jersey was a beautiful place to live and Philadelphia was an exciting, wonderful place to work but the winters were absolute torture for a southern farm boy like me. I was never able to comprehend why anybody would willingly live that far north. I'm sorry, I apologize to anybody who might have been born and raised there - and I suppose they would be equally miserable at my home in Arkansas - but it just was not good for me.

However, I was determined to continue my personal training regimen so, every workday at lunchtime, I would either work out in the basement gymnasium/weight room at the Supply Activity or I would go jogging through the beautiful city of Philadelphia. It wasn't easy working my way through the traffic so whenever I got caught by a street light, I developed the habit of dropping to the pavement and doing alternating one-arm pushups until the light turned green, then I would spring to my feet, flex, growl and take off running again. I ran through dozens of parks, jumped a lot of park benches and even a few fountains and I occasionally ran across the Ben Franklin Bridge into New Jersey and back.

When Sylvester Stallone started making the *Rocky Balboa* movies, I considered asking for royalties because he stole his training routine from me. He did the SAME things I had done when I was training on the streets of Philly. I had even run up those famous steps and did a little dancing and shadow boxing at the top, just like he did in the movies - but I did it all first. But I never went into a meat packing plant and punched the beef carcasses until the ribs were broken.

Anyway, I could have been rich and famous.

Fitness Report for 1 February 1975 through 31 July 1975

Section C: Performance of duty:
Regular duties   Excellent
Administrative duties   Excellent
Handling enlisted personnel Excellent

To what degree has he exhibited the following:
Personal appearance   Excellent
Military presence   Outstanding
Attention to duty   Outstanding
Cooperation   Outstanding
Initiative   Outstanding
Judgment   Excellent
Force   Excellent
Leadership   Excellent
Loyalty   Outstanding
Personal relations   Outstanding
Economy of management   Excellent
Growth potential   Excellent

Your estimate of this Marine's general value to the service:
Excellent to Outstanding

Considering the requirements of service in war, indicate your attitude toward having this Marine under your command:
Particularly desire to have

Narrative comments:
    S/Sgt Morris is alert, forceful, well groomed and has a pleasant personality. Calm and confident in manner, he is quite adept at dealing with personnel both in and out of the command. Highly motivated and interested in his work, he willingly accepts increased responsibility. S/Sgt Morris can be depended upon to put forth his best effort in any assignment and furnish the results on a timely basis. S/Sgt Morris is very effectively filling a Gunnery Sergeant's billet. He is well qualified

for promotion to the next higher grade. In the area of human relations, he works in total harmony with members of other races and creeds.

Reporting Officer
William D. Smith
Lieutenant Colonel USMC
Head, Readiness Office
Supply Operations Division

Staff NCO Academy

From 3 November 1975 through 17 December 1975, I was on temporary additional duty at the Staff Non-Commissioned Officers' Academy at Quantico, Virginia. This school was designed to enhance and fine-tune the leadership qualities of Marines who have advanced through the junior enlisted ranks (Private through Sergeant) and have thus embarked on a more definitive career path as Staff Sergeants. All Marines in the rank of Staff Sergeant (E-6) are ELIGIBLE to attend the school, although not all are CHOSEN to do so. Attendance at this school is reserved for those Staff Sergeants who presumably show definite promise of making significant future contributions to the advancement of the ideals, beliefs and traditions of the United States Marine Corps.

I was excited to be one of the chosen few and I was eager to attend this school. Successful completion of this course would mean that I had taken on yet another challenge and turned it into an opportunity to excel. In my opinion, it was just another phase of qualifying for membership in an exclusive category known as "Best of the Best". I was to be sorely disappointed by what I would learn about my fellow students.

While attending this six week school, I would still be actually assigned to the Marine Corps Supply Activity, Philadelphia, Pennsylvania, and would return to my regular duties there upon completion of the school. The school was designed to be a very intense, all-consuming training experience, mentally and physically demanding to an extreme limit and, while attending the school, I would be required to reside in the barracks set aside for Staff NCO Academy students on base at Quantico, so Juanita and I decided that she should simply remain in our apartment in Blackwood, New Jersey. We figured she might be able to come down to visit on a couple of the last two or three weekends of the school term and we might be able to spend Friday night and Saturday night at the Hostess House on base-that's sort of a military hotel.

There were 79 students in my class, divided into 7 sections with 11 or 12 students in each section. We lived in open squad bays, separated into small individual cubicles by partitions. Each student had a cot, a desk and a chair. Each section had a common social center with an exercise area where we could do sit-ups, chin-ups and simple exercises on an individual basis during our free time - what there was of that.

Each section had a "head", with commodes, sinks and a shower area. It was a Spartan existence, by some standards but, since I had spent my entire childhood living in houses with no electricity and no running water, it was as modern as I would have expected.

The Staff Academy had a highly competitive atmosphere. Class standings were posted on bulletin boards on a daily basis. If we were tested, physically or mentally, those test scores were posted. If we had been tasked with writing a book report on one of the books from the "required reading" list or with writing a thesis on leadership traits and principles (or on any other subject), the highest scoring thesis was posted. I might as well tell you, right now, that my material was always on the bulletin board and my test scores, in every category, were always at the top of the list. I would be the ultimate Academy student. My entire military career, my entire life, had been a full-time preparation period for this school. I lived and breathed the course materials of this school. I was utterly prepared. Listed next are two of my many winning selections.

Leadership Methods

If your Marines always know what they can expect from you, they'll be better motivated. If they always know what kind of attitude you're going to have in a given situation, there won't be so much apprehension in their minds when strained situations develop.

You can't set high standards and expect your Marines to conform to them unless you are a living example of the result of those standards. Everyone in your unit must know and understand what you expect and you must be such a good leader that your Marines will try to meet your standards, willingly.

If you are new to a unit, don't make drastic changes in routine unless they are absolutely necessary. If you are an established member of a command and have a steady routine of classes, training, physical exercise, etc., try not to vary too much from scheduled events. The troops will appreciate knowing what is going on from day to day and, most of the time, will be 'up' for it.

If you aren't consistent in your standards, your Marines will not know, from one week to the next, whether your inspections will be tough or easy, or whether your rewards and punishments will be worthwhile or insignificant, and they will begin to doubt whether or not you are worth listening to.

A good leader must be consistently fair in the tasks he assigns and in the standards he sets. Personal likes and dislikes should not determine which Marines get the undesirable assignments.

If you are a good leader, every Marine in your unit will strive to measure up favorably when comparing himself to you.

A leader may set out with the goal of simply having every member of his unit successfully pass the physical fitness test. He may realize that some of the troops may only be able to attain a minimum passing score but he will accept that as long as each person actually does pass. It is very gratifying to be able to say that your unit accomplished 100 per cent of any particular goal. Obviously, there may be at least one individual in the unit who has a personal goal of attaining the maximum score of 300 points on the PFT but, on the way to attempting to reach his personal goal, he will have already helped to reach the unit goal. If you are a good leader, you will be able to make it obvious to your troops that various unit goals are worth working for, even if they are merely to be used as stepping stones by an individual on the way to achieving his personal goals. And I just don't think a young individualist could get very motivated about accomplishing a unit goal if he thought nobody would show any appreciation for his efforts. If a particular goal is worth setting, and is worth the hard work required to attain it, it should be worth some recognition, even if you only slap a man across the back and say, "Good job, Marine. Thanks".

Of course, you should not set goals so high that even your most optimistic troops might think they are unattainable. Know your Marines. Learn as quickly as possible what they THINK their limitations are and set your goals just a little higher than that. As your unit reaches each level of success, you will be able to convince them that the NEXT higher level of achievement is really not so far away, after all. In a generally well-motivated unit, you must not allow a small group of underachievers (or even one single "slacker") to undermine your unit's overall effectiveness.

Leadership Traits

Assignment: Discuss five of the leadership traits you consider to be the most important.

All of the leadership traits are equally important. No matter how knowledgeable you may be, you will still not be an effective leader if you lack integrity. No matter how dependable you are, you still have to have good judgment. If you can hang around in the Corps long enough, you may actually get some promotions up through the ranks, almost in spite of your shortcomings. The main thing is not to try to get to be a leader but to try to get to be a GOOD leader. However, for the purpose of this assignment, I will simply choose and discuss five of the leadership traits, in no particular order.

Integrity: Basic honesty cannot be learned or acquired AFTER becoming a leader. Integrity is the reason that some public officials will separate themselves from private financial concerns if there is a chance that their private position might affect their performance of duty as public servants. Unfortunately, this type of self control is extremely rare, especially among politicians. But the actions of a military leader must be beyond reproach. Duty must be your first priority, and your duty is two-fold: (1) Accomplish the Mission. (2) Ensure the welfare of your troops. If your decisions are made on any other basis, you will not be an effective leader.

Dependability: It has always been a source of pride for me to know that any of the people who ever hired me to do a job could count on me to get the job done. As a Marine, I may not always agree with the things I am ordered to do but my seniors will always be able to depend on me to accomplish any lawful task.

Knowledge: The most important aspect of this trait is to be technically and tactically proficient in your own occupational specialty. Nobody of lesser rank should be more learned than I when specialized questions arise in my own field of expertise. Also, time honored tradition dictates that each and every Marine is *first and foremost* a Rifleman. Therefore, I should be able to fulfill not only the requirements of a Staff Sergeant in the supply field, but also the requirements of a Staff Sergeant in the infantry.

Judgment: In this day and age, many Marines of high rank are able to make lateral moves into other occupational specialties or transfer into situations in which they have limited experience. These individuals may be forced to question Marines of lesser rank in order to obtain sufficient facts or information in order to make a logical decision. An example of this might be a newly transferred Platoon Commander in a combat situation who accepts the recommendations and suggestions of the more experienced Sergeants and Corporals in his new platoon. Of course, it would not be a preferred course of action if you constantly have to rely on your junior Marines in such a manner but it would be infinitely worse judgment to make decisions based purely on your assumptions and speculations.

Bearing: A squared-away, clean-cut young Private fresh out of boot camp may have to go to work for a Staff Sergeant who has a beer belly, dirty brass and a sloppy haircut. There is no way that Private can have respect for that 'leader', no matter how good at his job that 'leader' may be. I want my subordinates to see me only at my best, so I always try to BE at my best. I want them to think of me as 'Super Sergeant'. Even when I have to discipline a subordinate, I want him to understand that I am only trying to help him to be a better Marine.

The preceding samples of my original drafts are typical of the type of my winning entries that were placed on the bulletin boards, from Day One at the Academy. Because of this, all of the other students in section 7 were continuously coming to me for help. It started with questions about spelling and quickly moved on to questions about grammar, sentence structure, traits and principles of leadership, study guides, study methods, thesis analysis, paragraph composition, transitional phrases, how to set up a sample lesson plan, procedures for presenting their subject matter when their turn would come to conduct a mock classroom exercise. During the early days at the Academy, I spent a lot of time in the lounge area, dispensing guidance and assistance for half a dozen students at a time. It did not bother me at all to give freely of my knowledge and my time to help my fellow students. And I never acted as if I resented the fact that they were so needy. However, things soon took a turn for the worse.

One morning, I awoke at 0515, before my alarm sounded. I was one of the very few students who had the foresight to bring a personal alarm clock so I never depended on being awakened by the Duty NCO holding reveille. It was still 15 minutes before reveille, so I went into the head to shave. Afterward, I showered. As I was drying off, my fellow students started coming into the head. They were really mad at me for not holding reveille. I hadn't thought much about the time but I also hadn't really considered holding reveille, either. That's the responsibility of the Duty NCO. Apparently, he had not done his job of turning on the squad bay lights, so everybody was running late - and they were acting as if it was MY fault. I hadn't even been aware that reveille had not been sounded. After all, I was in the shower - not in the squad bay. I was very upset by their attitudes so I said, "Hey, I'm not your big brother or your daddy or your keeper and I was not on duty so it isn't my fault. So shut up about it". Besides, all of those people really loved to stay in bed as long as possible, even after reveille, so if they needed a kick in the butt to get motivated, they didn't deserve the stripes on their sleeves, anyway. They said some very nasty things to me but I thought their anger was misplaced because it was the Duty NCO, not I, who had fallen down on the job.

After that, it was straight downhill for me. It seemed as though that one little incident had tainted my relationship with each and every one of them. It was as if everything about me that they had previously admired became something that they resented. Before the reveille incident occurred, I could do no wrong, in their opinions. Afterward, I could do nothing right. I became an instant outcast, through no fault of my own.

They made it quite clear that I was no longer welcome at the communal section table when we went to chow. I didn't really mind that, though, because I went there to eat, not to socialize.

During free time in the barracks, I tended to stay in my cubicle to study while the rest of the students sat around in the lounge area, telling jokes, gossiping and wasting their time. I chose to spend my time at something constructive, like doing my lessons, studying and exercising, so I was ostracized for being 'anti-social'. Also, even before the reveille misunderstanding, they could not understand why I did not want to go into town to hit the night spots. I had never been a bar hopper and I was not going to become one just to try to fit in with the crowd.

Another of the many things about me that irritated my fellow students was that I was much more athletic than any of them and my self-imposed physical training regimen really set them off. When they saw me in the exercise area, doing pushups between chairs, doing alternating one-arm pushups and doing one-arm chin-ups (without grabbing my wrist with my other hand), they made disparaging remarks, saying there must be a 'trick' to it because none of them could duplicate my feats.

My fellow students even showed anger over the fact that I had been recently selected for promotion to Gunnery Sergeant. I had received a letter of congratulations from Brigadier General M. C. Ashley, Director of the Education Center, Marine Corps Development and Education Command, Quantico, Virginia (a copy of which was put up on the bulletin board). When the promotion list was announced by Headquarters Marine Corps, the normal reaction of other Staff Sergeants should have been to grab my hand, shake it vigorously, slap me on the back and say something like, "Congratulations, future Gunny", but not my fellow students. None of them were on the promotion list and they acted as if I had done each of them a personal injustice by being selected. Some of them said things like, "Well, whose butt have you been kissing?"

But the one thing that REALLY infuriated my fellow students was the simple fact that I did not drink. One of my fellow students said, "I just don't trust a man who won't have a drink with me". I replied, "Well, I just don't trust a man who doesn't trust a man who won't drink with him". It took him a while to figure out what I said. He obviously was not a genius, by any stretch of the imagination. But my fellow students just could not understand or accept the fact that I simply did not imbibe, AT ALL. Out of 79 students in that particular class, I was the ONLY non-drinker. Those people wanted to just sit around a table in some bar and drink beer after beer after beer. What's the point of that? Water and soda pop are just fine with me but I was only a small child when I made the decision never to drink. But I have never adopted a 'holier than thou' attitude about it. And I have socialized on a great many occasions with people who drink and all of us got along just fine. It's just that I had never got started with alcohol and had no intention of starting, just in order to be 'one of the guys'.

I could conduct platoon drill better than my peers. I was academically superior to my peers. I was in much better physical condition than my peers. I was a better leader than my peers. My drill evaluation was over 96 %. My academic evaluation was over 96 %. My physical training evaluation was over 96 %. Out of 79 students, in every category, I was the closest to perfection.

I should have been the Honor Graduate out of 79 students but I didn't graduate at the top of the class. I didn't even place in the top 10 %. I graduated 19th out of 79 students. I was at the top of the class in every single category except one: Contemporary Leadership Evaluation. EVERYBODY in Section 7 placed me at the bottom of the list when they were listing their peers in order, according to their opinion of each person's leadership abilities. Every single one of my contemporary students in Section 7 indicated that I was their LAST choice in regard to being a leader. If the Contemporary Leadership Evaluation had been drafted during the first ten days of training, every one of my contemporaries would have placed me FIRST on the list.

At the Academy, the Contemporary Leadership Evaluation is figured in as part of the final grade. It has equal status along with drill, academics and physical conditioning. My extremely low peer evaluation rating pulled my overall grade point average down so low that I didn't have a 'snowball's chance in Hades' of graduating as the Honor Graduate, as I so richly deserved.

The Contemporary Leadership Evaluation gave my so-called 'peers' the perfect opportunity to stab me in the back, robbing me of my rightful place at the head of the class. I had been cheated out of being the Honor Graduate in boot camp, I had been cheated out of being the Honor Graduate in General Military Subjects School and now I was cheated out of being the Honor Graduate at the Staff Noncommissioned Officers Academy. I couldn't imagine why this sort of thing kept happening to me. Was I some sort of universal victim? Did I have a bull's eye painted on my back, or what? Hey, come on, Semper Fidelis, okay?

I suppose I may have been ranked higher by my student contemporaries if I had shown a bit more camaraderie, if I had tried a little harder to fit in, socially. After the reveille incident, perhaps I should have wrung my hands, cried crocodile tears and apologized profusely to my fellow students for not holding reveille in the place of the malingering Duty NCO. But I didn't attend the Academy to socialize, or to win a popularity contest, or to be 'one of the guys'. Instead, I went to the Academy to have my military abilities tested to the limit, to have my talents honed to a fine edge, to have my professionalism gauged by the best instructors in the business. I had been eager to face the challenge. But I can't defeat 'backstabbers'.

The lack of professionalism, indeed the immaturity, of my fellow students was apparent when they allowed their petty, childish attitudes of personal enmity toward me to affect the way they ranked me as a military leader. It was so obvious that the Contemporary Leadership Evaluation was nothing more than a popularity contest that I failed to see how the Academy faculty could overlook that fact. The Contemporary Leadership Evaluation may have been useful as an object lesson or as a simple exercise in judgment and objectivity but it should most certainly NOT have been considered as a portion of the overall final grade point determination for students.

The Academy lasted only six weeks. For such a short period, and especially for students, the Group Supervisor was not really required to write a formal fitness report on any of us other than to indicate that we had been present for duty and we had either passed or failed the course of instruction. However, 1st Lt Mayer apparently felt compelled to comment on my performance. He was aware that I was being ostracized by my fellow students, but he didn't know all of the reasons for it. Anyway, I appreciated the fact that he wanted to indicate his approval of my efforts in an official manner.

Also, Major Walker, who served as the Reviewing Officer for my fitness report, didn't have to make any sort of statement. He reviewed the fitness reports for all of the students from all of the Group Supervisors and he could have simply endorsed and forwarded it, just like all the rest. However, he also apparently felt the need to make a statement regarding my performance, even though he pointed out that his statement was not required by Marine Corps Orders covering the standard operating procedures for the Academy. As the Assistant Director of the Staff NCO Academy, I am sure he knew that I was the only student who had been selected for promotion to Gunnery Sergeant and I am sure that he conversed daily with the various Group Supervisors, so I believe he was probably aware of some of the troubles I was having with my fellow students, although he may not have been aware of all the reasons for those troubles. However, I feel sure that he knew my low standing among my contemporaries (as judged by my contemporaries) was not because of a failing on my part. My grades in every other training category were all well over 96 %. The student who graduated in first place had a grade point average of only 95.93. But since every one of my contemporary students placed me at the bottom of their list in regard to peer evaluation, my grade point average dropped from well over 96 down to 93.07. Because of the jealousy and spitefulness of my fellow students, I lost my spot as the honor graduate. But there were at least two people (First Lieutenant Mayer and Major Walker) who knew that I deserved a higher ranking than what I had received and that the ceremonial NCO Sword had been awarded to the wrong Honor Graduate. But that isn't really much consolation.

Staff Noncommissioned Officers Academy

Leadership Record of S/Sgt Roy L. Morris

Class standing	19th out of 79 students
Grade point average of student in 1st place	95.93
Grade point average of student in 19th place (S/Sgt Morris)	93.07
Shortfall that kept S/Sgt Morris out of 1st place	2.86
Grade point average needed to place in top 10 % of class	93.65
Grade point average of student in 19th place (S/Sgt Morris)	93.07
Shortfall that kept S/Sgt Morris out of top 10 % of class	0.58

Fitness Report for 3 November 1975 through 17 December 1975

Section C: Performance of duty:
Regular duties	Not graded
Additional duties	Not graded
Administrative duties	Not graded
Handling officers	Not graded
Handling enlisted personnel	Not graded

To what degree has he exhibited the following:
Endurance	Excellent
Personal appearance	Excellent
Military presence	Excellent
Attention to duty	Outstanding
Cooperation	Outstanding
Initiative	Excellent
Judgment	Excellent
Leadership	Excellent
Loyalty	Outstanding
Personal relations	Excellent

Narrative comments:

S/Sgt Morris completed the Staff NCO Academy. He demonstrated an excellent quality to assimilate instruction, an outstanding ability to express himself in writing and an excellent ability to express himself orally. He received twenty hours of leadership and human relations training. S/Sgt Morris graduated 19th out of 79 graduates with a final average of 93.07 %.

Reporting Officer
H. R. Mayer
First Lieutenant USMC
Group Supervisor
Staff NCO Academy

Statement of Reviewing Officer

MCO 1610.7A does not require a mark for regular duties (for a student). However, S/Sgt Morris' recorded daily performance was outstanding.

Reviewing Officer
L. D. Walker
Major USMC
Assistant Director
Staff NCO Academy
Quantico, Virginia

My supervisors back at the MCSA in Philadelphia were not dismayed by the fact that I had graduated only 19th out of 79. To the contrary, they seemed quite pleased that I had done so well. I suppose the fact that I had missed first place by less than 3 points helped, as did the fact that both the Reporting Officer and the Reviewing Officer had commented favorably on my performance even though they weren't required to comment, at all

I also learned that the Marine Corps Supply Activity in Philadelphia was being deactivated. All of the duties and responsibilities performed there were being transferred to the Marine Corps Supply Center at Albany, Georgia, which would subsequently be renamed the Marine Corps Logistics Support Base, Atlantic, (MCLSBLANT), Albany, Georgia. All military personnel working at MCSA, Philadelphia would receive transfer orders to Albany. And any civilian personnel currently working at MCSA in Philadelphia would be offered the opportunity to relocate. I was scheduled to be part of the advance party to be sent to Albany to set up shop and get things started at our new offices, so Juanita and I would be going to Georgia within two or three months.

When we had left Parris Island, South Carolina and were sent north to Pennsylvania instead of south to Albany, as I had requested, Headquarters obviously knew that I would eventually get my wish. That's why they sent me to Philadelphia, in the first place. I was astonished. The 'bigwigs' in Headquarters Marine Corps had actually done something logical. How about that!

I was barely back at Philadelphia from the Staff NCO Academy just a few days when I received my second recommendation for promotion to Warrant Officer. A copy of the letter of recommendation is provided, as follows:

UNITED STATES MARINE CORPS
Headquarters Battalion
Marine Corps Supply Activity
1100 South Broad Street
Philadelphia, Pa 19146

200:mlm
1040
9 Jan 1976

From: Commanding Officer
To: Commandant of the Marine Corps (Code MMRE-6)

Subj: Recommendation for appointment under the Fiscal Year 1977 Warrant Officer Program for Active Duty Personnel

The information contained in the basic application and enclosure (1) thereto has been verified with records on file in this Command and is correct. The applicant meets the basic eligibility requirements for the Fiscal Year 1977 Warrant Officer Program for Active Duty Personnel.

A completed letter of transmittal is included.

Staff Sergeant Morris is an industrious, resourceful, versatile and extremely dedicated Marine. He has demonstrated superior managerial skill, resourcefulness, enthusiasm and total competence in carrying out all of his duties. His exceptional knowledge of supply and related matters is especially noteworthy and enables him to provide invaluable guidance to both superiors and subordinates. This impressive Marine is intelligent, alert, well informed and possesses a keen, analytical and imaginative mind. He is a confident, level-headed individual who is completely trustworthy and honest.

Staff Sergeant Morris has a fine personality. He is tactful, diplomatic, courteous and always cheerful. He is thoughtful and considerate in his relationships with all people regardless of their race or creed.

Staff Sergeant Morris possesses every attitude and characteristic that defines the word Marine. He is highly motivated and thoroughly dependable. His impressive physique, bearing and impeccable appearance are indicative of the tremendous pride he takes in being a Marine.

Staff Sergeant Morris' leadership, desire to excel and superb performance in all he does place him among the top S/NCO's in the Marine Corps. He is a true professional with unlimited potential for advancement who was recently selected for promotion to Gunnery Sergeant.

Staff Sergeant Morris is enthusiastically recommended for the Fiscal Year 1977 Warrant Officer Program.

T. K. Lynch

Fitness Report for 1 August 1975 through 31 January 1976

Section C: Performance of duty:
Regular duties   Outstanding
Administrative duties   Outstanding
Handling enlisted personnel Outstanding

To what degree has he exhibited the following:
Personal appearance   Outstanding
Military presence   Outstanding
Attention to duty   Outstanding
Cooperation   Outstanding
Initiative   Outstanding
Judgment   Excellent
Force   Excellent
Leadership   Outstanding
Loyalty   Outstanding
Personal relations   Outstanding
Economy of management   Outstanding
Growth potential   Outstanding

Your estimate of the Marine's general value to the service:
Outstanding

Considering the requirements of service in war, indicate your attitude toward having this Marine under your command:
Particularly desire to have

Narrative comments:
  S/Sgt Morris is an industrious, resourceful, versatile and extremely dedicated Marine. He has demonstrated superior managerial skill, resourcefulness, enthusiasm and total competence in carrying out all of his duties. His exceptional knowledge of supply and related matters is especially noteworthy and enables him to provide invaluable guidance to both superiors and subordinates. This impressive Marine is intelligent, alert, well informed and possesses a keen, analytical and imaginative mind. He is a confident, level-headed individual who is completely

trustworthy and honest. S/Sgt Morris has a fine personality. He is tactful, diplomatic, courteous and always cheerful. S/Sgt Morris possesses every attitude and characteristic that defines the word "Marine". His impressive physique, bearing and impeccable appearance are indicative of the tremendous pride he takes in being a Marine. Staff Sergeant Morris' leadership, desire to excel and superb performance in all he does place him among the top S/NCO's in the Marine Corps. He is a true professional with unlimited potential for advancement who was recently selected for promotion to Gunnery Sergeant.

Reporting Officer
William D. Smith
Lieutenant Colonel USMC
Head, Readiness Office
Supply Operations Division

Roy Morris

Fitness Report for 1 February 1976 through 31 July 1976

Section C: Performance of duty:
Regular duties   Outstanding
Administrative duties   Excellent
Handling enlisted personnel   Excellent

To what degree has he exhibited the following:
Personal appearance   Outstanding
Military presence   Outstanding
Attention to duty   Outstanding
Cooperation   Outstanding
Initiative   Outstanding
Judgment   Outstanding
Force   Excellent
Leadership   Outstanding
Loyalty   Outstanding
Personal relations   Outstanding
Economy of management   Outstanding
Growth potential   Outstanding

Your estimate of this Marine's general value to the service:
Outstanding

Considering the requirements of service in war, indicate your attitude toward having this Marine under your command:
Particularly desire to have

Narrative comments:
   S/Sgt Morris works as a member of a three man team composed of a Captain, a civilian (GS-12) and himself. This project management team monitors and is concerned with the overall readiness of ALL Marine Corps Ordnance and Motor Transport combat essential items. This impressive Marine is intelligent, alert, well informed and possesses a keen, imaginative and analytical mind. He has demonstrated superior managerial skill, enthusiasm, resourcefulness and total competence in carrying out all of his duties. Above all, he is a confident, level headed

individual who is completely trustworthy and honest. I have found him to be tactful, diplomatic, courteous and always cheerful. Because he is in daily contact with Headquarters Marine Corps and the 'field', the previously mentioned traits are mandatory for his job. His impressive physique, bearing and impeccable appearance are indicative of the tremendous pride he takes in being a Marine. He daily displays a fine ability to communicate, both orally and in writing. S/Sgt Morris was especially picked for this demanding billet because of his leadership, desire to excel and superb performance in all that he does. Active in the civilian community, he has devoted many hours helping to organize a bowling league.

Reporting Officer
William D. Smith
Lieutenant Colonel USMC
Head, Readiness Office
Supply Operations Division

Roy Morris

Fitness Report for 1 August 1976 through 30 September 1976

Section C: Performance of duty:
Regular duties   Outstanding
Administrative duties   Outstanding
Handling enlisted personnel Outstanding

To what degree has he exhibited the following:
Personal appearance   Outstanding
Military presence   Outstanding
Attention to duty   Outstanding
Cooperation   Outstanding
Initiative   Outstanding
Force   Outstanding
Leadership   Outstanding
Loyalty   Outstanding
Personal relations   Outstanding
Economy of management   Outstanding
Growth potential   Outstanding

Your estimate of this Marine's general value to the service:
Outstanding

Considering the requirements of service in war, indicate your attitude toward having this Marine under your command:
Particularly desire to have

Narrative comments:
    S/Sgt Morris continues to work as a member of a three man team comprised of a Captain, a civilian (GS-12) and himself. This project management team monitors and is concerned with the overall readiness of ALL Marine Corps Ordnance and Motor Transport combat essential items. This impressive Marine is intelligent, alert, well informed and possesses a keen, analytical and imaginative mind. He has demonstrated superior managerial skill, resourcefulness, enthusiasm and total competence in carrying out all of his duties. Above all, he is a confident, level headed individual who is completely trustworthy and honest. I

have found him to be tactful, diplomatic, courteous and always cheerful. Because he is in daily contact with Headquarters Marine Corps and the 'field', the previously mentioned traits are mandatory. His impressive physique, bearing and impeccable appearance are indicative of the tremendous pride he takes in being a Marine. He daily displays a fine ability to communicate, both orally and in writing. S/Sgt Morris was especially picked for this billet because of his leadership, desire to excel and superb performance in all that he does. He continues to take an active part in community affairs.

Reporting Officer
William D. Smith
Lieutenant Colonel USMC
Head, Readiness Office
Supply Operations Division

My promotion to Gunnery Sergeant was effective on 1 October 1976. The actual promotion ceremony was held on 8 October 1976, one day before my 29th birthday. I had been in the Marine Corps for a total of 10 years, 2 months and 3 weeks and I was already a Gunnery Sergeant. There are a great many people who retire honorably after 20 years at the rank of only Staff Sergeant, so I was doing quite well, by any standard, especially considering the numerous occasions when my so-called peers and contemporaries had sabotaged my career because of their own jealousies and spitefulness. I overcame a lot of obstacles to become a "Gunny".

Fitness Report for 1 October 1976 through 30 November 1976

Section C: Performance of duty:
Regular Duties   Outstanding
Administrative duties   Excellent
Handling enlisted personnel   Excellent

To what degree has he exhibited the following:
Personal appearance   Outstanding
Military presence   Outstanding
Attention to duty   Outstanding
Cooperation   Outstanding
Initiative   Outstanding
Judgment   Excellent
Force   Outstanding
Leadership   Outstanding
Loyalty   Outstanding
Personal relations   Outstanding
Economy of management   Outstanding
Growth potential   Outstanding

Your estimate of this Marine's general value to the service:
Outstanding

Considering the requirements of service in war, indicate your attitude toward having this Marine under your command:
Particularly desire to have

Narrative comments:
    Gunnery Sergeant Morris continues to work as a member of a three man team comprised of a Captain, a civilian (GS-12) and himself. This project management team monitors and is concerned with the overall readiness of ALL Marine Corps Ordnance and Motor Transport combat essential items. This impressive Marine is intelligent, alert, well informed and possesses a keen, analytical and imaginative mind. He has demonstrated superior managerial skill, resourcefulness, enthusiasm and total competence in carrying out all of his duties. Above all, he is

a confident, level headed individual who is completely trustworthy and honest. I have found him to be tactful, diplomatic, courteous and always cheerful. Because he is in daily contact with Headquarters Marine Corps and the "field", the previously mentioned traits are mandatory. His impressive physique, bearing and impeccable appearance are indicative of the tremendous pride he takes in being a Marine. He daily displays a fine ability to communicate, both orally and in writing. Gy/Sgt Morris was especially picked for this billet because of his leadership, desire to excel and superb performance in all that he does.

Reporting Officer
William D. Smith
Lieutenant Colonel USMC
Head, Readiness Office
Supply Operations Division

UNITED STATES MARINE CORPS
Supply Operations Division
Marine Corps Logistics Support Base, Atlantic
Albany, Georgia 31704

P820:JLM:amt
1040
15 Feb 1977

From: Director
To: MCLSBLant Fiscal Year 1978 Warrant Officer Screening Board
Subj: Recommendation for Fiscal Year 1978 Warrant Officer Program for Active Duty Personnel; case of Gunnery Sergeant Roy L. Morris

Gunnery Sergeant Roy L. Morris is recommended with enthusiasm for the subject program.

Gunnery Sergeant Morris possesses, without doubt, the well rounded professional attributes required of a Warrant Officer of Marines. He is mentally alert, physically fit and honestly committed in his desire for selection to Warrant Officer.

Gunnery Sergeant Morris' current assignment as an Equipment Specialist demands the capability to effectively manage the full spectrum of Motor Transport equipment relative to the Marine Corps. This assignment further requires the capability to communicate, on a daily basis, with not only senior military officers but also with customers in the field, manufacturers and various other interested parties. Gunnery Sergeant Morris unquestionably possesses these capabilities and excels in their use.

Gunnery Sergeant Morris has the required background and experience in varied supply and warehousing billets for MOS 3050 (Warehousing Officer). He has continually received awards of proficiency pay for superior performance in those areas and has five years of actual assignments in warehousing billets.

Gunnery Sergeant Morris consistently scores a High First Class rating in the Physical Fitness Test and is qualified as High Expert with both the rifle and pistol. Additionally, he has qualified for Presidential

Sports Awards in such varied categories as karate, weight training, jogging and bowling.

Gunnery Sergeant Morris is enrolled in the Albany Junior College and displays a unique ability to express himself through a well developed command of vocabulary.

A married man of high moral character, devoted loyalty and total dedication to the Corps, Gunnery Sergeant Morris will find no difficulty in transition to Warrant Officer and will most definitely be an asset to the Marine Corps Officer ranks in any given task.

> W. G. Carson, Jr.
> Colonel USMC

It was my third recommendation for promotion to Warrant Officer and, as the saying goes, *third time's the charm.* The official message from Headquarters Marine Corps was issued on 6 July 1977, listing all of the enlisted Marines who had been selected for promotion. This was followed by an article in the *Navy Times* dated 18 July 1977. The actual promotion ceremony would not be performed until 12 January 1978 so I had to survive for six months as a Gunnery Sergeant, with everybody knowing that I would soon become an officer. There were only three selectees who were stationed at Albany so we were a rare breed - and we all knew we would have to stay just about perfect, in every respect. There was a lot of peer pressure. Some of our peers took our selections well and some did not.

Fitness Report from 1 December 1976 through 31 May 1977

Section C: Performance of duty:
Regular duties	Outstanding
Administrative duties	Excellent
Handling enlisted personnel	Excellent
Training personnel	Excellent

To what degree has he exhibited the following:
Personal appearance	Excellent
Military presence	Excellent
Attention to duty	Outstanding
Cooperation	Outstanding
Initiative	Outstanding
Judgment	Excellent
Force	Excellent
Leadership	Excellent
Loyalty	Outstanding
Personal relations	Outstanding
Economy of management	Excellent
Growth potential	Outstanding

Your estimate of this Marine's general value to the service:
Excellent to Outstanding

Considering the requirement of service in war, indicate your attitude toward having this Marine under your command:
Particularly desire to have

Narrative comments:
    Gy/Sgt Morris is an intelligent, dedicated Staff NCO. He is responsible for monitoring Motor Transport readiness throughout the Marine Corps. He works with enthusiasm and has demonstrated a high

degree of initiative and skill in his efforts to improve readiness in the Motor Transport functional areas. Gy/Sgt Morris is enrolled in Albany Junior College, working toward an associate's degree.

Reporting Officer
H. R. Raines
Lieutenant Colonel USMC
Head, Engineering/Motor Transport
Supply Operations Division

Fitness Report for 1 June 1977 through 7 November 1977

Section C: Performance of duty:
Regular duties	Excellent
Administrative duties	Excellent
Handling enlisted personnel	Outstanding
Training personnel	Outstanding

To what degree has he exhibited the following:
Personal appearance	Outstanding
Military presence	Outstanding
Attention to duty	Excellent
Cooperation	Outstanding
Initiative	Outstanding
Judgment	Excellent
Force	Excellent
Leadership	Outstanding
Loyalty	Outstanding
Personal relations	Outstanding
Economy of management	Excellent
Growth potential	Outstanding

Your estimate of this Marine's general value to the service:
Excellent to Outstanding

Considering the requirements of service in war, indicate your attitude toward having this Marine under your command:
Particularly desire to have

Narrative comments:
    Gy/Sgt Morris is an intelligent, well informed Staff NCO. He is well versed in all aspects of supply and the computer programs that support the Marine Corps logistical readiness effort. His positive "can

do" attitude is contagious and he has been a major factor in maintaining high Branch morale. He attends Albany Junior College in his off-duty hours and is the Scoutmaster for the Base Boy Scout Troop.

Reporting Officer
H. R. Raines
Lieutenant Colonel USMC
Head, Engineer/Motor Transport
Supply Operations Division

Fitness Report for 8 November 1977 through 11 January 1978

Section C: Performance of duty:
Regular duties   Outstanding
Administrative duties   Outstanding

To what degree has he exhibited the following:
Personal appearance   Outstanding
Military presence   Outstanding
Attention to duty   Outstanding
Cooperation   Excellent
Initiative   Outstanding
Judgment   Excellent
Force   Excellent
Leadership   Excellent
Personal relations   Excellent
Growth potential   Outstanding

Your estimate of this Marine's general value to the service:
Excellent to Outstanding

Considering the requirements of service in war, indicate your attitude toward having this Marine under your command:
Particularly desire to have

Narrative comments:
Gy/Sgt Morris is a quiet, friendly, intelligent and thoroughly dedicated Marine who is extremely interested in his job and the people he works with. It is realized that 60 days is a relatively short period to justify an outstanding rating in regular duties; however, Gy/Sgt Morris has demonstrated an exceptional degree of proficiency and professionalism in performing his duties. He possesses many positive attributes that will enable him to become an outstanding Warrant Officer. In addition to his regular duties, Gy/Sgt Morris takes an interest in numerous community activities. He served as the Scout Leader for Troop # 12 for the past eight months, Assistant Coach/Instructor for the Base Junior Bowlers, and is President of the Base Intramural League. He has actively sought

self-improvement by completing several college level courses and is currently enrolled in the Basic Officers Extension Course from the Marine Corps Institute. His appearance in uniform is impeccable and he consistently scores high first class on the physical fitness test.

Reporting Officer
F. L. Jones
Major USMC
Head
Engineer/Motor Transport/General Property
Supply Operations Division

During my entire enlisted career, I had continued my military education by reading the various manuals that were available and by enrolling in correspondence courses available from the Marine Corps Institute. Over the years, I have lost some of my completion certificates but listed below are some of the many courses which I completed:

Marine Corps Stock Lists
Basic Organic Accounting
Marine Noncommissioned Officer
Financial Management
Individual Protective Measures
3.5 inch Rocket Launcher
Portable Flamethrower
Military Functions in Civil Disturbances and Disasters
Marine Corps Stock Lists (updated version)
Organic Property Control
Fundamentals of Map Reading
Functions of the Infantry Staff Noncommissioned Officer
Punctuation

My choice of reading materials included the obvious daily newspapers and periodicals so that I could sustain up-to-date general knowledge of world events but also included the following:

Leatherneck Magazine
Guidebook for Marines
The Rifle Platoon in the Offense
The Rifle Platoon in the Defense

And many other articles and manuals covering individual and unit combat tactical maneuvers

During my off-duty hours, I also qualified for Presidential Sports Awards in the following categories:

Bowling
Running
Weight Training
Jogging
Gymnastics
Martial Arts

I also attended evening classes in many diverse subjects at colleges wherever I might be stationed.

All of the above examples of off-duty interests combined to establish a well-rounded and focused background which enhanced my value as a United States Marine.

An Officer of Marines

On 12 January 1978, I was promoted to Warrant Officer during the mid-afternoon. It was a Thursday, so my first full day in the Marine Corps as an officer would be Friday the 13th. That has always been my lucky number and my luckiest day. It was to be a great and momentous day.

But first, I had to survive the anxiety and nervousness of the 12th.

The past few months had been hectic for Juanita. She had a regular job off-base, she served as a den mother for my troop of boy scouts, she still did occasional repairs on uniform clothing for some of our friends and she made the alterations on my uniform. There are not a LOT of differences between the enlisted uniform and the officers' uniform. They are subtle but they are significant. First of all, she had to educate herself regarding what those differences were. Then she had to figure out how to make those alterations. My full-dress uniforms were relatively new so there was no need to buy new uniforms when mine were perfectly serviceable.

Furthermore, she had to walk a fine line between currently being the wife of a Staff NCO and being the wife of a future officer. We had a wide network of friends and acquaintances, from our involvement in bowling and the scouting program, from both of our jobs and from the fact that many of our friends were long-term friends who had transferred with us from Philadelphia when the Supply Activity was relocated to Albany.

Fortunately, Juanita was the type of person who never changed. She treated the wife of the lowest private with the same dignity and courtesy that she displayed toward the wife of my Company Commander. My upcoming promotion did not change her attitude toward our friends.

She was still the same caring, giving, gracious person she had always been and she never embarrassed anybody with anything she said or did.

However, we return to the moment at hand. During the morning of the 12th, Juanita and I had a lot of paperwork to be done. The Battalion Adjutant was instrumental in streamlining the process of making the transition from enlisted status to officer status for both of us. He was a Chief Warrant Officer (W-3) and had served as my witness back in November, when I had signed an extension of my current enlistment in order to have sufficient obligated service to accept the promotion to officer status. After becoming an officer, I would not have a designated release date. I would serve until retirement or until I resigned, whichever came first. Or until I might get kicked out.

For me, the morning of the 12th was traumatic. My honorable discharge from the Marine Corps as a Gunnery Sergeant had been effective as of 11 January 1978, the day before but I had to conduct all of our business on the 12th in full-dress uniform. My uniforms had been altered and my Gunnery Sergeant stripes had been removed. I could not yet wear Warrant Officer's bars because I had not yet taken the oath of acceptance as an officer. So, until about 1500 (that's 3:00 pm for civilians), I had to walk around looking like a Private, wearing neither stripes nor bars.

I received a lot of curious stares from people everywhere we went that day. Everybody was probably wondering how a Private could have earned all of the ribbons and badges I was wearing or what I might have done to get 'busted' all the way down to Private.

At my work section, I took a lot of good-natured joking about being a 'slick sleeve' from my FORMER fellow Staff NCO's. They said they wanted to get their kicks in while they all still outranked me. Juanita seemed to be quite amused by my predicament. However, I pointed out that she was really 'getting around' because, within a 24 hour time period, she would have been kissed by a Gunnery Sergeant, a civilian, a Private and a Warrant Officer. OOH-RAH!

Finally, it was about time. All of the pre-promotion paperwork had been done (thanks to Chief Warrant Officer J. D. Henry), the various members of the promotion ceremony were assembled in the Battalion Commander's conference room, the visitors and guests had been gathered and the public affairs office photographer was in position.

My Battalion Commander, Colonel G. S. Aspenwall, administered the oath of acceptance as I recited it, word for word. He pinned a Warrant Officer bar on my right shoulder and 'the love of my life' pinned a bar on my left shoulder. There were various handshakes and congratulations all around. The gang from my work section went back to the office while Juanita and I went down the hall to the administration office to pick up our new identification cards. That was when we both started to believe that this fairy tale dream just might be real.

How and Why

How did I manage to be selected for promotion? And why would I give up the stripes of a Gunnery Sergeant? And what IS a Warrant Officer, anyway?

I think the best way to explain what a Warrant Officer is might be to describe what it takes to become one. In the first place, you have to have a high degree of intelligence. The average level of intelligence of human beings is 100. That's classified as the norm. In order to become a Marine Corps Officer, you must have an IQ of 110, or higher. That requirement applies, whether you go through ROTC in college or move up from the enlisted ranks. My personal IQ is either 129 or 132, depending on which test you consider to be valid. I took an IQ test while I was in boot camp and another while I was being considered for embassy duty. As it turned out, I was not selected for embassy duty because I was too short. However, I was not at all interested, anyway, in being a security guard for some idiot politician, no matter where his embassy might have been located. So, that was just as well.

Another prerequisite for promotion to Warrant Officer is at least four years of exemplary service as an enlisted Marine. My rating of Class V (the highest rating possible) on the physical fitness test, my rating of High Expert with both the rifle and the pistol, and my consistent awards of proficiency pay for superior performance all indicated that my enlisted service was, indeed, exemplary. Apparently, I was eminently qualified to be a Warrant Officer.

In 1978, there were 4,106 applicants for promotion. Out of all the enlisted Marines in the Corps, those were the ones who honestly believed that they were qualified and had a chance to win a promotion. Furthermore, it also means that the senior officers who were responsible for those enlisted Marines also believed that they were qualified - otherwise, the officers would not have forwarded those applications with their favorable endorsements - and those 4,106 enlisted applicants would not even have been considered by the Headquarters Marine Corps Selection Committee.

Even so, there were only 233 Marines selected for promotion to Warrant Officer. That's only about 5.7 % of those who were qualified. Without any doubt, these were truly the 'Best of the Best'. I felt sincerely and deeply honored to be one of those 'Chosen Few'.

Marine Corps Warrant Officers are generally addressed as 'Gunner' by both enlisted Marines and commissioned officers, alike, in much the same manner that Marine Corps Captains are addressed as 'Skipper'. Both of these titles denote considerable respect and admiration for the officer thus addressed but they also imply at least some degree of familiarity or camaraderie with that officer. For example, when a Captain or a Warrant Officer gives a command to an enlisted Marine, that Marine will usually respond with either "Yes, Sir" or "Aye Aye, Sir" as he goes about obeying or complying with that command, especially in a formal situation. However, in casual situations or during routine operations in the 'work-a-day' world, a Marine might sometimes respond with "Okay, Skipper" or "Okay, Gunner".

There are four grades within the Warrant Officer ranks. To explain the responsibilities, duties and authority levels of each, it would be easiest to compare these grades to their equivalent grades within the commissioned officer ranks. Even civilians are generally familiar with the names of the various grades within the commissioned officer ranks, and they are usually able to imagine the routine assignments which might be given to those various ranks so, when you hear the grade of a Warrant Officer, just imagine the grade to which it corresponds within the commissioned officer ranks and you will have some idea of where that particular Warrant Officer stands within the hierarchy of the officer corps.

Commissioned Officer rank and pay grade	Warrant Officer rank and pay grade
Second Lieutenant (O-1)	Warrant Officer (W-1)
First Lieutenant (O-2)	Warrant Officer (W-1)
Captain (O-3)	Chief Warrant Officer (W-2)
Major (O-4)	Chief Warrant Officer (W-3)
Lieutenant Colonel (O-5)	Chief Warrant Officer (W-4)
Colonel (O-6)	Chief Warrant Officer (W-4)

As you see, a Warrant Officer (W-1) may be comparable to either a Second Lieutenant or a First Lieutenant, depending on his or her particular job assignment at any given time. By the same token, a Chief Warrant Officer (W-4) may be comparable to a Lieutenant Colonel or a Colonel.

The pay that is given to a Marine depends not only on his rank but also on his length of service. For example, as a brand new Warrant Officer (W-1), I was earning more than the average First Lieutenant, and more than many Captains, because of my twelve years of prior service as an enlisted Marine.

Anyway, my promotion moved me into a category that was quite unique. Not only was I a former enlisted Marine who had become a Marine Officer, but I had joined the ranks of the rarest breed of all - a Marine Warrant Officer. Proving my professionalism every step of the way, I had earned the right to wear bars on my collar the same way I had earned every single stripe that had ever been sewn on my sleeves, by working hard, by using my God-given intelligence and my military knowledge and by honing my natural skills and abilities to perfection.

Marine Officers who have the privilege and distinction of prior service in the enlisted ranks are known as Mustangs. Envision a stallion on the open plains. Envision a wild spirit that may be changed but may not be tamed. These are the truest of Marines - the Best of the Best. These are Marine Corps Mustangs.

A Promise to Keep

Upon becoming a Marine Corps Officer, I made one solemn vow to myself that I would always try to do right for the enlisted Marines who would come under my authority. My reason for this was very simple - during all those years that I served as an enlisted Marine, there were a great many officers in various positions of authority over me. Many of them were of mediocre quality, lackadaisical in the performance of their duties and generally unmindful, if not actually uncaring, of the responsibility that goes along with the authority of their rank. They were Marine Corps Officers simply because they had managed to wangle a degree of some sort from some rinky-dink college, thereby qualifying for service as an officer. To put it bluntly, those people just simply weren't good enough to be in a leadership billet over ME. They comprised about 50 % of the officer corps. Then there were some officers who were considerably below average, people who had no business, whatsoever, being Marine Corps Officers. They were despicable, self-serving, backstabbing prima donnas. Those comprised about 20 % of the officer corps. Luckily, there were also a few people who met, or exceeded, the standards expected of Marine Corps Officers, people who I considered to be worthy of being appointed to positions of authority over me. In fact, I was very proud to serve with many of them. Those people made up about 30 % of the officer corps.

A Marine Corps Officer has two main guidelines in the performance of his duties:

Accomplish the mission

Ensure the welfare of the troops

It makes absolutely no difference what the mission actually is, whether you are at peace or at war or whether you are in garrison or in the field. If your mission is to manage a warehouse full of military gear or to lead a platoon in battle, the principal guidelines remain the same.

For example, in combat, your mission might be to occupy and hold a defensive position, using individual and unit tactics and maneuvers to establish fire superiority against an enemy force, If you properly establish fields of fire for your automatic weapons, position your riflemen in support of those crew-served weapons and establish communication with supporting units so that you can arrange for air strikes and artillery barrages outside your perimeter, then you might have a chance to accomplish that mission.

But it isn't all that simple. That's only half your job as an officer. In order to ensure the welfare of your troops, you need to arrange for the treatment or evacuation of dead and wounded, arrange for resupply of rations, water and ammunition, arrange for proper health and medical treatment, arrange for proper administrative and logistical procedures and control a multitude of incidental factors which might affect the troops.

For instance, in regard to health and medical treatment, the troops need clean, dry socks and serviceable footwear to avoid getting 'immersion foot' (or jungle rot, as it is sometimes called), they will need salt tablets if the climate is hot, one or more of them might be allergic to penicillin or other drugs - those troops need to be identified so that the corpsmen won't give the wrong medication in case of wounds or sickness.

In regard to administrative and logistical procedures, some of the troops may have pay problems that need to be resolved before you start a ten-day operation or patrol in the 'bush'. (Granted, they won't need any money in their pockets while on an operation but they may have dependents back home depending on an allotment check that may not be delivered if the paperwork isn't done before you head out of your base camp).

And you may have some troops who are eligible and qualified for promotion and that should be settled before going back out into 'dark territory' because the benefits available to a Sergeant might be infinitely different from the benefits available to a Corporal if he is wounded and winds up permanently disabled. This would be especially significant to the benefits that might be available to his dependents if he is captured and becomes a prisoner of war.

I want to stress one more aspect of 'ensuring the welfare of the troops'. If a Marine performs his duty in a manner that would earn him a decoration or an award, his Platoon Commander absolutely MUST be willing to take the time and make the effort to document that Marine's performance. Otherwise, no commendation will ever be given and that Marine will never receive the recognition he deserves. If it isn't recorded and reported, then it's the same as if it never happened. Conversely, if an incorrect entry is put into the record, even if it is absolutely an outright lie, it will forevermore be automatically accepted as a fact simply because it is in the official record. Officers are responsible for regularly reviewing the service records of the Marines under their control but many of them simply disregard and neglect this duty.

I wanted to be the kind of officer that any enlisted Marine would be proud to serve with. I was determined that no junior Marine would ever have to say, "I got cheated by the system because Gunner Morris didn't do what he was supposed to do".

So, yes, I would accomplish the mission - but I would also leave no stone unturned in order to ensure the welfare of my troops.

The quality of the Marines in any given platoon will vary greatly. I have often heard some other officers complain, saying, "I have to spend 90 % of my time with 10 % of my people". I have a different attitude about that. I am perfectly willing to spend that 90 % of my time dealing with the slackers, drunks, jerks and malcontents as long as I have the privilege, the pleasure and the honor of spending the other 10 % of my time with the superior Marines.

Now, To Work

I did quite well in Warrant Officer Basic School. I did so well, in fact, that I was given my first choice of duty stations upon graduation. I chose a three year accompanied tour on Okinawa. It was the perfect way for Juanita to travel abroad and see other countries and we deserved a break. It was also the perfect way to ensure that I could have her all to myself by getting her as far away as possible from her family.

Juanita was the oldest of nine children. She had practically raised her younger brothers and sisters and she had a highly developed sense of duty and responsibility. Her family, including her parents, had never learned to turn loose and let her live a separate life with me. Family ties are strong - I understand and appreciate that. Family bonding is important to me, too. My first published book, *Thicker than Water*, clearly establishes my strong feelings for my family. But it also clearly shows that I am also an individualist and I made my own way in the world. That's all I wanted Juanita's family to do - to go their own way without depending quite so heavily on her. Anyway, this was a Great Adventure, a new life, and we would be able to share it together.

Upon arrival on Okinawa, I was assigned as the Base Subsistence Officer for Marine Corps Base. We supported twenty-nine Marine Corps dining facilities all over Okinawa and it was the largest military food service operation in the entire Corps. I replaced First Lieutenant Loy, who departed the day after I arrived. This job was not actually within my specific area of expertise, since I had been promoted to Warrant Officer as a Warehousing Officer. The Subsistence Section did not actually 'warehouse' any subsistence. We received foodstuffs from the suppliers on a daily basis and doled it out to the Marine dining facilities. So I guess it was close enough.

As I settled in to learn my new job, I came to realize that I had a group of phenomenal people working for me. Sure, there were a few malcontents and slackers but they were offset by a lot of hard-charging, dedicated and very professional Marines, from the lowest ranks right up through the Staff NCOs.

Among the 'stand-outs' within the junior ranks were Lance Corporals J. Jones, Jr., J. R. Toothaker, Gregory D. Gobell, James E. White and Thomas G. Zusan, Corporal Keith D. Martens and Sergeants Stanley W. Montgomery and Keith J. Berman.

There were several really great Staff NCOs, although the three who were absolutely the very best were Staff Sergeant David M. Harrell, Gunnery Sergeant Francis E. Gembicki and Master Sergeant Jose R. Mora. In fact, during the time they served with me, S/Sgt Harrell and Gy/Sgt Gembicki were both recommended to receive Meritorious Masts. Both were also recommended to receive the Meritorious Service Medal (the highest peacetime medal that can be awarded) and finally, both were recommended for promotion to Warrant Officer. M/Sgt Mora was also recommended to receive a Meritorious Mast and was highly recommended for promotion to Master Gunnery Sergeant. I know all of those details because I was the one who drafted all of those recommendations. I was a very lucky Warrant Officer to be surrounded by such notable Marines who were scattered all through the enlisted ranks within my work section. I was the only officer in the Marine Corps Base Subsistence Section.

Roy Morris 127

Fitness Report for 31 August 1978 through 28 February 1979

Section C: Performance of duty:
Regular duties　　　　　　Outstanding
Administrative duties　　　Excellent
Handling enlisted personnel　Outstanding
Training personnel　　　　Excellent

To what degree has he exhibited the following:
Personal appearance　　　Outstanding
Military presence　　　　Outstanding
Attention to duty　　　　Excellent
Cooperation　　　　　　Outstanding
Initiative　　　　　　　Excellent
Judgment　　　　　　　Excellent
Force　　　　　　　　　Excellent
Leadership　　　　　　　Excellent
Loyalty　　　　　　　　Outstanding
Personal relations　　　　Outstanding
Economy of management　Outstanding
Growth potential　　　　Outstanding

Your estimate of this Marine's general value to the service:
Excellent to Outstanding

Considering the requirements of service in war, indicate your attitude toward having this Marine under your command:
Particularly desire to have

Narrative comments:
　　This energetic, dedicated Marine Officer displays great growth potential. WO Morris is professionally well qualified and highly capable. He is diligent, conscientious and hard working and takes a great deal of pride in himself and his work. He can be relied upon to accomplish his tasks in a highly acceptable manner with very little supervision required. WO Morris carries out his duties in a highly enthusiastic and cheerful manner and maintains a cooperative spirit, being well liked by all for

his sure, easy, unfailing manner in getting things done. WO Morris has been delegated duties as Officer in Charge of the Base Food Service Subsistence Branch, a task which requires thoroughness, management capability, good judgment and conscientiousness. The variety of increasingly complex duties he has assumed indicates his ability to absorb knowledge and to progress to work of increasing difficulty and responsibility. WO Morris eagerly renders assistance to all personnel without regard to race or creed.

Reporting Officer
Jerry W. Sullivan
Captain USMC
Base Food Service Officer
Marine Corps Base

The Simple Truth

Friday the 13th has always been my luckiest day of the year but on Friday, 13 April 1979, my beloved wife, Juanita, deserted me. She was going back to the States to visit with her family. Two of her sisters had been injured in a car wreck and she wanted to be with them. They weren't seriously injured. There were no broken bones. They had been treated and released from the hospital. There was really no reason for Juanita to go home but she went, anyway. It was too early in our tour of duty on Okinawa for the government to pay for her travel so I had to borrow money from the bank to pay for her ticket.

It was only three days before her 30th birthday. That is an important milestone and I wanted to share it with her but it was not to be. She left me alone but she got to spend her birthday with the people she really loved the most, her family.

While making the transition from Gunnery Sergeant to Warrant Officer in Warrant Officer Basic School at Quantico, Virginia, I had done so well that I was awarded my first choice of duty assignments so I had chosen an accompanied tour on Okinawa. I thought I would be guaranteed to have her all to myself for three years on Okinawa, thousands of miles away from her family, without any interruptions or interference. I was mistaken. While I was watching her fly away, I somehow knew that she was taking a step that would change our lives in a most horrible way. There was an unmistakable sense of doom.

When Juanita returned to Okinawa many, many weeks later, she found out I'd had an affair with another woman. I'd been lonely. It had been my turn to have her all to myself but she had given my time to her family when she went home. When she learned of my affair, she kicked me out of the house and I had to get a room at the Bachelor Officers' Quarters. She returned to the States (again) and divorced me in very short order.

It wasn't fair. I'd had to share her with her family for years. Whenever they wanted her, she would go. It cost a lot of money, catering to the wants and needs of her family but that didn't bother me at all. What did bother me was the time together we lost because of them.

There were many times when my military duties had separated us, when I would have duty at the base overnight, when I would be in the field on tactical maneuvers. And there were several major, long-term separations. (1) When I went back to Viet-Nam the second time after we got married. She stayed in Oregon with her parents while I was gone. (2) When I was a Sergeant at the Marine Corps Base in Albany, Georgia, I was sent to Okinawa for 13 months in a duty status that did not allow her to accompany me. She decided to remain in our mobile home where we had been living in a trailer park just a mile or so out the back gate of the base. (3) When I was a Staff Sergeant, I was sent to Quantico, Virginia to attend the Staff Noncommissioned Officer's Academy for three months. She stayed in our apartment in Blackwood, New Jersey because I would be returning to duty at the Marine Corps Supply Activity in Philadelphia, Pennsylvania after completing the Academy. (4) When I was promoted from Gunnery Sergeant to Warrant Officer, while stationed again at Albany, Georgia, I was sent to The Basic School (TBS) for Officers (Warrant Officer's Basic Course) at Quantico, Virginia for four months. She stayed in our base housing quarters at Albany, waiting to find out where my next duty station would be after completing TBS. Those were expected separations, part of my life in the Marine Corps, part of my life in my chosen profession and therefore, they were acceptable separations. Not enjoyable separations (not for me, anyway) but at least acceptable.

But the separations that existed between us when we were together were not acceptable. She got plenty of "mini-vacations" from me, from having to put up with me. In many of my duty assignments, I was unable to go home during my lunch break so she had plenty of days when she didn't have to put up with me at all from 7:00 in the morning until 5:00 or even 6:00 in the evening. She would often have all day to herself. So what was the problem?

I offer no excuses for my mistake. I am just a man, just a human being. I was the best there was in so many different categories on a professional military level but I answer to the same drives and longings as every other person on earth. I never smoked, drank or used drugs in my entire life and I gave Juanita the best life that I could possibly give her. But sometimes, you see, a person's best is good enough and sometimes it isn't. Well, actually, I must admit that I was also a very demanding male, as males go. I was a very intense, healthy and active individual and I guess she finally just got tired of putting up with me and my needs.

But, you know, nobody is perfect. I was wrong and I was terribly sorry. She made a mistake, too, but that's another story, I suppose. The thing is - there are actually very few 'Angels' among the human race but, you know, there are also very few 'Demons' among us. We are all basically the same. It's a simple fact. Some of us can accept that and some can't.

When Juanita divorced me, I couldn't understand why the earth kept turning. The very fabric of the universe should have been ripped apart when she threw me away. There should have been a complete disruption of the space/time continuum. I wish I could have made her feel about me the way I felt about her. Being with her was like living a beautiful dream. Touching her was wonderful. Hugging her was magical. Kissing her made my heart sing. Loving her gave my soul wings. But it's over. It's been over for almost four decades. It still hurts so much it might as well have been yesterday.

I loved Juanita more dearly than I have ever loved anyone in all my 69+ years. I started loving her from the first moment we met. I will always love her. I will go to my grave loving her. With my dying breath, I will whisper her name. But that doesn't make any difference to anybody else. That will never matter to anybody except me. And that's the simple truth.

I went on with my military existence. I went on trying to be the best that I could be.

Fitness Report for 1 March 1979 through 27 July 1979

Section C: Performance of duty:
Regular duties	Outstanding
Administrative duties	Excellent
Handling enlisted personnel	Outstanding
Training personnel	Excellent

To what degree has he exhibited the following:
Personal appearance	Outstanding
Military presence	Outstanding
Attention to duty	Outstanding
Cooperation	Outstanding
Initiative	Excellent
Judgment	Excellent
Force	Outstanding
Leadership	Outstanding
Loyalty	Outstanding
Personal relations	Excellent
Economy of management	Outstanding
Growth potential	Outstanding

Your estimate of this Marine's general value to the service:
Excellent to Outstanding

Considering the requirements of service in war, indicate your attitude toward having this Marine under your command:
Particularly desire to have

Narrative comments:
    WO Morris is the Subsistence Officer for the Marine Corps Base Consolidated Food Service System. He is directly responsible for the supervision, accountability and ensuring that subsistence supplies are delivered to twenty-nine operational dining facilities. WO Morris has established a system which enables him to perform his daily duties with a minimum of effort and a maximum of efficiency, revising procedures as necessary to ensure complete accuracy of records and accounts. WO

Morris has displayed good judgment, initiative, a problem-solving attitude, integrity and dependability in the performance of his duties and by so doing, has contributed greatly to the efficient operation of this section.

Reporting Officer
Jerry W. Sullivan
Captain USMC
Base Food Service Officer
Marine Corps Base

Comments of Reviewing Officer
During the timeframe of this report, the losses and gains (monthly) of the inventory were drastically reduced. It was the efforts of WO Morris which significantly contributed to this positive effort.

Reviewing Officer
J. A. Poland
Colonel USMC
Assistant Chief of Staff (G-4)
Marine Corps Base
Camp Smedley D. Butler
Okinawa, Japan

Backstabbing

On 27 July 1979, I was replaced as the Base Subsistence Officer by a Woman Marine Captain newly-arrived on Okinawa. She actually was a Subsistence Supply Officer and the job was ideal for her. That was not the backstabbing part. That simply was as it should have been. The actual backstabbing came later, in my new job.

I was to be the new Officer in Charge, Bulk Storage Section, Storage Operations, Third Force Service Support Group. Simultaneously, I was also to be the new Officer in Charge, Material Handling Equipment Section, Storage Operations, Third Force Service Support Group.

The Bulk Storage Section filled Warehouse 500 in the Makiminato Service Area. There were also several acres of open storage adjacent to the warehouse, surrounded by a security fence. The warehouse was quite large, longer than a regular city block. It was separated into four bays. It also held the Bulk Storage Section office. The material handling equipment (forklifts, warehouse tractors, cargo trailers, etc.) was kept in one of the bays.

I spent the weekend and the first three days of the week touring the warehouse and the open storage area, going over my new area of responsibility and analyzing the situation. The place was a madhouse. The former Officer in Charge of Bulk Storage had departed more than six weeks previously and he had quite obviously had no idea of what he was supposed to be doing, anyway, so opening the door of Warehouse 500 was quite similar to opening the door to a maze for which there was no diagram, no theme, no blueprint.

On 2 August 1979, I gave a letter to the Officer in Charge of Storage Operations, listing just a few of the more obvious problems and offering suggestions which would remedy some of those problems. I wanted to see what kind of reaction I would get so that I could gauge how easy or how difficult my immediate supervisor might be to work with. The OIC of Storage Operations was Chief Warrant Officer (W-4) R. C. Stricklin and I would soon learn that, not only would he be difficult to work with, he would be IMPOSSIBLE to work with. Anyway, my letter was as follows.

UNITED STATES MARINE CORPS
Bulk Storage Section
Storage Operations

RLM/st
2 Aug 1979

From: Officer in Charge, Bulk Storage Section/
Material Handling Equipment Section
To: Officer in Charge, Storage Operations

Subj: A sampling of Bulk Storage problems

Bay One
Problem: This bay houses, among other things, the security cage. A Corporal is in charge of the cage but he doesn't have a key. At the start of the work day, he has to go (on foot) to Battalion Headquarters to get the security cage key from the Battalion Staff Duty NCO. However, he rarely sees the Staff Duty NCO. Usually, he is given the key by the Duty Clerk, who is generally a PFC or Lance Corporal. At the end of the day, he has to return the key (on foot) to Battalion Headquarters. This is not only a waste of time, it is a stupid procedure.
Solution: Allow me to set up a key locker within my office at Warehouse 500. In this locker, we can store all of the internal keys peculiar to the various sections within the bulk storage area. One of my NCOs or Staff NCOs will control the issue of the various keys to appropriate personnel, as required.

Bay Two
Problem: The floor plan (for the storage racks) does not comply with MCO P4450.7C, the Marine Corps Warehousing Manual. Forklifts have access to secondary aisles ONLY from the central aisle. This restricts movement and storage of material and prevents the efficient and logical use of material handling equipment. I don't know who set up the floor plan but he obviously had no knowledge or experience of warehousing procedures.

Solution: Allow me to reconfigure the floor plan to facilitate the use of forklifts and to comply with MCO P4450.7C, page 2-15.

Problem: Locations assigned to the shelving do not comply with MCO P4450.7C. The compartment location assignments are not set up in progressive alpha/numeric sequence. This has resulted in frequent incorrect assignments of locations for incoming shipments of material. Further, bulk storage personnel have had numerous failures to find specific items when they are trying to find stock to fill outstanding requisitions because they are trying to look for the locations in accordance with the training they received in basic warehousing school.
Solution: Allow me to reconfigure the location system and conduct a subsequent location verification inventory to establish a legitimate location for stock on hand and in order to comply with MCO P4450.7C, page 2-17.

Problem: The bulk storage warehouse should be used only for large, unwieldy and/or bulky items which would not qualify for storage in the Medium/Bin Storage Warehouse (Warehouse 400). The Bulk Storage Warehouse is also an acceptable storage area for items which would ordinarily be stored in medium or bin storage, but which require bulk storage simply because there might be an extremely large quantity of the item on hand. However, there are NUMEROUS items in the Bulk Storage Warehouse which properly belong in medium/bin storage, but which were 'dumped' into Warehouse 500 when the move from Camp Foster to Makiminato was made (several months before I took over Bulk Storage).
Solution: Allow me to interject some logical reasoning into the determination of where the stock in my warehouse actually belongs and allow me to make the transfers when the situation is appropriate.

Bay Three
Problem: This bay is designated as a receiving/issuing section. However, there is not sufficient floor space allowed for these two functions to be performed. Receipts are staged in various aisles, where they are continually in the way of every other warehousing operation being performed.

Solution: Allow me to move some of the medium/bin sized stock to Warehouse 400, where it belongs, so that we will have room to establish an area in which we can stage incoming receipts. Furthermore, have medium/bin sized receipts unloaded directly at Warehouse 400, where they are supposed to go, anyway.

Bay Four
Problem: The configuration of the 'grid' storage locations set up in here is not in compliance with MCO P4450.7C. Bulk storage personnel are unable to reconcile this system with what they were taught in basic warehousing school or with systems used anywhere else in the Marine Corps.
Solution: Allow me to reconfigure the floor plan to establish a logical and proper location system and to comply with MCO P4450.7C, page 2-14.

Since my arrival here last Friday, I have noted that morale is at an extremely low ebb. Both of my crews are working ten hour shifts, six days a week and my key personnel are usually here on Sunday, too. The troops are very well aware of all the problems which exist here and they can see the efforts we are making to attempt to remedy these problems ('We' being myself and my Staff NCOs) but they can also see that nothing is being accomplished. The general consensus inside Warehouse 500 is that nobody OUTSIDE Warehouse 500 cares about the problems that exist here. Is this a correct assumption? Perhaps many of the problems are unsolvable at this particular point in time. However, it would really be a definite boost for morale if the Officer in Charge of the SASSY Management Unit, Lieutenant Colonel Hitzelberger, could visit the warehouse and spend a little time with the troops to let them know that he is at least aware of their problems. Or perhaps, the Battalion Commander or the Sergeant Major could at least walk through the work areas.

Warehouse 500 is a disaster area. It did not get this way over an extended period of time and it did not get this way because of any lack of professionalism or expertise on the part of anybody who works in here. Recently, SASSY Management Unit assets were moved from

Camp Foster to the Makiminato Service Area. Seven medium-sized warehouses were emptied and all of their stock was 'dumped' into Warehouse 500. I was not involved in preparation for the move. I was not involved in the actual move. I was not involved in the placement of the stock when it was brought into the warehouse. In fact, most of my troops were not even assigned here when the move took place. Generally speaking, we inherited this warehouse and everything that is in it. Every day, we open many 50-cube boxes to find all categories of stock piled inside. My Staff NCOs and my troops are working very hard to bring order out of this chaos and they deserve some show of appreciation and some recognition for their outstanding efforts.

Roy L. Morris
WO   USMC

The preceding letter was one I wrote that addressed only some of the actual warehousing problems in the Bulk Storage Section. I naively assumed that CWO Stricklin and I could handle these problems between ourselves. After all, we were both Warehousing Officers.

The problems I found with the forklifts, warehouse tractors and cargo trailers were infinitely different, much more diverse and much more complex. I intended to address these problems in a letter I drafted as the Officer in Charge of the Material Handling Equipment Section. The solutions to these problems could only be approved and/or implemented by higher authority than either CWO Stricklin or I had, so I addressed the letter to the Commanding Officer, 3rd Supply Battalion, via the Officer in Charge of Storage Operations (CWO Stricklin) and via the Officer in Charge of the SASSY Management Unit (Lt/Col Hitzelberger). If both of them agreed with my assessments, they could forward the letter up through the chain of command with their own endorsements. And if either of them disagreed with my assessments, they could indicate the reasons for their disagreements in writing as they forwarded my letter.

Actually, I knew that the letter would eventually have to go even higher up the chain of command, at least as far as the Commanding General, 3rd Force Service Support Group because the problems I had found were so severe that corrective action would require action by units outside our chain of command.

However, when I took the letter to CWO Stricklin, he would not allow me to send it through. When I asked him what was wrong with it, he said there was probably nothing seriously wrong with it but he did not want me to be the signer of the letter, even though I had written it. I tried to assure him that if he disagreed with anything I said, he could include his opinions in his endorsement when he forwarded the letter.

He just simply absolutely would not allow it. He told me, point blank, that if the letter was going through, it could ONLY go through with HIS signature, not mine. He got very agitated about it and he seemed to be quite paranoid about it. We had strong words between us and I swear I could actually imagine that he was having difficulty restraining himself from foaming at the mouth.

My main goal was to get this information into the hands of people who could authorize the proper corrective action so I finally agreed to draft the letter for his signature. However, I left my initials (as the drafter) in the identification code in the upper right hand corner of the letter so that I would receive at least partial credit for the original thinking.

Later on, one of the clerks in CWO Stricklin's office told me that he had ordered her to replace my initials with his so that he would appear to be the drafter. She retyped the letter but left my initials in place and gave the letter to him with a whole stack of other letters to be signed and he didn't notice what she had done.

Another clerk told me that CWO Stricklin had previously informed many senior officers that no significant problems existed within the MHE Section and he was appalled when I discovered so many problems within just a few days of my arrival. He realized he COULD NOT allow me to be the one who advised the senior officers of the true situation. He could only 'save face' if he was the one who 'found' and reported the problems.

I had only been in the organization less than a week and I was already antagonizing my immediate supervisor. I didn't mean to be adversarial but I have never been a 'Yes' man and there was no reason to start at that point. Frankly, I believe CWO Stricklin was astonished by the fact that I had accomplished so much and had initiated so many improvements in such a short time. He most certainly wasn't going to admit that I was of higher quality than he. But the main reason this kind of information was whispered to me by his subordinates was the fact that none of the clerks in the Storage Operations office had any respect for him. They all seemed to like me and they all let me know, individually, at one time or another, that they could tell I was 'one of the good officers' and they could see that I was actually trying to solve problems and take care of the troops. I appreciated that.

Anyway, the following document is a copy of the letter that I drafted, however reluctantly, for HIS signature. Even if you have no experience in the maintenance field and don't understand all of the military jargon, you will easily be able to see that I had literally 'opened a can of worms'.

UNITED STATES MARINE CORPS
Storage Operations
SASSY Management Unit
3rd Supply Battalion
3rd Force Service Support Group

850/RLM/pam
4790
2 August 1979

From: Officer in Charge
To: Commanding Officer, 3rd Supply Battalion, 3rd Force Service Support Group
Via: Officer in Charge, SASSY Management Unit

Subj: Material Handling Equipment

The following problems and proposed solutions pertaining to MHE are forwarded:

Problem:
Equipment operators, both in the Storage Operations section and in the supported units are not following prescribed procedures for safe operation of equipment. Equipment operators are not performing required first echelon maintenance, such as the before, during and after operation checks. For example, operating equipment with low fluid levels may cause internal damage. Further, operating equipment with faulty clutch, brakes, etc. may result in physical damage to the equipment or to the operator.

Solution:
The NCOIC of Material Handling Equipment has been ordered to conduct a training program for the equipment operators within the Storage Operations Section. Subjects covered will include safe and proper handling of equipment, procedures for performing first echelon maintenance and reasons for this maintenance, and the proper method of completing the trip tickets. The scope of this program will be broadened within thirty (30) days to ensure that all operators from the

Storage Operations Section and all operators from supported sections and units receive complete instructions regarding material handling equipment, after which time nobody will be allowed to operate MHE unless he has an endorsement on his operator's license verifying that he has attended the appropriate training. Also, the NCOIC of MHE will have the authority to issue citations for unsafe and/or improper use of MHE and will monitor operators from all supported sections and units.

Problem:
Because of the shortage of material handling equipment and because of the high 'dead line' rate of existing equipment, the Bulk Storage Section is currently operating two shifts. This is necessary to ensure maximum utilization of personnel who would otherwise be unable to perform their missions while waiting for equipment to become available. This produces a SEEMINGLY higher rate of equipment failure due to increased usage within a single 24-hour period. For example, a forklift which will operate for 500 hours before requiring shop maintenance might possibly be operated for about twelve to thirteen weeks before it must be sent in for shop maintenance if it is used only during one single work shift on a given day. However, if it is available for use by two separate work shifts in a single 24-hour period, it will accumulate 500 hours of operation in only about six weeks. A great deal of the work in the Bulk Storage section REQUIRES the use of a forklift and if all of the bulk storage personnel were to be at work during the same work shift period, some of them would be wasting production time while waiting for forklift assets to become available.

Two of the model 1704 gas 4,000 pound forklifts are approximately fifteen (15) years old. Most of the model 1706 gas 4,000 pound forklifts are between eight (8) and ten (10) years old. The average age of the model 1806 electric 4.000 pound forklifts is six (6) years. Four forklifts have been 'surveyed' without replacement. This has an extremely adverse effect on our capability to accomplish our mission and to provide equipment support to other units.

Solution:
A review of material handling equipment requirements is currently being conducted within the Storage Operations Section by the new

Officer in Charge of MHE (namely, WO Morris). Upon completion, results and recommendations will be forwarded. Liaison with the Base Motor Transport Officer and the Base Motor Transport Maintenance Chief indicate that very limited forklift assets are available to replace equipment which is 'surveyed' due to age and that disposition instructions have been requested for the four forklifts which have recently been 'surveyed'.

Problem:
There is currently no Base tire repair shop at the Makiminato Service Area. There is only one tire machine at the Base Motor Transport Maintenance Section at Camp Foster, with only one Local Japanese Civilian assigned to repair flat tires. Transportation support is inadequate to shuttle flat tires to and from Camp Foster in a timely manner. Many times, personal vehicles have been used to transport flat tires to preclude excessive 'down time' for the MHE.

Solution:
A tire repair shop should be established at the Makiminato Service Area within the Base Motor Transport Maintenance Facility Subunit. Liaison with the Base Motor Transport Maintenance Chief indicates that the tire machine at Camp Foster is the only one available and that a 24-48 hour turnaround is his projected time frame for repairing flat tires. The new Officer in Charge of MHE (WO Morris) has dictated that personal vehicles will no longer be used to transport flat tires between MSA and Camp Foster, reasoning that this transportation is the responsibility of Base Motor Transport and if we continue to relieve them of this burden by circumventing the system, then the need for improved service in this area will never be made apparent to senior officers who are in a position to take corrective action.

Problem:
There is no charger available in Warehouse 500 for the model 1805 electric 4,000 pound forklift. Currently, nine of these forklifts are situated elsewhere with the supported units and sections, where chargers are available. The one remaining forklift of this type, which is located at Warehouse 500, the bulk storage warehouse, is 'down' because the

nearest compatible charger is located in warehouse 506. This forklift is the indoor type and cannot be driven on the roadways in order to gain access to a charger. When bulk storage assets and material were moved from seven (7) warehouses at Camp Foster to Warehouse 500 at MSA, no provision was made, at the time, to provide a charger for this type of forklift at the ONE warehouse where it would be MOST needed--Warehouse 500.

Solution:
Additional assets of the charger required for the model 1805 electric 4,000 pound forklift have been requested by the Base Motor Transport Section through the Property Control Office and Direct Support Stock Control Branch (DSSC). We have no projected availability date, at this time.

Problem:
There is currently no contact team operating from the Base Motor Transport maintenance facility. Without personnel available to perform onsite maintenance, many minor repair jobs are causing excessive 'down time' for MHE simply because the equipment must be removed to the Base Motor Transport maintenance facility at Camp Foster, or to the maintenance subunit at MSA for completion of required repairs.

Solution:
The Base Motor Transport Maintenance Facility contact teams should be reestablished with the capability to complete minor repairs onsite so that 'down time' for MHE will be reduced to a minimum. The Base Motor Transport Maintenance Chief stated that there is no provision for reestablishing the contact team, at this time.

Problem:
The system of recordkeeping in regard to trip tickets, daily dispatching record of MHE and maintenance schedules is inadequate.
Solution:
Both the Responsible Officer of each supported unit or section and the NCOIC of MHE will review trip tickets and the dispatching record daily to ensure that the procedures taught to operators are being followed. The

NCOIC of MHE will report any discrepancies to the new OIC of Material Handling Equipment, Warrant Officer Morris. Preventive maintenance schedules are controlled by Base Motor Transport, so the 250 and 500 hour maintenance cycles will be based on monthly reports submitted by the NCOIC of Material Handling Equipment. The Responsible Officer of each supported unit or section will ensure that this maintenance cycle is followed.

R. C. Stricklin
CWO USMC

After I drafted the first MHE letter for CWO Stricklin's signature (at his insistence), he ordered me to draft an endorsement to that letter for Lieutenant Colonel Hitzelberger's signature. When I asked him how I was supposed to know what the Colonel would want to say, he told me, "Just do it".

When I wrote the endorsement, I again listed my initials in the upper right hand corner and used the words I would want the Colonel to say in support of my basic letter. I figured, if he didn't like what I wanted him to say, he could make up his own words.

It was right about that period of time that I had been informed that CWO Stricklin had ordered his clerk to remove my initials and replace them with his so that it would appear that Stricklin, rather than Morris, had done the original thinking and had drafted the letter. At that time, I had no idea of the extent to which CWO Stricklin would go in order to make me look bad just so that he could make himself look good. When I had grated on his nerves that very first time, I simply did not realize what a 'hornet's nest' I had kicked over. His paranoia was complete. He simply could not live with the knowledge that one of his subordinates was obviously so much more intelligent than he was and he would eventually stoop to absolutely ANYTHING to 'put me in my place'. I had only been dealing with him a few days so I still had no idea what an absolute backstabbing jerk he really was.

There were some really fine junior enlisted Marines assigned to the bulk storage section. The Assistant NCOIC of Bulk Storage, Sergeant

James D. Brooks, brought three of these men to my attention. I had been impressed with Sergeant Brooks so, based on his opinion, I recommended the following men for meritorious promotion from Private First Class to Lance Corporal:

S. M. Bell,
L. G. Clark
D. Martin.

UNITED STATES MARINE CORPS
3rd Supply Battalion
3rd Force Service Support Group
Fleet Marine Force Pacific

1/JAC/ver
4790
16 August 1979

From: Commanding Officer
To: Commanding General, 3rd Force Service Support Group
Subj: Maintenance and Operation of Commercial Forklifts
Ref: (a) CG, MCB Camp Smedley D. Butler l
tr 4/DRH/gb 4790 of 11 Jul 79
Encl: (1) OIC Storage Operations,
SMU ltr 850/RLM/pam 4790 of 2 Aug 79

In response to reference (a), a study of established operating and maintenance procedures for the commercial forklifts assigned to the Battalion was conducted, as per enclosure (1). The study indicated that the discrepancies noted by FSMAO were accurate and were the result of inadequate procedures and insufficient attention at the operator level, and indifference at the management level. To correct the cited discrepancies and to prevent recurrence, the following actions have been taken.

Delineate line of responsibility. The Storage Officer, SMU, is now accountable to the Battalion SOC for the utilization and maintenance of the forklifts. A new Responsible Officer, Warrant Officer R. L. Morris, has been appointed to replace the incumbent.

Increase visibility and timely readiness reporting. The Battalion MMO will now report on commercial assets, tractors and forklifts, commencing in September. The Group Equipment Readiness Briefing will serve as the vehicle to ensure continuing command interest.

Improve communications with the Base Motor Transport Maintenance Facility. The problems and the means to resolve them have been discussed with the base facility. I have personally discussed this matter with the Base MMO and feel confident that base support for the commercial fleet will also improve.

Implement an effective training program to include operators' maintenance, safety, and record keeping procedures. This is obviously fundamental to the success of any maintenance program. To ensure the quality of the program, assistance, in the form of review and recommendations, from the Group MMO will be requested.

The above enumerated actions will be aggressively monitored to guarantee that this long-standing problem is, in fact, solved.

J. A. Caputa
Lt/Col USMC

The preceding letter from Lt/Col Caputa, the Battalion Commander, gave a real lift to my spirits. For one thing, it assured me that the letter I drafted for Stricklin had actually made it into the hands of some senior officers and had the attention of the Commanding General of 3rd FSSG and the Commanding General of Marine Corps Base. So I did have at least some hope of accomplishing something.

The Battalion CO was talking about MY study. And I now knew, for sure, why Stricklin didn't want anybody to know that I had drafted the letter he had insisted on signing and I knew the clerks had been telling me the truth about Stricklin having previously told the senior officers there were no significant problems with MHE. I bet he was horrified at all the attention MHE was getting from the Generals. If I had somehow been allowed to sign that letter, it would have been obvious to everybody that he had previously done inadequate research into the situation and he would have been exposed as both an idiot and a liar.

Lt/Col Caputa's letter also dictated that a training program would have to be implemented, to include operators' maintenance, safety and record keeping procedures. I assumed, correctly, that the training sessions would be conducted by either the Officer in Charge of MHE (namely, me) or by my assistant.

Therefore, I drafted a form letter to be sent to the commanders of every unit which was supported by my MHE section, requesting information on the forklift operators who would be attending the training sessions. I needed to be able to arrange for classroom facilities, training aids, lesson plans, testing materials, and a lot of other details. The Battalion Commander wanted a training program and I was going to give him a good one.

CWO Stricklin didn't approve of my original draft of the form letter, so I redrafted it. Then I resubmitted the form letter. After a considerable time had passed, I asked him about getting the letter sent out. He told me that it wasn't going to be sent out and that I had no business requesting the information, in the first place. I told him he was hindering me in my efforts to correct the problems in the MHE Section and that I needed the cooperation of those unit commanders in order to accomplish the mission I had been assigned when I had inherited the 'can of worms' called the MHE Section.

He became highly irate that I had the nerve to even SUGGEST that he was a hindrance to me. He said that my job was to do EXACTLY what he told me to do and that any other action on my part would constitute disrespect and disobedience. He had become very excited, telling me that I had better start acting like a 'team player' and that, if I didn't, he would see to it that corrective action would be taken. He was absolutely adamant about being completely in control and not having ANYBODY question his judgment.

At the time, I wasn't quite sure how I was going to be able to get the required training accomplished without his support, or at least without his permission. I suppose, if I could have arranged to allow him to pretend it was his idea, he might have allowed the plan to proceed. But I could see no reason why I should be forced to stroke the ego of a paranoid, self-serving control freak such as he was.

UNITED STATES MARINE CORPS
Storage Operations
3rd Supply Battalion
3rd Force Service Support Group

RLM/st
5 Sept 1979

From: Officer in Charge,
Bulk Storage Section/Material Handling Equipment Section
To: Officer in Charge, SASSY Management Unit
Via: Officer in Charge, Storage Operations

Subj: Material Handling Equipment

Ref: (a) OIC Storage Operations letter 850/RLM/pam over 4790 dated 2 Aug 79

Encl: (1) Status of MHE assets
(2) MHE personnel roster

The mission of the Material Handling Equipment Section to provide MHE support to using units within Third FSSG has been seriously impaired by the lack of serviceable assets and by a critical shortage of personnel.

Enclosure (1) reflects the availability and serviceability of existing assets at the Makiminato Service Area.

Enclosure (2) reflects the current status of personnel assigned within the MHE section. L/Cpl Sanders will be leaving within two months. Receipt of a replacement for him as soon as possible is imperative. L/Cpl B. C. Stewart has been designated (by CWO Stricklin) as a permanent member of the Supply Company working party to fill an obligation of the Third Platoon (Bins Storage Section). There has been no replacement from the Third Platoon to assume L/Cpl Sanders' duties in the MHE Section and I have been informed that a replacement will NEVER be provided. Out of only seven (7) billets in the MHE Section, three of those billets have been vacant ever since I have been assigned simultaneously as OIC of Bulk Storage and OIC of MHE.

With L/Cpl Sanders' billet vacant because of CWO Stricklin's arbitrary decision, the MHE Section is at less than 43 %, personnel-wise. This has placed a severe strain on the ability of the MHE Section to accomplish its mission.

Although there are certain priority projects with which I am tasked as OIC of the Bulk Storage Section, I have also been required to obligate forklifts and personnel, on a higher priority basis, to other sections (Bins Storage Section and Medium Storage Section) within Storage Operations in order to provide maximum support to those sections. The loss of essential equipment and personnel in this manner has seriously impaired my Bulk Storage Section in accomplishing our own mission. I am currently requiring my day crew to work ten (10) hours per day and I am operating a night crew under the same conditions. This plan of action, coupled with working a skeleton crew on weekends, has somewhat alleviated the problems related to operating without adequate available material handling equipment. However, working long hours without proper equipment has had a detrimental effect on morale.

When I drafted reference (a) for CWO Stricklin's signature, I proposed several possible solutions to the more pressing problems. I do not foresee a substantial improvement in the near future unless maintenance and repair of material handling equipment is improved significantly and unless the current personnel problems can be resolved.

The Bulk Storage Section will continue to operate two shifts on extended hours to accomplish our assigned priorities. I will transfer one Marine from my Bulk Storage Section to my Material Handling Equipment Section to replace the man who was taken to cover the Third Platoon (Bins Section) working party requirement.

Roy L. Morris
WO   USMC

Enclosure (1)
Status of Material Handling Equipment physically designated at Makiminato Service Area

Electric forklifts assigned   40
Electric forklifts dead lined   24
Electric forklifts available   16

Gas forklifts assigned   16
Gas forklifts dead lined   6
Gas forklifts available   10

Warehouse tractors assigned   4
Warehouse tractors dead lined   4
Warehouse tractors available   0

Enclosure (2)
Material Handling Equipment Table of Organization Personnel Roster

T/O #	TITLE	T/O RANK	RANK	NAME	STATUS
72	NCOIC	S/Sgt	S/Sgt	Moore, J.	Assigned
80	Asst NCOIC/ Forklift Operator	Sgt	L/Cpl	Sanders, R.	Assigned/to leave within 60 days
74	Operator	L/Cpl	L/Cpl	Stewart, C.	Assigned
74	Operator	L/Cpl	L/Cpl	Stewart, B. C.	On permanent working party filling 3rd Plt. (Bin Storage Section) Slot
74	Operator				Vacant
76	Operator				Vacant
84	Operator				Vacant

The preceding letter is one that I drafted after I had travelled all over the island, reviewing the material handling equipment situation. I believe I found every piece of equipment and determined the correct status of each piece. It took three days because I often had to return to MSA to take care of problems. I used my personal vehicle.

When I drafted this letter, I listed myself as the signer. By this time, I was tired of playing politics with CWO Stricklin. I wanted this information to be noted. I wanted the Officer in Charge of the SMU (Lt/Col Hitzelberger) and the Battalion Commander (Lt/Col Caputa) to know exactly how bad the situation was. And I had reached the point that I wanted them both to know that I was the one doing the work, doing the thinking and doing the writing. I knew there would be hell to pay when I took this letter to Stricklin. But even after all I had gone through with him, up to that point, I still didn't realize just how really dangerous he could be.

After he read the letter, he accused me of trying to undermine his authority, of attempting character assassination, of trying to blame my troubles on the 3rd Platoon Commander because I mentioned, in the letter, that I was required to provide one man to fill a 3rd Platoon working party requirement. As if I was trying to blame all my troubles on the loss of a single worker.

Stricklin was totally off the grid with anger. He was slamming things around in his office. The only reason the clerks didn't bust in on us to prevent manslaughter was because they knew that I had studied martial arts and that I was really in no serious danger from that madman.

He said that if I tried to go 'over his head' to give this letter to ANYBODY, he would file charges against me for disrespect, disobedience, insubordination and anything else he could think of. Mostly, he was scared of being exposed as an idiot because he had previously told the senior officers that no serious problems existed with MHE.

Then he started trying to make it seem that I was unable to master the situation because the situation was beyond my limited capabilities. But the truth is that the only reason I had been unable to resolve many of the problems I had inherited when I was assigned simultaneously as both the Officer in Charge of Bulk Storage AND Officer in Charge of Material Handling Equipment was because he blocked every effort I made to clean up the mess he had given me.

And part of my problems with CWO Stricklin had nothing at all to do with the professional performance of my duties. The very first weekend I was assigned, he wanted me to attend what he considered 'Officers' Call', so I could get together with his other junior officers and him at the Officers' Club or at his bachelor officers quarters. He wanted us all to sit around, drinking beer and talking. Well, that first time, I showed up and ordered a soda pop (he was quite disconcerted to discover that I was a total non-drinker). I stayed and talked with them for a while, as long as the conversation was work-related, but when Stricklin started telling stories and the episode turned into a 'bull' session, I excused myself and said I had work to do. He got very upset that he was losing the newest member of his audience but I let him know (without actually saying so) that I had better things to do than sit there for hours while he tried to impress us with a list of his 'accomplishments'. I wasn't discourteous and I didn't try to embarrass him in any way, but I really and truly did have better things to do.

Well, since I had failed to get that previous letter past him, I redrafted it and changed the format. And I set it up for HIS signature. But he just would not sign it. He did not want that information to go anywhere and, again, he threatened me with charges if I tried to get around him in any way. His problem was that my research placed all of the information about MHE in one package, so it would be obvious that the problems were much more serious and much more widespread than anyone had previously believed - and, once again, it proved that his previous 'investigation' into MHE had been slipshod and haphazard and his results had, of course, been totally inaccurate.

Then it was time to write fitness reports on the Staff NCOs under my command. Stricklin wanted me to backdate the fitness reports to the date the previous Officer in Charge of Bulk Storage had departed but that had been over six weeks before I had been assigned. He just didn't want a gap to exist between my predecessor and myself. We had some severe arguments over this situation but as usual, the guidelines - the regulations - were in my favor. Our disagreement was so heated and so prolonged that I decided to make it a matter of record by sending him an official memorandum on the subject. A copy of the memo is listed next.

Memorandum for the Record dated 15 September 1979

From: Officer in Charge,
       Bulk Storage Section/Material Handling Equipment Section
To: Officer in Charge, Storage Operations

Subj: Fitness Reports

    Sir, you have ordered me to write fitness reports for the Staff NCOs assigned to the Bulk Storage Section and to the Material Handling Equipment Section. I am willing to do so, as I am their reporting senior but I do not agree with the time period you want cited on the fitness reports. I cannot sign a document to cover the period of time after the last OIC departed and before I arrived. He was gone for six weeks before I was assigned here.

    My date of detachment from Marine Corps Base, my old command, was 27 July 1979. The starting date for any fitness report which I can legally sign for any personnel in 3rd Force Service Support Group, my new command, is 28 July 1979.

    I know you're going to say that I am being disloyal and disrespectful but you can't order me to do something that we both know is illegal. You are trying to get me to make a false official statement on a government document. That would be a violation of my oath. I will not do it.

                                                 Roy L. Morris
                                                 WO   USMC

Last Resort
31 October 1979

On this day, I stood formally relieved of my simultaneous assignment as Officer in Charge of Bulk Storage and Officer in Charge of Material Handling Equipment and was being transferred out of the Storage Operations Section and I didn't really have much to lose so I drafted my final communiqué as a member of Storage Operations. CWO Stricklin had finally realized that he was never going to be able to bend me to his will and turn me into one of his 'Yes' men, so he searched the island until he found someone who was eligible to replace me and had me reassigned to another section which was still in the SASSY Management Unit but outside of Storage Operations (his personal domain).

CWO Stricklin had a dilemma. He could not have me 'relieved for cause' because I would have the right to demand a hearing by a tribunal of senior officers to fight the charges against me. If that happened, he knew that I would bring to light all of his mistakes, his errors of judgment, and the many ways he had sabotaged me in my efforts to correct the problems I had discovered, so he simply had me transferred to a lesser position as if he was doing me a favor by 'reducing the pressures I had been facing'.

I had finally come to a decision. It was a momentous decision. I realized that I was going to have to go around the chain of command. For a Marine, especially a Marine of my caliber, the chain of command was practically a sacred concept. A concept that I was being forced to violate. The only way the Officer in Charge of the SMU, Lt/Col Hitzelberger, was going to find out the truth about the situation that existed between Stricklin and me was if I bypassed Stricklin and personally provided the truth to the Colonel.

As on so many occasions before, I was depressed by the lack of professionalism and the lack of leadership qualities displayed by one of my fellow Marines. CWO Stricklin was the WORST example of a Marine Corps Officer I ever encountered. He was an absolute Master at kissing up to his seniors and running roughshod over his juniors. He was an expert at the art of character assassination through snide remarks, innuendos and outright lying. His skill was second to none at taking credit for the efforts of his subordinates and placing blame on them for his own failures. He would have made a wonderful politician.

Memorandum for the Record dated 31 October 1979

From: Warrant Officer Roy L. Morris
To: Lt/Col D. A. Hitzelberger

Subj: Performance of Duty

When I first assumed duty as OIC of Bulk Storage and simultaneously as OIC of Material Handling Equipment, Warehouse 500 was a disaster area. I toured the area the very first time on 25 July 1979.

The previous OIC of Bulk Storage had vacated the position six weeks before I arrived. The warehouse office was empty. The front doors of Bay Two and Bay Three were wide open and there was only one man to be found in the warehouse when I walked in. That was Master Gunnery Sergeant Fiorello, who was driving a forklift putting away receipts. I was astonished. There are many times when this sort of 'hands on' leadership might be appropriate, and even necessary, but he was alone and not providing guidance and leadership to anybody. He was doing a PFC's job.

There wasn't a full ten square feet of open floor space in any section of the warehouse. In some instances, it was difficult to distinguish the aisles from the rows of stock. There were no specific areas set aside for processing receipts and issues. Items to be researched by the Technical & Research Section were positioned indiscriminately in various aisles of the warehouse.

In my first day on the job, I counted more than sixty (60) safety violations. I am referring to the method and manner in which boxes were stacked and the way storage racks and locations were set up.

The open storage lot behind Warehouse 500 was almost hopeless. There were at least thirty-five 50-cube boxes full of gear mixed in with boxes of trash all over the lot. The trash bins were filled with trash and they were surrounded by piles of trash.

Warehouse security was virtually nonexistent. People from other units and sections were constantly going through Bay Three to get to the MHE Section. There was absolutely no control over the gate opening into the back lot so that other sections were constantly bringing their trash and dropping it out by the truckload.

Troop morale was at the lowest point that I have ever observed in my career (I knew people who were happier while I was in Viet-Nam). The troops were treated badly by almost all of their seniors. The NCOIC of Bulk Storage was a strict disciplinarian who used very little tact or thoughtfulness in dealing with the troops.

The troops had, at one time, been placed on tropical hours, meaning that they came to work at 0600 and got off work at 1430 to avoid the worst heat of the day. However, the heat had been disregarded when the work hours had been extended from 0600 to 1700.

The Company and Battalion leaders were constantly making demands on the troops without routing those demands through the proper channels. I discovered that, on many occasions, the troops were being contacted directly by Company and Battalion officers and Staff NCOs to conduct administrative and disciplinary functions. One night, while I was at the warehouse with the night crew, we received a call from the First Sergeant, telling us that a certain Marine had to report to the Company Office immediately to face non-judicial punishment for a period of unauthorized absence. I went to the Company Office with this Marine, partially because I felt it was my duty to be present while he faced his charges and partially to ask the First Sergeant why I had not been informed that this Marine's hearing had been scheduled. Imagine my surprise when I walked into the Company Office to find another of my Marines being advised of his rights by the First Sergeant in preparation to face punishment. I told the First Sergeant, in no uncertain terms, that I wanted to be present for any hearings to be held on any of my Marines for any reason and that I wanted to receive some advance notification of future administrative matters in time to plan my schedule around them.

There are many ways in which leaders in the SASSY Management Unit are failing the troops. Morale is at a record low because they are convinced that almost everyone in a leadership billet is screwed up and that the few decent leaders have their hands tied by a screwed up 'system'.

Along with my responsibilities as Officer in Charge of Bulk Storage, I was also assigned as Officer in Charge of Material Handling Equipment. All of the officers and Staff NCOs who spoke with me on the subject of MHE told me that the status of MHE was well past the critical stage and that I had literally inherited a veritable 'can of worms' and, in fact, all of the people who talked with me told me they were very surprised to hear that I had been assigned to fill both billets simultaneously and that they fully expected that I would most certainly not be able to satisfactorily accomplish both jobs at the same time.

When I took over MHE, the entire section consisted of one Staff Sergeant and two Lance Corporals. These people, incidentally, were deducted from the manpower assets within my Bulk Storage Section.

Neither the NCOIC of MHE nor anyone else within Third FSSG could tell me what I was actually responsible for, in regard to material assets. I went directly to the Marine Corps Base Motor Transport Section. They could not give me a list of all MHE assets which had been or should be assigned to Third FSSG. Their equipment custody record cards had not been updated during the past five months. I also learned that the former Third FSSG Responsible Officer who had signed those ECR cards had departed from Okinawa without being properly relieved.

I used my personal vehicle to travel to all Marine camps on Okinawa to conduct an overall inspection/inventory of all MHE which might possibly come under my control. After I determined what I believed to be a complete list of all MHE for which I might be responsible, I gave the list to the Supply Battalion S-4 Section. They accepted my list as being accurate. I could only hope that I had found everything.

Shortly prior to my assignment, the Field Supply Maintenance Analysis Office had conducted a safety/serviceability inspection on MHE. The results of that inspection indicated that our MHE was totally unsatisfactory. Within one week of the day I assumed duty as OIC of MHE, I had established a program to improve the status of MHE. However, I had also decided that correcting everything that was wrong with MHE was going to take a lot more 'horsepower' than I had as a lowly Warrant Officer, so I drafted a letter covering some of the problems and solutions I wanted to pursue. I had several serious setbacks in this effort because CWO Stricklin disagreed with me on my drafted response to the FSMAO results.

Our differences were eventually worked out, although I took umbrage over CWO Stricklin's insistence that the letter be written as if it was coming from the OIC of Storage Operations (himself) rather than from me, as the OIC of Material Handling Equipment. He was absolutely determined that all correspondence that I originated would have Stricklin listed as the signer, regardless of the subject or content of the correspondence.

Something that was extremely puzzling to me was the fact that he ordered me to draft the endorsement to my own letter. I disagreed. That would defeat the whole purpose of making an endorsement. If I wanted to write a letter, in the first place, it should come from me as the signer. As the next senior officer over me, he would be the first via. The OIC of the SMU would be the second via. If either of those individuals wanted to concur with my ideas and opinions, they could do so through their endorsement. If they disagreed with any of my suggestions or recommendations, they could present their own opinions through their endorsement.

Considering the mission priorities and requirements with which I was faced at the time, I felt that one particular act on CWO Stricklin's part was retaliatory in nature and actually rather childish. My platoon, the fourth, was required to fill a third platoon road trash work party requirement without receiving a replacement. I fully realize the critical personnel shortage which existed within all of Storage, but this decision was a bad one in that many Marines in the fourth platoon (and elsewhere) knew of the problems that I was having with CWO Stricklin and they felt that he was using his seniority to take advantage of us. The clerks in Stricklin's office knew of our many arguments and they were putting the word out that I was not 'buckling under' to Stricklin's pressure.

In my other new position as OIC of Bulk Storage, I inherited the responsibility for ensuring that Meritorious Masts were given to the personnel who had been involved in moving Storage from Camp Foster to Makiminato. It doesn't matter that the move resulted in such a total mess at Warehouse 500 (Bulk Storage). The administrative details of the move had been the responsibility of the officers and Staff NCOs involved. The troops involved in doing the actual work had put forth their best effort and had spent many long, arduous hours of labor in getting the job done. The manner in which I learned of the Meritorious Masts was that some of the troops approached me and asked about them. When I asked CWO Stricklin about the Meritorious Masts, he said it was being taken care of. A week later, I asked him again. He seemed quite upset that I was 'badgering' him about it but he told me that he would have WO Elggren, of the third platoon, take care of it. And he did, eventually. Meritorious Masts were given out....but ONLY to the members of WO Elggren's third platoon. I don't know if Elggren left out my people, on purpose, but I would bet my last dollar that Stricklin arranged to have it done that way. He's such a spiteful individual. So, I drafted a letter to get the awards arranged for my people. I had to pull a few strings with the admin people at Battalion Headquarters, but I didn't make the mistake of going through Stricklin. I took my letter and my list of names to one of the enlisted people at Battalion and we pretended that I was merely updating WO Elggren's list, adding just a few names that had been inadvertently left off the list. I'll never give the name of the enlisted Marine that 'fixed' the list for me, but we got it done. The awards were made, finally, to my people in the 4th Platoon.

During early September, I was advised of another unique problem by Sgt Brooks, the NCOIC of the night crew. His Marines were being forced to walk a great distance unnecessarily each night at the end of their shift because there was only one gate left unlocked leading from the warehouse area into the barracks area, this being the gate at the end of the entire block of warehouses (the gate nearest to building 107). The night crew had to walk four kilometers from the warehouse to the barracks when they used that gate. However, there was a personnel gate at the end of Warehouse 500 (our warehouse). If the troops were allowed to use that gate, they would only have to walk 300 meters. When I asked Stricklin if we could have a key to that personnel gate, he replied that it would be a security risk. I could not see the logic in that, and I made the mistake of telling that to CWO Stricklin - If Sgt Brooks unlocked the gate only long enough to let his night crew through, then locked the gate behind them, how could that be a security risk? Stricklin gave me quite a lecture on security. He didn't actually SAY that I didn't know the first thing about security but he made it pretty clear that, in his opinion, I didn't know the first thing about security. Then I asked him about the gate that is left open at the end of the warehouse area by building 107, the gate my workers were forced to go through. There were no security cameras there. There was no guard there, not even during the hours of darkness. There was not even a sign saying 'restricted area - all unauthorized personnel keep out'. When I asked him if that was his interpretation of security, I knew that I was right on the borderline of having charges filed against me for insubordination or disrespect, but by that time in the course of my assignment within the Storage Section, I had already been on that borderline with him on many occasions, before. Anyway, we were never allowed to open that personnel gate.

In mid-September, command attention was focused on warehouse security. A letter was drafted in Storage Operations and forwarded to Supply Battalion, listing various personnel to be authorized to pick up warehouse keys from the Battalion Staff Duty. I was not consulted ahead of time regarding the personnel I wanted to be listed, so I drafted a letter to correct discrepancies on the list. When I took my letter to Stricklin, he said that he was personally drafting a letter to correct the list for ALL of Storage and that he would extract the appropriate information from the draft of my letter. As late as 22 October 1979, I reviewed the key access list at the Staff Duty's office. My proposed corrections had never been made.

I want to point out that I had many lively discussions with Stricklin regarding the night crew. He was against the very idea of having a night crew, while I was convinced that the work performed by the night crew was the only thing that enabled Bulk Storage to effectively function. There are several important points to remember when considering the advantages of having a night crew. (1) These people never had to be excused from work to attend to administrative details, or to go to sickbay or to go to clothing cash sales, as this sort of business was taken care of during their free time during the day. (2) While the day crew had to share forklifts with the Cyclic Inventory Section and with other sections, the night crew was able to utilize all forklift assets for OUR purposes. (3) While the day crew lost a lot of production time because of company formations, training, priority walk-through requisitions, customers, official visitors, etc., the night crew was able to dedicate all of their duty hours toward the accomplishment of Bulk Storage Section goals.

I completely disagreed with Stricklin's plan to establish grid locations in Bay 4 of my warehouse. I told him that the setup of a grid system in the same bay with an aisle and row system was in violation of MCO P4450.7C, the Marine Corps Warehousing Manual, but he wasn't interested in hearing what I had to say, especially when I offered to show him the manual. He was absolutely furious that I would even DARE to suggest that his idea was not in conformance with the warehousing manual.

I have absolutely no understanding of why CWO Stricklin wanted the rows in Bay Two to be turned to run north-south instead of east-west. Again, his new plan for the location system was not compatible with the Marine Corps Warehousing Manual and the very idea of changing the direction of the rows was illogical and contrary to common sense. The aisle in HIS new location system was only nine feet wide. It was virtually impossible to work in that area with anything except a model E4 'reach fork' forklift.

CWO Stricklin dictated that the same system be started in Bay One as he had started in Bay Four. He had aisles 1 and 2 deleted and started grid locations in there. However, since I had objected so strenuously before against his plans for my warehouse, and because I had based my arguments on my knowledge of the Marine Corps Warehousing Manual, he didn't call it re-warehousing. He called it 'realignment' and assumed that made it alright.

When it was time to write fitness reports on the Staff NCOs in Bulk Storage, CWO Stricklin wanted me to include the six week period between the relief of the former OIC of Bulk Storage and my assignment to duty as OIC of Bulk Storage. I told him I could not do that because I was still assigned to Marine Corps Base during that period of time and I could not write reports on people who I did not even know during that time. He just kept insisting that I do so, until I was finally forced to actually REFUSE, in WRITING, to do what he was ordering me to do because it was illegal and I could not knowingly make a false statement on an official government document. Only then did he finally stop trying to coerce me into it. Even so, his actions, his manner, his comments to me and about me indicated that he was totally disgusted with what he called my obstinate and disrespectful refusal to obey orders.

When Gy/Sgt Torres was transferred to Warehouse 400, I was prepared to write a "not observed" fitness report on him for the short period of time that he worked for me. However, CWO Stricklin told me he wanted to write a fitness report on the Gunny, himself, to cover the entire period since his last report and he asked me if I could simply write a sample rough draft fitness report on Gunny Torres, based on my limited observations which might help him in writing a Section C narrative statement of his own. This was not actually a totally unreasonable request, especially coming from CWO Stricklin, so I prepared what I considered a valid statement and assigned sample Section B markings on a rough copy of a fitness report, based on my very limited observations and conclusions during the short time I had worked with Gy/Sgt Torres. I fully expected CWO Stricklin to take my markings and comments with the proverbial 'grain of salt' and make a rewrite based on his own observations, using my notes only as background data. He did not do that. He changed only one of my markings in Section B and quoted my remarks EXACTLY in Section C, the narrative section. This was unworthy of CWO Stricklin and very unfair to Gy/Sgt Torres. CWO Stricklin was too lazy to write the fitness report based on his own observations and, as usual, he plagiarized my work to make things easy on himself. In my humble opinion, CWO Stricklin lied to me.

CWO Stricklin dictated projects and priorities in such a haphazard manner that we were continuously forced to switch from one task to another, hardly ever being able to complete one assignment before having to start another. He repeatedly committed my personnel to whichever special project he had in mind at the moment without once considering any projects which I might have underway. He required me to accompany him on mandatory tours around the warehouse as many as three times a day, showing me changes he wanted made, although I repeatedly assured him that I had already decided what needed to be done. I already knew what the problem areas were and had decided on various courses of action and I really must say that my priorities and projects made a lot more sense than his did.

From the very outset of my experience at Bulk Storage, I was never able to please CWO Stricklin with anything that I accomplished, and I had accomplished a great deal. While continually processing receipts and issues within expected time frames, I had also cleared all aisles of loose material, which was a gargantuan task, in itself. I had set aside specific areas to be used for issues, receipts and technical research.

Security had been established and maintained. Thousands of 'location-load' documents had been processed for gear which was previously 'lost', resulting in an increase of accountable material assets worth hundreds of thousands of dollars. The safety violations had been virtually eliminated. A significant portion of the material which had been 'thrown into' Bay Five during the move from Camp Foster (which occurred before my time) had been consolidated and re-warehoused into the other bays where we had already established locations for the material involved. There had been an extensive general consolidation project underway ever since I took over and established the proper guidelines. Great progress had been made in clearing up (and cleaning up) the open storage back lot. There had been countless other improvements within Bulk Storage which can't really be chronicled here. It was not because of CWO Stricklin's so- called 'guidance' that I had been able to accomplish all these things. On the contrary, I had accomplished all these things IN SPITE OF his interference.

On 3 October 1979, I attended a meeting with OICs and NCOICs of units supported by Material Handling Equipment. I had been summarily relieved of duty as OIC of MHE but it was no fault of my own. Because of CWO Stricklin's interference, because of his refusal to allow me to take the necessary actions, because of his refusal to forward my requests for action to higher headquarters and because he had actively conducted a character assassination campaign against me with innuendos, with snide remarks, with disparaging comments about my abilities and with outright lies, I had been unable to make enough appreciable improvements in the status of MHE.

At that meeting, the Battalion Executive Officer stated that, within sixty (60) days, all MHE assets would be brought up to a 95 % ready rate with a dead lined rate of only 5 %. When he said that, I burst out laughing. I couldn't help it. Because of the solemnity of the situation, it was rude of me to laugh but he didn't look like 'Merlin the Magician' and he didn't have a magic wand. And after all, I had just been fired. First Lieutenant Anderson was introduced as the new OIC of MHE. This was to be his only duty. He didn't realize it but he was extremely lucky that he was not going to be saddled with the additional responsibility for Bulk Storage. That would have been an immediate 'kiss of death'. Also, he was to be officially part of the Battalion Staff, so he would not have to work with CWO Stricklin. That would have been an insurmountable stumbling block for him. He would be able to take his problems, his suggestions and his requests for assistance DIRECTLY to Lt/Col Caputa, the Battalion Commander, so he would have all the 'horsepower' he needed to accomplish his new mission.

My MHE people (all three of them) had been transferred to Lt Anderson's control so that he could get his own new crew of MHE personnel trained. On Monday, 29 October 1979, when I attended a meeting with Lt/Col Caputa and Lt Anderson, I was advised that my MHE personnel would not be returned to me at Bulk Storage until 15 November 1979. Both Lt/Col Caputa and I expressed surprise that he would still need so much more time to get his own MHE people properly trained but we agreed that he needed and deserved every opportunity to succeed. After all, he had been committed, by the Battalion Executive Officer, to get all MHE up to 95 % ready in 60 days. Twenty-six of those days were already gone and there was, as yet, no improvement so maybe he was starting to feel the pressure.

I had already tried to explain to Lt/Col Caputa that there were many elements involved in repairing a dead lined forklift: (1) A contact team of qualified mechanics has to check out the forklift to determine exactly what is broken; (2) The Supply Operations Division has to order the parts required to repair the forklift; (3) If the parts are not available on-island, they will have to be ordered from the States; (4) The parts have to be received from the source of supply; (5) Base Motor Transport Maintenance Section has to schedule a date and time when that forklift can be worked on; (6) Arrangements have to be made to move the forklift from wherever on the island it may be located to the appropriate repair facility; (7) The actual repair process has to be successfully completed; (8) And if the forklift has to be surveyed (or in other words, if it is 'totaled'), a replacement forklift has to be ordered from the manufacturer. These are some of the reasons why I had burst out laughing when the Battalion Executive Officer had stated that all MHE would be 95 % ready in sixty (60) days at the meeting on 3 October. He just seemed to be so incredibly naïve, if not incredibly stupid. He had no idea what he was committing himself to.

But in the final analysis, Lt/Col Caputa's opinion of my knowledge, experience and expertise had been so thoroughly 'tainted' by CWO Stricklin that he did not pay the least bit of attention to my efforts to enlighten him. CWO Stricklin's attempt at character assassination had been supremely successful.

Although my past experience had been made light of by CWO Stricklin, I had accumulated several successful years of warehousing experience and I was perfectly capable of determining what could and should be done to improve the efficiency and appearance of a warehousing operation. My abilities and expertise were attested to by the 'outstanding' fitness reports, the accolades and the awards which I had received from a multitude of many different senior officers in my past assignments.

But I had never been, and will never be, a 'Yes' man. That made me immediately unpopular with CWO Stricklin. If I feel that a discrepancy has occurred, I will not hesitate to point out and try to correct that discrepancy, regardless of the fact that my actions may not be popular with some other people. If somebody tries to force me, or to coerce me, to follow a course of action which is contrary to logic or Marine Corps guidelines, I will voice my opinion, regardless of the impact it may have on my relationship with my immediate senior. Rank does not make Right.

I do not drink and I have very rarely voluntarily placed myself in the company of those who do, or rather I should say in the company of those who drink to excess (visiting with friends who have a few social drinks is perfectly acceptable). And I very rarely socialize. This tends to make me appear to be an outsider, or even a renegade, but this has no bearing on my professional performance of duty. My attitude toward drinking caused my very first problem with CWO Stricklin. During the first couple of days of my new assignment, he wanted me to get together with him (and the rest of his junior officers) at the club to 'talk shop' over a few beers. At that time, I was willing to attend because I believed that the encouragement, guidance and helpful hints I might receive would actually be quite beneficial to me in my new very challenging dual assignments as OIC of Bulk Storage and OIC of Material Handling Equipment. I drank a Dr Pepper and ate chips. At first, it wasn't so bad. We actually did 'talk shop' for a few minutes. But after I realized that the meeting had quickly deteriorated into a 'bull' session and drinking party, I excused myself. Later, CWO Stricklin tried to counsel me about my behavior and he didn't like it when I told him that I would gladly attend any meeting he scheduled, anywhere, as long as it dealt with either warehousing or material handling equipment but when the meeting deteriorated into a 'bull' session, then I would consider the 'official' part of the meeting to be over, and I would again excuse myself.

However, CWO Stricklin got his revenge on 31 October 1979, when he arranged for me to be relieved of duty and transferred to Camp Hansen, thirty miles away near the north end of the island where I was assigned as the Assistant Officer in Charge and Warehousing Officer of Consolidated Issue Point # 1.

I regret that circumstances prevent me from continuing my duties as the Officer in Charge of the Bulk Storage Section and as the Officer in Charge of the Material Handling Equipment Section because I considered those jobs to be very formidable challenges, worthy of my talents, especially considering that I was performing them simultaneously. I had many things in mind to be accomplished there during the remainder of my tour. I know that I did an excellent job there, in spite of CWO Stricklin's interference, because I would never have accepted anything less than perfection from myself. I honestly feel that no other officer could have done any better job, given the same situation, personnel and equipment, especially if he had to work with CWO Stricklin. That statement is not intended to belittle the abilities of any of my fellow officers. It's just that I am very well aware of, and am supremely confident in, my own knowledge, expertise experience, intelligence and leadership.

Roy L. Morris
WO   USMC

Fitness Report for 28 July 1979 through 31 October 1979

Section C: Performance of Duty:
Regular duties	Above Average
Additional duties	Not observed
Administrative duties	Above Average
Handling officers	Not observed
Handling enlisted personnel	Above Average
Training personnel	Not observed
Tactical handling of troops	Not observed

To what degree has he exhibited the following:
Endurance	Not observed
Personal appearance	Excellent
Military presence	Outstanding
Attention to duty	Above Average
Cooperation	Excellent
Initiative	Above Average
Judgment	Above Average
Presence of mind	Not observed
Force	Not observed
Leadership	Above Average
Loyalty	Outstanding
Personal relations	Excellent
Economy of management	Above Average
Growth potential	Excellent

Your estimate of this Marine's general value to the service:
Above Average

Considering the requirements of service in war, indicate your attitude toward having this Marine under your command:
Be glad to have

Narrative comments:
    Warrant Officer Morris is a personable officer who enthusiastically performs his duties. Although not totally proficient in all areas of

warehousing, he is demonstrating continual progress towards improving his technical proficiency. For this reason, Warrant Officer Morris has been reassigned to a less dynamic organization where he can apply and demonstrate the techniques and basics of warehousing on a lesser scale but over a wider range of application. In time, Warrant Officer Morris should develop into an efficient and effective officer. This report is late due to the administrative oversight of the reporting senior.

Reporting Officer
F. C. Williams, Jr
Major USMC
Officer in Charge
General Account
SASSY Management Unit

Reviewing Officer
D. B. James
Lieutenant Colonel USMC
Officer in Charge
SASSY Management Unit

    The preceding fitness report was actually written by CWO Stricklin, although Major Williams is listed as the reporting officer. I never met Major Williams. I have no idea who he was, so I don't know how he got listed as my reporting officer. The reviewing officer is listed as Lt/Col James. I never met him, either. That jerk, CWO Stricklin, had stabbed me in the back many times with his innuendos, his snide remarks, his disparaging comments and his outright lies about me and he was determined to stab me in the back one last time and he knew the best way to do that was through my fitness report. He was perfectly willing to sabotage the professional career of a fellow officer in order to preserve his own image in the eyes of our senior officers.

    I signed the blank original of my fitness report at the time of my transfer, 31 October 1979. That's the way it's done. The person being reported on signs a blank fitness report. Then the reporting officer fills it in and signs it. After that, the reviewing officer signs it and sends it to Headquarters, Marine Corps. The person being reported on does not generally see the completed fitness report.

Although I had signed the blank original form on 31 October, 1979, when I was officially transferred, it was not filled in until 17 December 1979, after which it was signed by the reporting officer, Major Williams (the officer I never met). And it was also signed on 17 December 1979 by the reviewing officer, Lt/Col James (the other officer I never met).

The last sentence in the narrative comments section said that the fitness report was submitted late due to the administrative oversight of the reporting officer. That is an absolute, bald-faced lie. The real reason CWO Stricklin didn't get it signed until 17 December was because he had to wait for almost seven (7) weeks until Lt/Col Hitzelberger had completed his tour of duty as Officer in Charge of the SMU and had moved on to his new job. Then CWO Stricklin could get Major Williams, the new OIC of the General Account, to sign as the reporting officer and Lt/Col James, the new OIC of the SASSY Management Unit, to sign as the reviewing officer and Lt/Col Hitzelberger would not be aware of what CWO Stricklin had done to me. Or at least, that is what CWO Stricklin obviously thought because he did not know that I had written that 9-page memorandum for the record about my performance of duty and about the way CWO Stricklin had fought me at every turn or that I had gone around the chain of command to personally give the memo to Lt/Col Hitzelberger. It was not a classified document and did not contain any vital military information that would be injurious to my country and I was the original author so I decided it would be within my rights to give a copy of the memo to Lt/Col Hitzelberger. The things that CWO Stricklin had done and said in order to destroy me went beyond devious and underhanded - they were clearly symptoms of a twisted psyche and a paranoid, self-delusional personality. In the final analysis, I considered him to be a thoroughly evil person who felt no compunction whatsoever about destroying a fellow officer's career in any way possible in order to embellish his own career. That is why I felt justified in going around the chain of command.

CWO Stricklin had been very careful in filling out my fitness report. He couldn't record any markings which were unsatisfactory and he couldn't make any statements in the narrative comments which would be considered unquestionably derogatory because that would make the fitness report subject to review by the person being reported on (namely, me). He knew that the act of putting 'Above Average' or 'not observed' markings on my performance grades and that putting mostly 'Above Average' and 'not observed' markings on my traits and principles grades would be detrimental to my career – without those remarks being flagged as being derogatory - because he obviously intended to mark his other junior officers (my peers) much higher.

And in the narrative comments section, he used such phrases as "Although not totally proficient in all areas of warehousing", and "has been reassigned to a less dynamic organization" and "In time, Warrant Officer Morris should develop". He wanted to make it appear that I was in way over my head and didn't really have any idea how to run a warehouse and needed to be guided along, that I didn't have the knowledge or the expertise needed to survive in an active working situation, and that the job I had been given was just simply too big for me to handle, too complex of an operation for me to grasp all the intricacies, and that I had to be transferred into a smaller, less demanding job so that my poor brain could handle it.

Actually, he was afraid that, sooner or later, all of the troubles between us would come to the attention of someone REALLY high up in the chain of command, someone whose opinions could not be poisoned against me by his lies. Then some very probing questions would be asked and the truth would come out. He was paranoid about his insecurities and he could not afford to have that happen, so he arranged to have me 'transferred to a less demanding assignment'.

However, he made one small miscalculation with my fitness report. The markings and the comments on this fitness report, which BARELY covered a three-month period, were such a drastic departure from the MUCH HIGHER excellent and outstanding markings and comments that had appeared on every other fitness report I had ever received over the past TEN YEARS from a significant number of different reporting seniors since the day I was promoted to Sergeant, that THIS fitness report was automatically flagged by the monitors at Headquarters Marine Corps as being a derogatory fitness report. I guess somebody in Washington just didn't believe I could have become so stupid, so incapable and so unqualified in such a short period of time. The fitness report was returned to me on 5 January 1980 and I was given the chance to make a rebuttal statement - to defend myself against what THEY (at Headquarters Marine Corps) considered a derogatory fitness report. That's how I found out what CWO Stricklin had tried to do to me. All I had to do was return the fitness report to Headquarters Marine Corps, along with a copy of the 9-page memo I had previously written for Lt/Col Hitzelberger describing my own performance and outlining the difficulties I had encountered with that backstabbing jerk, CWO Stricklin. I can safely assume that my memo was an adequate response to this derogatory fitness report because, later on, I was promoted to the rank of Chief Warrant Officer (W-2) ahead of many of my contemporaries with whom I had graduated from Warrant Officer Basic School.

A Fresh Start

So, 1 November 1979 was my first day as Assistant Officer in Charge/ Warehousing Officer of Consolidated Issue Point # 1 at Camp Hansen. I spent most of the day reviewing the service records of the people in my new section. And of course, I was their new Platoon Commander. I had two Gunnery Sergeants, two Staff Sergeants and 35 troops (Sergeant and below). And there was also Captain Skelding, the Officer in Charge of the CIP but he didn't count because I was not supposed to have to train him.

That was the worst platoon I had ever encountered. They were quite a mob. Those people had no unity and no discipline. Their uniforms could not pass an inspection if their lives depended on it. The warehouse was a shambles. At 1600, I left the Captain in charge of an empty warehouse and took EVERYBODY out for physical training and a 3-mile run. I knew I would be able to turn them loose in time so they would not miss their evening meal, although some of them might not be able to keep it down after going for a little outing with me.

Of course, I already knew why they were such a sorry lot. There was a serious lack of good leadership, for one thing. That would be easy to correct, especially after I could have a private meeting with the four Staff NCOs.

The other reason for their poor attitudes was that they were very far removed from the Company and Battalion headquarters and were treated as 'unwanted step children' by their own administrative sections. I had immediately found a lot of discrepancies in their service records and there was no excuse for that because, even though Captain Skelding had been failing to do his job in some regards, the Company and Battalion admin sections were still supposed to have periodic reviews of all assigned personnel, even though they were physically removed from the headquarters area and were living and working almost at the far end of the island. For example, there was one Marine with 25 months time in grade as a Lance Corporal, waiting for promotion to Corporal, even though there were no adverse counseling sessions and no disciplinary actions against him. Those people needed somebody who was willing to fight for them. Basically, they needed me.

Captain Skelding and I got along splendidly. He was a good-natured, happy-go-lucky kind of guy but he wasn't much of a Leader type and he wasn't really very good at dealing with the administrative problems that came along so he let me handle those two areas, including anything dealing with warehousing. He stayed in the office.

The best thing about him was that he did not like CWO Stricklin, at all. When he found out that CWO Stricklin had fired me, he said, "Well, if you couldn't get along with Stricklin, then you must be a really good guy".

Captain Skelding and I started to make changes at CIP # 1 and they were the kind of changes the troops really appreciated. Our Company and Battalion headquarters were thirty miles away at Makiminato and it wasn't easy to accomplish even the simplest administrative tasks but the clerks in the admin offices already knew me because of all the turmoil CWO Stricklin and Lt/Col Caputa had caused me and they knew I wouldn't back down from a situation until it got fixed.

For my new platoon, I fought with Battalion over lost paychecks, delays with correspondence courses, problems with allotments to families back in the States, delayed promotions and legal problems that just seemed to drag on and on.

I drafted a lot of correspondence for Captain Skelding and I did it willingly for two reasons. One reason was that the troops needed someone who could speak the language of the admin people at Company and Battalion headquarters. The other reason was that Captain Skelding simply asked me to. He quickly realized that I was a better writer than he was and he didn't mind admitting it. We made a great team.

From the very start, we recommended two Meritorious Masts, one for Corporal J. L. Hicks and one for L/Cpl L. H. Hobson. We recommended two Marines for assignment of an additional MOS (Military Occupational Specialty). They were L/Cpl S. Leshenski and L/Cpl N. Laguna. We arranged long-overdue promotions to Private First Class for Privates C. M. Barley and B. L. Croft.

The Hard Way

For any civilians who may someday read this: Each morning at 0800 and each evening at official sundown, the flag is raised and/or lowered in front of the headquarters building on every military base in the world. A bugle sounds the start and end of the 'colors' ceremony. Any Marine who is outside when he hears the bugle faces the direction of the flag and stands at the position of attention. If he is in uniform, he also salutes.

On the evening of 16 November 1979, personnel of CIP # 1 were involved in a platoon party in and around a covered patio in a park area of Camp Hansen. The patio was covered but there were no walls so it was essentially an open area. When the bugle for evening 'colors' sounded, all personnel present came to attention. All, that is, except for L/Cpl Johnson. He was sitting on one of the tables under the patio shed. He remained seated and said, "F--- that, I'm under cover!"

Gy/Sgt Sarka, who was facing away from the patio (toward the flag) called over his shoulder, "Everybody had better be at attention". When I glanced back over my shoulder, I saw that L/Cpl Johnson was still sitting and that a Major from another party at an adjacent patio was headed our way.

I stepped over to Johnson, grabbed his belt with one hand and his collar with my other hand, lifted him over my head and threw him from the patio table to the grassy area surrounding the concrete patio and said, "Now you're definitely not under cover, you jerk, so get your ass straightened up right now".

After the final bugle sounded, the Major chewed out Johnson for failing to show the proper courtesy and respect for the flag. I assured the Major that I would personally give Johnson an attitude adjustment. I guess he hadn't been in my platoon long enough to know he was going to have to really 'toe the mark' if he wanted to get along with me. He learned the hard way.

The Daily Grind

On 13 December 1979, I had the pleasure of promoting L/Cpl Hobson to Corporal. Captain Skelding was gone so I got to do the honors. Hobson had a year in grade as a Lance Corporal with no problems on his record. This was one of many cases over which I had gone around and around with the senior members of the Supply Battalion admin staff. I just simply had to badger the hell out of them to get things done for the people at Camp Hansen.

Hobson's promotion warrant was dated 1 November 1979 but it hadn't been signed until 20 November and we still didn't receive it at Camp Hansen until 13 December. After I promoted Hobson, I went to MSA and had a talk with Staff Sergeant Gibbs. She was the Battalion Admin Chief and she had repeatedly assured me that all paperwork of any kind had only a 48-hour turn-around time through the battalion office. When I talked with her that afternoon, I reminded her of that claim in regard to efficiency and said, "Well, if that's true, why did it take your people over a week to find PFC Santa Cruz's last paycheck and why did Corporal Hobson's warrant get dated on 1 November, then get signed on 20 November, then not arrive at Camp Hansen until 13 December?

She and I had passed some other words between us but we were alone in a conference room at battalion headquarters, so we figured we could dispense with some of the formalities that would ordinarily have been observed between members of our respective ranks and that we could be frank and forthright with each other, even though she still obviously felt somewhat restrained because of my status as an officer.

During that conversation, I pointed out quite a few other instances where the battalion staff had been somewhat less than efficient in their handling of administrative matters, at least in regard to the people at Camp Hansen. However, I finally convinced her that I was not on a "headhunting" expedition but that I only wanted better service for my people. I believe we had a better understanding about each other, after that. I finally assured her that I liked her very much as a person and that

I actually had a high regard for her as a professional but that I would not pull any punches if I thought my people were being treated unfairly or incorrectly, regardless of my personal likes or dislikes.

Four days later, on 17 December 1979, Captain Skelding promoted L/Cpl Fernandez to Corporal. It had been the same situation with him as it had been with Corporal Hobson. When I had taken over the platoon on 1 November, I had reviewed the service records for all my new people and started 'lighting fires' under the battalion admin staff. I shouldn't have been forced to make an absolute nuisance out of myself to get stuff like this done. Service records were supposed to be reviewed periodically to ensure that things like this don't happen. It's a shame that I had to do so many other leaders' jobs for them. What if I hadn't been sent to this unit? How long would these problems have existed, if not for me? And what about all the other junior Marines in all the other commands who did not have somebody like me to fight their battles for them? Every day and in every way, Marine leaders throughout the Corps were failing to ensure the well-being of the troops. I considered that to be a Cardinal Sin for Marine Corps Officers.

Faith like a Mustard Seed

30 November 1979

At that point, PFC Cole had been in my section (and my platoon) for a couple of days but he had already been charged with assault and battery on another Marine while he was in the incoming transient (unassigned) barracks, undergoing initial training and orientation as a new member of the command.

Here's Cole's story: In the wee hours of the morning, the Marines in the next cubicle came in drunk and noisy. The men in Cole's cubicle complained about the noise. Some of them exchanged verbal insults. Cole and two other men went over to the next cubicle. PFC Wilkins and another man were arguing. Wilkins pushed the other man. At this point, Cole stepped between them. Wilkins got hit by a punch that was thrown over Cole's shoulder by the other man. Wilkins was under the impression that Cole was the one who had hit him.

Captain Randel, the CO of Supply Company, wanted Cole to be at the company office in the Makiminato Service Area for 'office hours' (non-judicial punishment) that afternoon, so I took him down there in my truck. It turned out that the CO had been called away and he wasn't expected back that day. So we went back to Camp Hansen. At 1630, Captain Randel called and said to come back down.

Wilkins was there and told his story. Then Cole told his story. Even though I had known Cole for only a couple of days, I was impressed by his absolute faith in justice, so I asked the CO for a chance to find a couple more witnesses. Surprisingly, the CO agreed.

4 December 1979

That morning, Captain Randel came up to Camp Hansen to conclude the 'office hours' on Cole because two more witnesses had been found and they were assigned to other units at Camp Hansen. Based on their testimony, I could not have found Cole guilty but the CO did. While the CO was announcing his guilty verdict, Cole interrupted him and asked for a court martial instead of accepting non-judicial punishment. That is one of the rights of the accused and it brought the proceedings to an immediate halt. However, Captain Randel gave Cole a pretty rough 'dressing down' for his decision and for his attitude toward authority. He said some pretty harsh things about the way Cole was obviously brought up and told him he couldn't solve all his problems with his fists. I felt that Captain Randel should not have talked to Cole that way.

26 December 1979

Supply Battalion was really dragging their feet regarding Cole's court martial. When I called, I was told that Captain Leonardo had been assigned as Court Officer and that he wanted to hold court on Friday at Camp Hansen. I called 9th Engineer Battalion to make sure that the witnesses, PFC Dixon and PFC Briggs, would be available.

28 December 1979

Captain Leonardo came up to Camp Hansen to hear the testimony of Briggs and Dixon, but we had a surprise for him. Just the night before, Cole had found PFC D. R. Sherman, who is the man who actually hit Wilkins. None of the CID investigators had found Sherman, possibly because they thought Cole was guilty and was just making up the story about another person being involved. Captain Leonardo was willing to withhold any decisions until he could hear what Sherman might have to say. I appreciated that and wanted Cole to win. He was an excellent worker, conscientious, industrious - he didn't even smoke or drink.

31 December 1979

Cole's court martial would be concluded at Makiminato. Sherman actually did confess and described how Cole had stepped in between them just when Sherman swung at Wilkins, so it appeared that Cole had thrown the punch. Sherman told the truth, even though he knew that he would be facing charges himself. I told Sherman I greatly admired him for telling the truth and for helping Cole get off the hook. I also told him that when he had to face his own charges, I would be glad to come in and remind the Court of the way he had accepted the responsibility of testifying for Cole. It turned out that he had never known about Cole getting in trouble over the altercation until Cole found him a couple of nights before. He assured me he would have come forward a long time ago, if he had known.

There was also another man at the court martial willing to speak up for Cole. Sergeant Friend (that's his real name) had been at the transient barracks that night when the altercation occurred. He had not witnessed the actual event but he heard Sherman talking about the incident in the barracks. Sgt Friend didn't know who Cole actually was but he found out about the court martial from Briggs and Dixon, who were with him in 9th Engineer Battalion at Camp Hansen.

It's about 30 miles from Camp Hansen to Makiminato and, even though he wouldn't have any way to get back to Camp Hansen after the court martial, Sergeant Friend made his way down there on his own, anyway, because he thought he might be able to do Cole some good simply by telling about the conversation he had overheard. He also didn't know that Cole had found Sherman. Sgt Friend is the kind of NCO who will do what he can to look out for the troops, even if they aren't HIS troops. I greatly admire that and I told him so.

The court martial was not concluded in time for anybody to catch the last military bus going north, so nobody had a way to get back to Camp Hansen unless they had Japanese yen available to ride the civilian bus system. I didn't want them to have to face that expense, so I loaded Sgt Friend, Briggs, Dixon, Cole, and even Sherman into my truck. I took them over to the Makiminato Special Services Cafeteria and bought burgers, fries and cokes for everybody. Then I drove them back to Camp Hansen. They had all missed the midday meal at their respective chow halls and they were going to miss the evening meal because the chow halls would be closed by the time we could get back to Camp Hansen. It was getting late on New Year's Eve and I wanted to let them know that I appreciated what they had all done for my platoon member, PFC Cole.

Cole had never lost his faith during the entire process. He had truly believed that justice would eventually prevail and for ONCE, it did. It was a good way to finish out the year.

Roy Morris

Fitness Report for 1 November 1979 through 25 January 1980

Section C: Performance of Duty:
Regular duties	Outstanding
Administrative	Excellent
Handling Officers	Excellent
Handling enlisted personnel	Outstanding
Training personnel	Excellent

To what degree has he exhibited the following:
Personal appearance	Outstanding
Military presence	Excellent
Attention to duty	Excellent
Cooperation	Outstanding
Initiative	Excellent
Judgment	Excellent
Force	Excellent
Leadership	Outstanding
Loyalty	Outstanding
Personal relations	Excellent
Economy of management	Excellent
Growth potential	Outstanding

Your estimate of this Marine's general value to the service:
Excellent to Outstanding

Considering the requirements of service in war, indicate your attitude toward having this Marine under your command:
Particularly desire to have

Narrative comments:
    WO Morris is a mature, dependable, hard working Marine. He presents a well-groomed appearance, possesses sound judgment and is able to motivate others. Quick to learn, he is able to organize his work load so as to produce accurate results in a minimum amount of time. It

is the opinion of this officer that WO Morris has been and will continue to be an asset to his organization and the Marine Corps

    Reporting Officer
    J. T. Skelding
    Captain USMC
    Officer in Charge
    Consolidated Issue Point
    SASSY Management Unit
    Camp Hansen, Okinawa

UNITED STATES MARINE CORPS
3rd Marine Division (-) (Reinforced)
Fleet Marine Force

21/FXH/gcs
4400
13 Feb 1980

From: Commanding General
To: Commanding General, Third Force Service Support Group, FMF, FPO San Francisco 96602 (Attn: AC/S Operations)

Subj: Monthly Consolidated Issue Point (CIP) Fill Rate; request for

The recent improvement in Class IX repair parts support provided at the Camp Hansen CIP is noted with pleasure. It is evident that the outstanding efforts of Captain J. T. Skelding and his CIP personnel are beginning to pay important dividends. His re-warehousing program and other procedural refinements should continue the upward trend in supply effectiveness and the downward trend in B-13 exception processing.

In order to periodically advise the Division and subordinate commanders of the supply performance of the CIP, it is requested that the Camp Hansen fill rate be provided each month. If data are available which portray the fill rate for individual Division units, that would be especially helpful.

Your cooperation in this regard will be greatly appreciated.

D. K. Dickey
By direction

The preceding letter from the Commanding General of 3rd Marine Division speaks glowingly about the RECENT improvements at the Camp Hansen Consolidated Issue Point and heaps praise on Captain Skelding and his CIP personnel but it didn't mention me by name, although I was the sole reason for those recent improvements.

Captain Skelding had been running that warehouse for a year and it was a disaster area. I got there on 1 November 1979 and by 13 February 1980, the CIP had improved so much that we received this congratulatory letter from the Commanding General of the 3rd Marine Division. It was no secret that I was the one who had been the cause of the improvement, but nobody wanted to admit it, except for Captain Skelding. Honestly, he was very embarrassed about the fact that I had not received credit for the improvements.

It was MY re-warehousing program and those were MY procedural refinements that were causing the upward trend in effectiveness. I had conducted many classes on receiving, issuing, location verification and inventory control. I had even taught everybody how to operate the forklift. And I was doing everything in accordance with the Marine Corps Warehousing Manual and the Marine Corps Supply Manual, two documents I knew well. I could quote chapter and verse for any given supply-related or warehouse-related situation, the same way that an old-time preacher could quote chapter and verse from the Bible.

And it wasn't just the procedures in the warehouse and the streamlined methods of controlling the receiving and issuing processes (two major supply functions) that were involved in improving the situation at the CIP. The troops had come to realize that I wasn't going to allow the Company and Battalion admin sections to treat them poorly just because they were stationed 30 miles away. If one of our people had a problem, he or she couldn't just pop on over to the admin office, sign some paperwork and be back at work in half an hour. It was different for us.

None of our junior troops had personal vehicles, so they couldn't just drive down to Makiminato at their convenience, even if the Captain could let them go. There was an inter-camp military shuttle system but it was very intermittent. Sometimes, our people had to use the Japanese civilian bus system and, of course, they had to pay for the bus ride out of their own pocket. Not only that, they had to pay in Japanese currency, so everybody had to keep a few dollars worth of yen available. And if one of our people had to go to the Company or Battalion headquarters, even if it was just to sign one piece of paper, he or she would be gone all day.

The CIP didn't even have a section vehicle so I assigned my most trustworthy PFC as the section driver and gave him a key to my truck. He took documentation to the Stock Control Branch, picked up paperwork and paychecks from the admin offices and shuttled people where they needed to go. And he occasionally transported supplies.

I was doing anything and everything that needed to be done. I was fulfilling the promise I had made to myself the first time I pinned on officer's bars. At every command, in every position of authority (even when I had to try to work around CWO Stricklin), I was pursuing only two goals: (1) Accomplish the mission; (2) Ensure the welfare of the troops. Everything else was gravy.

Inspector/instructor Duty

In April 1980, I was chosen to be a member of an Inspector/Instructor Team. This was a very special honor. In order to be chosen as an I/I Team member, you have to be recognized as an absolute master in your occupational specialty. I didn't have any false modesty about it. I had a very high opinion of my abilities as a Supply Officer and as a Warehousing Officer but being chosen meant that somebody VERY HIGH in the chain of command had the same opinion, or I would not have been chosen.

I soon found out who that person was: Lieutenant Colonel Hitzelberger, who had been the Officer in Charge of SASSY Management Unit, over Chief Warrant Officer Stricklin, who had been the Officer in Charge of Storage Operations, over me when I had been assigned simultaneously as the Officer in Charge of Bulk Storage and as the Officer in Charge of Material Handling Equipment.

Before he left the SMU, Lt/Col Hitzelberger became aware of some of the difficulties I had been having with CWO Stricklin. Of course, all he had heard directly was what CWO Stricklin had told him, all of which was bad, especially after CWO Stricklin realized that I wasn't going to be one of his 'yes' men. And then I had given Lt/Col Hitzelberger the memorandum I had written, detailing some of the battles that I'd had with that idiot, CWO Stricklin. So he knew some of the stories BEHIND some of the stories.

Not only that, but Lt/Col Hitzelberger had found out about the high praises the Commanding General of the 3rd Marine Division had given for the drastic improvements that had taken place in the supply procedures and in the warehousing operations of the Consolidated Issue Point at Camp Hansen (improvements which had taken place only after I was assigned there).

So, when the Commanding General of 3rd Force Service Support Group told Lt/Col Hitzelberger that he wanted him to take an I/I Team to Japan to find out what all was wrong with LSU 3 / 4, and that he could pick anybody he wanted for the team, Lt/Col Hitzelberger chose Captain McTeague to handle maintenance problems and he chose me to handle supply and warehousing problems (and some fiscal, administrative and personnel problems). I was deeply honored. Lt/Col Hitzelberger could have chosen any officer on Okinawa. He could have chosen CWO Stricklin but he didn't. He needed the best available so he chose me. It was an awesome challenge and an awesome responsibility. For me, it was just one more opportunity to excel.

LSU 3 / 4 means Landing Support Unit, Third Battalion, Fourth Marine Regiment. We didn't know anything about this unit. But we were going to walk in there and, in a couple of days, we were not only going to find out what all was wrong with their operation but we were going to figure out how to fix all of their problems. Then, we were going to instruct them on how to carry out the fixes we decided on.

Of course, I took the latest copies of the Marine Corps Supply Manual and the Marine Corps Warehousing Manual with me, even though I could recite them both, from front to rear, from memory. I just wanted to be able to show those folks, if necessary, that whatever I was telling them was straight out of the book.

20 April 1980

We went to Futenma Air Base at 0800 for the first leg of our journey. We flew out on a C117 cargo plane. It had only a few seats. Major General Robinson, the Commanding General of 3rd Marine Division, and his wife were also passengers. I was surprised that they would ride on such a roughshod aircraft but it saved a lot of money for the Marine Corps, using space available instead of making another flight. We took off at 1000.

It was a thrill to fly again. The flight made me a little sick but it was still wonderful. I had forgotten how very beautiful the earth looks from up here. Some of the clouds looked like simple hazes between us and the earth but some of them looked so solid, so complete, that I felt that I could step out and walk on them. We flew mostly over water, of course, but the occasional islands I glimpsed looked very beautiful. Some of them could have qualified as island paradises.

We landed at 1530 at Atsugi, Japan and rode a military bus to Camp Fuji, not far from Mount Fuji, an extinct volcano. Major General Robinson and his wife had a staff car waiting for them at the airfield.

The first thing we did was find a place to leave our belongings. They put all three of us in the same hut. There were already six officers living in the hut. It was pretty primitive but it was a roof over our heads and there were a couple of kerosene stoves, so it was alright. The next thing we did was find the chow hall. The food was terrible. It was even worse than the garbage that had been served to us in boot camp.

After chow, we walked up to the supply area to look around before dark. Major Pankey, the Commanding Officer of LSU 3 / 4 and First Lieutenant Brown, the Supply Officer, walked with us. Everybody walked everywhere at Camp Fuji.

My first impression of the supply section was quite bad. The only inside storage was a trailer van for the small bin-sized items. Everything else was in 30-cube boxes lined up outside. Some of the boxes were covered with a tarpaulin. The boxes were not waterproofed. They were placed on very uneven ground and many of the boxes were warped. None of the boxes had the tops (or the fronts) affixed.

21 April 1980

We (the I/I Team) were up at 0530. We shaved and had breakfast. Nobody else in the tent was up, yet. Captain McTeague and I went over to the LSU admin office at 0700. We were just sitting there looking over the 'read' board when we heard someone in the back section. It was Captain Gurley, the LSU Executive Officer. He came into the front section, wearing a jogging suit. Captain McTeague said, "We're just looking for a place to park our bodies, temporarily". Captain Gurley just looked at us for a moment, said, "Welcome here, go ahead". Then he turned and went into the back section. At 0720, people were starting to get out of bed. Everybody seemed rather lethargic. They probably had a right to be. This was a pretty dismal place. The living conditions were very primitive. For example, the hut we were in was a block away from the head and showers.

21 April, 22 April & 23 April 1980

Lt/Col Hitzelberger spent these days with the headquarters section, Captain McTeague was with the maintenance and motor transport sections and I was mostly in the warehousing and supply sections, although Lt/Col Hitzelberger had suggested that I also look into administrative, fiscal and personnel matters. We all started quite early and worked very late.

24 April 1980

Today at lunch, I couldn't believe it. The food was actually reasonably good. The tables had clean tablecloths on them. The mess men were all wearing mess whites. It was the best meal I had eaten since I had been there. Then, I found out why. The General ate there that day. I mean Major General Robinson, Commanding General of 3rd Marine Division, who had flown from Okinawa on the plane with us.

During the afternoon, the General toured the LSU area. When he came into the supply tent, Lt/Col Hitzelberger and I were there. Major Pankey accompanied him. After a few minutes of small talk, General Robinson found an opportunity to compare the setup he was now looking at with a supply and warehousing operation he had reviewed in the recent past. He started telling us about the Consolidated Issue Point at Camp Hansen. He said, and I quote exactly, "That is the finest supply and warehousing operation I have ever seen". He went on to say that he had talked with the Marines working there and he had been very highly impressed with their appearance, their attitudes and their professionalism.

Of course, the General already knew Lt/Col Hitzelberger and he was aware that I was part of the Colonel's I/I team from Okinawa but, while he was going around shaking everybody's hand, he looked at me closely, and said, "I know you, don't I, Gunner?" I replied, "Yes, Sir. I run the supply and warehousing operation at the CIP at Camp Hansen". He smiled and then he spoke for a few more minutes about the great job I had been doing on Okinawa and told everybody to listen closely to any guidance that I might have to offer. Then he left with Major Pankey and Lt/Col Hitzelberger. A two-star General had spoken highly of me. My star was shining brightly.

26 April 1980

Well, this little trip was almost over. I had spent numerous hours each day inspecting and instructing such varied subjects as supply, warehousing, first echelon (user) maintenance of material handling equipment, forklift operation, fiscal accounting and administration.

At noontime, we went to the air terminal at Atsugi to confirm arrangements for our flight back to Okinawa. During the afternoon, we moved from the quarters of LSU 3 / 4 to quarters in the base camp area at Camp Fuji. The living conditions for the permanent personnel at Camp Fuji were infinitely different from the living conditions at LSU 3 / 4. Everybody at the base camp lives well. The Staff NCOs and officers each have one end of a permanent wood hut to themselves (no tents or crowded conditions). Each room has a stove and real furniture. The dining facility at the base camp was a wonder to see. It was actually clean and the food was wonderful. It was like a restaurant.

There were so many differences between the two areas, I found it hard to believe they were only about a mile apart. Actually, they're both part of the same base. But the people at the base camp were considered 'permanent personnel' and were assigned from the States directly to Japan for a regular one year tour. The people at the LSU were temporary and were sent from Okinawa to Camp Fuji, Japan on a supposedly 'temporary additional duty' status, presumably for six months at a time, except that wasn't always the case. Some of the people at the LSU in a TAD status had been at Camp Fuji for over nine months and their parent commands didn't intend to move them back to Okinawa until almost time for them to return to the States. That situation caused many of them to feel as if they had been abandoned.

The following memo is my after-action report to Lt/Col Hitzelberger regarding our I/I trip.

Memorandum for the Record dated 27 April 1980

From: Chief Warrant Officer Roy L. Morris
To: Lt/Col Hitzelberger

Subj: LSU 3 / 4

Encl: (1) Observations regarding LSU 3 / 4
(2) Recommendations regarding LSU 3 / 4

I am very dissatisfied with the conditions I have found in the supply and warehousing sections of LSU 3 / 4. Lack of organization is rampant and lack of supervision is the keynote in many of the problems existing there. A lackadaisical, slipshod attitude toward the daily routine, in general, and toward supply support, in particular, is painfully evident at almost every level of the chain of command.

I worked very closely with Sergeant Patrick Weir on a daily basis. He responded favorably and immediately to my every criticism or recommendation. I saw positive improvement in his performance and believe we may see an improvement in his particular area of responsibility. I wish I could say the same for the personnel who are senior to him.

I want to point out that many of the junior Marines assigned from Okinawa to this unit are grossly misled about the living and working conditions they can expect here and it appears that their parent commands might actually be lying to them about the length of time they will be spending in the 'temporary' assignment.

Since you instructed us (Capt McTeague and myself) to be totally blunt and straightforward with our observations and recommendations, enclosures (1) and (2) may be couched in terms and expressions which may not find favor with senior members of the chain of command.

On enclosure (2), besides my recommendations pertaining to supply and warehousing matters, I have included an addendum containing my recommendations regarding those other situations you told me to notice.

Roy L. Morris
CWO USMC

Observations regarding LSU 3 / 4 supply and warehousing operations. (Enclosure 1)

There is no organization, no cross-training of available personnel, no on-the-job training for newly arrived personnel, no set procedures for the various receiving and issuing actions which occur.

Partially because of the quasi-temporary nature of the organization here, there are no data processing facilities available locally and all transactions must be accomplished by courier flights to Okinawa. Obviously, such flights might be affected by typhoons and other weather conditions so stock status is generally maintained by manual methods on hand printed cards.

There are currently 480 backorders on the stock number demand list. This is an extremely large number for a support unit of this size.

The number of backorders on the stock number demand list which are suspected of being invalid: 185.

A sampling of 100 backorders was checked. Of these, 47 had stock locations listed on the location deck (a manually maintained card file). 20 of these had multiple locations. If these requests had been properly reviewed, and if stock was actually available on the listed locations, then the items should not have been backordered. The assets should have been issued and unit readiness would have been enhanced.

I checked 80 items from the actual physical locations to the locator deck. Of these, 43 items of stock had locator cards in the deck. 37 items were on location but had no corresponding locator card on file. These 37 items, therefore, were 'lost' and would have resulted in backorders, unnecessarily, if requested by the using units.

I checked 195 stock items from the locator deck to the actual physical stock locations. Of these, only 128 were found to be correct.

There is no firm method of determining if a substitute item is available when a requested item is not in stock.

In the supply tent, there are no areas set aside for staging receipts and issues, no area for staging items requiring research and no area set aside for set assembly. Receipts were lying all over the place. Pending issues were haphazardly placed throughout the tent.

The only inside storage available for stock items was a semi-trailer van with a wall of pull-out bin boxes. The overhead lighting inside the trailer was inadequate, even with the doors open at midday.

Medium and bulk storage consisted of 56 thirty-cube boxes randomly placed outside. None of the boxes had the tops (or fronts, in some cases) attached. Some of the bulk assets were simply placed on open pallets. Some of the boxes were covered with tarpaulins. None of the boxes were waterproofed.

Recommendations regarding LSU 3 / 4. (Enclosure 2)

A Standard Operating Procedure for each supply and/or warehousing activity should be established. On-the-job training should be instituted. In the future, personnel assigned to serve in supply and/or warehousing billets in this unit should be school-trained in the supply or warehousing fields. The nature of the mission of this unit does not allow time to cross train an engineer, or truck driver or infantryman in the various intricacies of supply and/or warehousing procedures through on-the-job training.

However, cross training of available personnel already present should be conducted, so that a stock clerk involved in receiving can move over to the issue section with no loss of efficiency or effectiveness, or so that a stock clerk involved in maintaining the stock locator deck can move over to the fiscal accounting section, to state a couple of examples.

Repair or replace the lighting inside the semi-trailer van where the bin storage boxes are located, so that the locations listed on the face of the bin box and the identification tags on the stock items can be read. At the very least, make some flashlights available for use in the van.

Conduct a complete location verification program. This should be a two-way process, first from the locator deck to the physical stock location, then from the actual stock items on location to the locator deck.

Ensure that acceptable substitute items are listed on the locator cards. This can be done on a gradual basis. Each time an item is researched, the findings should be noted on the locator cards.

Consolidate locations for stock items having two or more locations listed.

Conduct a reconciliation/review with all supported units to determine validity of backorders.

The medium and bulk storage boxes should be relocated to a flat area, preferably with a base of steel matting. At any rate, all of the boxes should be placed on pallets.

The rows of stacked storage boxes should be reinforced and affixed to each other by a framework of boards or by banding.

The tops (or fronts) of the storage boxes should be affixed to the box with hinges so that the boxes can be closed (and perhaps locked).

A permanent covering should be erected over the storage boxes. This covering should allow access to all boxes for the stock pickers while providing maximum protection from the elements for the stock.

Take action to identify and rollback excess stock.

Investigate the possibility of establishing a data processing unit at Camp Fuji. I know it would not be feasible to place it at the LSU 'forward area' because only tents are available but there are permanent structures at the base camp area.

Ensure that the parent commands on Okinawa send only qualified personnel to fill billets at Camp Fuji. The LSU should not be considered as a 'dumping area' for people who are considered to be incompetent, or malcontents, or troublemakers, or otherwise undesirable.

Furthermore, ensure that assigned personnel understand, from the very first, that this assignment might be considered to be a hardship tour, in comparison to conditions at the parent command on Okinawa, or even at the Camp Fuji base camp. This might preclude at least some of the problems with troop morale that are prevalent in this command.

The dining facility should be cleaned up. The dining facility manager should be fired. The cooks assigned to work there should be school trained. This is not the place to be learning how to cook through on-the-job training. The mess men should wear clean clothes. The portions are too small. The quality of the food is poor but people should be allowed to ask for seconds, if they can stand to eat it. (Remember, the only decent meal we had while we were there was on the day when General Robinson was scheduled to eat at the LSU dining facility).

I didn't have time to watch an entire movie when I checked on the troop entertainment category, but I saw enough of two of them to be able to make the following recommendations: The movies that were shown were definitely of the low-grade, 'B' movie variety, so the quality of entertainment, in that regard could easily be improved. The sound system should be replaced, as I could barely make out what the actors were saying through all of the scratching, buzzing, whistling, static and white noise coming through the speakers.

There were no special services facilities available. Granted, you can't expect much when you are already living in tents but there were no outside basketball courts, no areas set aside for football or baseball. Some people, like me, might even have welcomed the availability of an obstacle course, just for something constructive to do. There was no library available. There was not even a tent set aside where people could go to play chess, checkers, dominoes or monopoly.

Sir, I knew of some units that treated their troops better in Viet-Nam.

Roy age 14.

Roy's toys as a teenager.

Roy's old hay truck (brother Danny in back).

Roy's car 1950 Ford Custom (the first car Juanita and I rode in).

Roy age 16 yr 11 mo, brother Steve Junior and neighbor Kenneth Ennis.

Proof of insanity.

Roy's vacation home in Viet-Nam.

Roy's promotion to black belt Shorin Ryu Karate.

Roy age 26.

Promotion to Warrant Officer by CO and wife Juanita.

Roy practicing with nunchucks.

Roy practicing with double nunchucks.

Ruddell & Proper Motor Pool Art.

Rolling On.

Keep on Trucking.

More proof of insanity.

(Macho Man) the older version.

Roy demonstration at brother Dan's Tae Kwon Do class.

Roy demonstration continues.

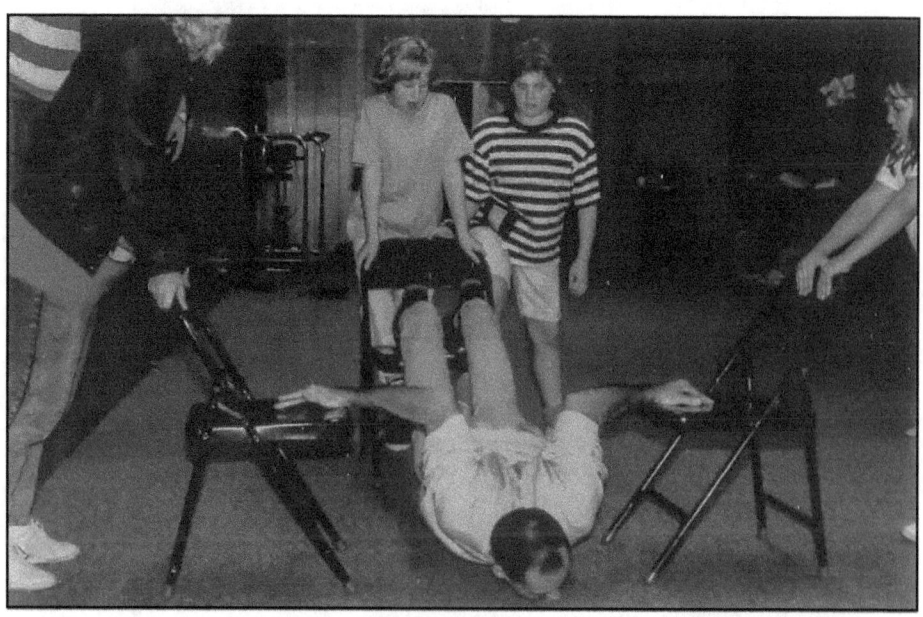

Roy demonstration continues.

Roy demonstration continues.

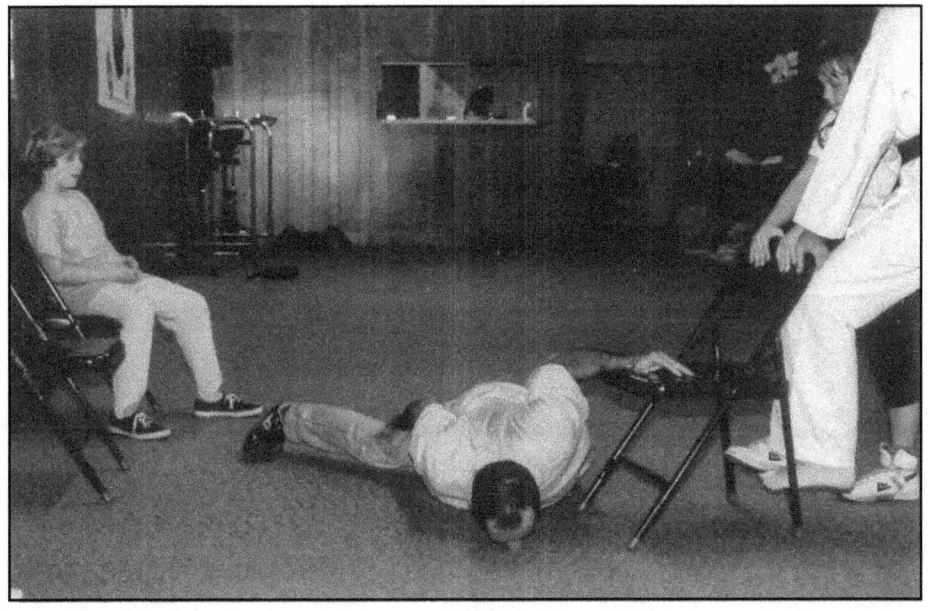

Roy demonstration continues.

Business as Usual

Back on Okinawa, on 10 May 1980, I had the privilege and the pleasure of presenting a Meritorious Mast to PFC Myron A. Alexander. Colonel Shroyer, the Commanding Officer of the 3rd Supply Battalion, had it typed up exactly as I had originally drafted it.

It's moments like that that help to make what I do worthwhile. Three days later, a situation went in exactly the opposite direction. On 13 May 1980, PFC J. V. Bailey was absent from work. At 0800, PFC D. R. McMullan told Captain Skelding that Bailey was at her house, where she lived with an Okinawan civilian. He was sitting outside when she came out to leave for work. He had obviously been drinking heavily.

He told her he had the day off and wanted to stay at her house but she wouldn't let him in because she didn't know him very well. I went out and picked him up. I told him Captain Skelding had filed charges against him. He had previously been demoted from Lance Corporal to Private First Class for public drunkenness. I dropped him off at the barracks and told him to get into uniform and be at the warehouse in 20 minutes.

Captain Skelding called the company commander. The CO said he would vacate the suspension of Bailey's sentence for some prior charges and that he would be sent immediately to Correctional Custody (the brig).

I had Bailey's platoon sergeant take him back to the barracks to inventory his belongings. Everything goes into storage while a person is in the brig. Then he was taken to the company office at Makiminato.

That evening, the CO called to tell me that he was sending Bailey back because the brig was full (60 people). I couldn't believe it - we had to make a reservation to send somebody to the brig???

So, he would be on barracks restriction. That meant he would go to work and to the dining facility and nowhere else. And when he isn't working, he would have to sign in with the Battalion Officer of the Day every two hours.

Oh, well, leadership has its little peaks and valleys, doesn't it?

No Choice

On 28 May 1980, at 4:51 pm, Cindy Frances Oates gave birth to my daughter, Brandie Lynn Morris at Kuwae Naval Hospital on Okinawa. This was a very momentous occasion. For over 11 years, Juanita and I had very carefully avoided the possibility of becoming parents. My reason was simple: I wanted to keep Juanita all to myself and didn't want to share her with anybody, not even my own child. I had been forced to share her attentions with her family because they were already there but I did not intend to add to the number of people who would be competing with me for her time and her companionship. Not voluntarily. Juanita's reason for not wanting a child was probably more practical. She had been the oldest child of a very large family so she had already done her share of raising kids. Besides, she already had to contend with me. She would have had no time or energy for a child.

With Cindy, my preferences were completely ignored. She made the decision to have a baby and then stopped taking precautions to avoid a pregnancy....without telling me. At first, I was terribly upset. I had NEVER wanted to become a father but if I had, I would have made a baby with Juanita, the only woman I had ever truly loved. Luckily, Brandie Lynn was the absolute perfect child and she stole my heart the first moment I saw her. What a great young'un!

On the military side of my life, things were going very well. I dealt with the occasional malcontent and troublemaker, as any Section Leader/Platoon Commander will but I had a great abundance of high quality people around me, too.

For example, there was L/Cpl D. Hall, who I recommended for meritorious promotion to Corporal. There was L/Cpl J. E. Cole, who I recommended for Marine of the Month. L/Cpl Anita Y. Farrow received a Meritorious Mast, printed exactly as I had drafted it when I made the recommendation. L/Cpl J. E. Cole also received a Meritorious Mast, under the same conditions. PFC M. A. Alexander was recommended for Marine of the Month. PFC P. E. Calloway received a Meritorious Mast.

Fitness Report for 26 January 1980 through 14 July 1980

Section C: Performance of duty
Regular duties   Outstanding
Administrative duties   Excellent
Handling officers   Excellent
Handling enlisted personnel   Outstanding
Training personnel   Excellent

To what degree has he exhibited the following:
Personal appearance   Outstanding
Military presence   Excellent
Attention to duty   Excellent
Cooperation   Outstanding
Initiative   Outstanding
Judgment   Excellent
Force   Excellent
Leadership   Outstanding
Loyalty   Outstanding
Personal relations   Outstanding
Economy of management   Excellent
Growth potential   Excellent

Your estimate of this Marine's general value to the service:
Excellent to Outstanding

Considering the requirements of service in war, indicate your attitude toward having this Marine under your command:
Particularly desire to have

Narrative comments:
    Since being assigned to this section, CWO Morris has proven himself to be exceptionally hard working. He is extremely motivated, highly dedicated and very versatile. He is a self-starter who takes a great deal of pride in himself and his work. He can be counted on to produce accurate results in a minimum amount of time. He has consistently exercised executive ability, good judgment, loyalty, unquestioned

integrity and is indeed a credit to the supply field and the United States Marine Corps.

    Reporting Officer
    J. T. Skelding
    Captain USMC
    Officer in Charge
    Consolidated Issue Point
    SASSY Management Unit
    Camp Hansen, Okinawa

UNITED STATES MARINE CORPS
Consolidated Issue Point # 1
SASSY Management Unit
3rd Supply Battalion
3rd Force Service Support Group

838/
RLM/st
4600
15 July 1980

From: Chief Warrant Officer Roy L. Morris
To: Officer in Charge, SASSY Management Unit
Via: Officer in Charge, Consolidated Issue Point # 1

Subj: CIP # 1 Vehicle

    CIP # 1 was previously authorized the use of a military vehicle in order to conduct liaison with SMU, with Supply Company and with 3rd Supply Battalion sections at Camp Kinser and Makiminato Service Area
    This vehicle was used to transport documentation for computer updates at the SMU, to pick up and deliver paperwork to the company and battalion administrative sections, to pick up supplies, to make self-service runs and to transport personnel to and from Camp Kinser and MSA for functions such as administrative matters, unit training, personnel matters, weapons cleaning, etc.
    CIP # 1 has been operating without a vehicle since the last week of May, when the jeep was dead lined for brake repair. When it was repaired, it was used by 3rd Supply Battalion as a training vehicle instead of being returned to us. Now, I have been informed that the vehicle is again dead lined.
    For the time period when we have been without a vehicle, I have allowed my section driver to use my personal vehicle, a pickup truck, in order to conduct our official business. Occasionally, our section driver used a rented Japanese vehicle when I was not able to allow him to use my truck. At those times, I gave him enough cash for gasoline and

other expenses so that he would not have out-of-pocket expenses for government business.

On some occasions, when our Marines had to conduct official business at Camp Kinser or MSA, they had to either ride the military inter-camp bus service, or use the Japanese civilian bus service when the schedule of the military bus service would not suffice. Whenever they were forced to use the civilian bus service, I gave them enough Japanese currency to cover their expenses.

However, it is 60 miles, round trip, from here to Makiminato and, although I am willing to continue to suffer these out-of-pocket personal expenses in order to support our mission and to ensure the welfare of my troops, I do wish to point out that all of the other SMU, Company and Battalion sections HAVE vehicles available, even though they are all RIGHT THERE, generally within easy walking distance of every place of business where any of their personnel might be required to go while we, thirty miles away, have no military vehicle support at all.

We are not subordinate to any of the units stationed here at Camp Hansen, so we cannot rely on any of them for logistical support of this kind. This situation has been quite detrimental to the morale of my troops. The overwhelmingly prevalent opinion among these junior Marines is that we are being treated as 'castaways', or even 'bastard children', so to speak.

Therefore, I hereby request that a replacement military vehicle be made available to CIP # 1 to conduct official business.

Roy L. Morris
CWO USMC

The following letter is an exact reproduction of a letter which constituted Lt/Col James' endorsement to my request for a military vehicle. It is reprinted exactly with the grammatical errors left in place. I was pleased that Lt/Col James, the OIC of the SMU, readily endorsed my letter regarding our need for a vehicle. Amazed, also, but still pleased. He actually saw the logic of my reasoning. Either that or somebody on his staff was able to convince him of the logic of my reasoning.

However, I wished he would either learn how to use proper English and punctuation in the drafting of his correspondence or that whoever drafted his endorsement for him would learn how to use proper English and punctuation. Well, I know that his initials in the upper right corner indicate that he drafted this endorsement but the presence of his initials there doesn't necessarily mean that he actually DID draft it. I know, from personal experience, that some people are perfectly willing to take credit for work performed by someone else. But there are so many errors on this particular endorsement, I surely would not want to take credit for having drafted it.

Anyway, if he drafted it, he made a lot of grammatical errors. And if he did not draft it, then he failed to catch the errors when he proofread it, if he even bothered to proofread it. In any case, he signed it so he is still ultimately responsible for the errors. I will list the errors:

Example: 'Responding timely to administrative requirements from both battalion and company from Camp Hansen has and continues to be a problem'.

Should read: 'Responding in a timely manner (from Camp Hansen) to administrative requirements from both battalion and company headquarters has been and continues to be a problem'.

Example: 'The fact is for both administrative and operational requirements a reliance is made on personal vehicles'.

Should read: 'The fact is that for both administrative and operational requirements, the CIP personnel often rely on the use of personal vehicles or on costly public transportation'.

Example: 'It is requested this requirement be expedited'.

Should read: 'It is requested that the resolution of this requirement be expedited'.

Even though I had still never met him, I already knew that Lt/Col James was a bosom buddy of CWO Stricklin, my backstabbing former boss. Judging by the grammatical mistakes and the punctuation errors made on the endorsement that Lt/Col James was willing to sign his name to, he seemed to be about the same caliber of officer that CWO Stricklin was. Maybe that's why they got along with each other.

UNITED STATES MARINE CORPS
SASSY Management Unit
3rd Supply Battalion (-) (Rein)
3rd Force Service Support Group
Fleet Marine Force, Pacific
FPO San Francisco 96602

800/DBJ/mab
4400
22 July 1980

FIRST ENDORSEMENT on Consolidated Issue Point No. 1 ltr 838/RLM/st over 4600 dtd 15 July 80

From: Officer in Charge, SASSY Management Uint
To: Commanding Officer, Third Supply Battalion

Subj: Consolidated Issue Point (CIP No. 1) Vehicle

Ref: (a) OIC SMU ltr 813/CJB/mab over 4400 dtd 1 Jul 80

Readdressed and forwarded.

    Consolidated Issue Point No. 1 is normally staffed with twenty-five to thirty Marines. Responding timely to administrative requirements from both battalion and company from Camp Hansen has and continues to be a problem. The fact is for both administrative and operational requirements a reliance is made on personal vehicles.

    By previous correspondence, reference (a), a vehicle for CIP operations has been requested. It is requested this requirement be expedited.

D. B. James

Copy to:
OIC, CIP Camp Hansen

Security Patrol

Standing duty as a member of the Village Security Patrol was an additional duty that the male Marines at Camp Hansen got stuck with from time to time. Kin Village was right outside the gate. It was not a large village but there were a great many bars where military personnel could go to drink and flirt with the numerous waitresses who worked at the bars and provided company to the men while they were drinking. Naturally, many of the men got too drunk and wound up getting their pockets picked while they paid exorbitant prices for alcohol.

When they came out of the bars and tried to make their drunken way back to the base, it was the job of the Security Patrol to try to sort of steer them in the right direction while attempting to keep them out of the hands of the Japanese Police. The main reason we tried to get them back to the base before the JPs got involved was because on Okinawa in those days, there was no such thing as excessive force or police brutality. Oh, well, I mean, sure, it happened but it was not acknowledged as such. Most of the JPs were martial arts experts (after all, Okinawa was the birthplace of Shorin-Ryu Karate) and they all carried batons, with which they were highly skilled.

So, it was in the best interests of the drunks to be apprehended by the military Security Patrol rather than by the JPs. Being charged by military authority with public drunkenness or unbecoming conduct is a cakewalk compared to doing time in a Japanese prison for resisting arrest. Just thinking about it makes me cringe. But the Security Patrol was not designed as a disciplinary unit. Our primary goal was to get the drunks back through the gates and onto the base as quickly and quietly as possible and we tolerated a lot of bad behavior from the drunks that we would not have accepted under any other circumstances, all in the interests of keeping them out of Japanese jails. And I must say that the Security Patrol helped hundreds of young Marines from suffering entanglements with local law enforcement. Additionally, by removing the drunks from the civilian public areas, we were also promoting goodwill between military and civilian components.

However, some of the drunks didn't see the logic of what the Security Patrol was trying to accomplish so problems did arise, occasionally. Alcohol kills brain cells. So, lack of judgment, not to mention colossal stupidity, were common side effects for the drunks. To illustrate, I offer the following examples of encounters I had while serving as Officer in Charge of the Village Security Patrol or as the Officer of the Day dealing with the Security Patrol:

Example: At or about 0029 (that's 12:29 am) on 17 April 1980, while I was serving as Battalion Officer of the Day, a drunk Marine was delivered to me by the Security Patrol. He was PFC S. L. Fitzgerald of A Company, 9th Engineer Support Battalion, 3rd Force Service Support Group. His liberty had been secured by the Officer in Charge of the Security Patrol. The guards gave me his ID card and his liberty card.

I took him to the Bridge Platoon barracks and turned him over to the Duty NCO. Then I reminded PFC Fitzgerald that his liberty was secured and told him he could pick up his ID card and liberty card from the battalion office at 0800 in the morning. He started insisting that I give his cards back. I repeated my instructions and said, "Now, you should mind your manners". As I turned away, he shouted, "That's f----d up.

As I turned back toward him, the Duty NCO, assisted by two other Marines, grabbed him and pushed him toward his rack. They didn't want me to be forced to subdue him because he would automatically be charged with assault on an officer because he would obviously have tried to resist. Luckily for him, he was charged only with disobedience of a direct order and disrespect.

Example: I was approached at the Guard Station by a Japanese civilian at about 0030 (that's about 12:30 am) on 8 May 1980. At the time, I was the only one present who could understand even a little Japanese, so I dealt with the gentleman. He said there was a man sleeping on the steps of his house. At this point, he did not wish to involve the JPs, so he had come to us, asking only that the man be removed.

Accompanied by a member of the Guard, I followed the gentleman to his house, which was only about three blocks away. We found the man sleeping on his back, apparently passed out drunk. With some difficulty, we roused him enough so that he could walk. After thanking the Japanese gentleman, we took him to the Guard Station, took his ID card and learned his identity. He was L/Cpl Timothy P. Streits of Communications Company, 7th Communications Battalion.

A member of the Camp Guard stated that this same Marine had been found sleeping in the road by Gate # 2 one night in the very recent past. From my limited observations and from the information received, it was obvious that L/Cpl Streits was unable to control his use of whatever substance it was which had rendered him physically and mentally unable to conduct himself in a proper manner, so I charged him with public drunkenness, disturbing the peace, creating a public nuisance and conduct unbecoming to a Marine.

Example: At approximately 2115 (9:15 pm) on 3 August 1980, while on duty as Officer in Charge of the Kin Village Security Patrol, I was making the rounds with two members of the Security Patrol when I observed two men wrestling around with each other in the street. One of them was obviously drunk and the other was trying to control him.

We separated them. I asked the drunk for his ID card. He replied, "Get f----d". Then he twisted away and started to run up the street. Gy/Sgt Johnson, who was leading another patrol, met him at the corner. They tackled him and put him on the ground. We handcuffed him and started back to the base.

On the way, he was constantly jumping around quite a bit and trying to twist away from us, even though he was still handcuffed. And we were starting to get some interference from the other man because he was repeatedly trying to push my team aside and grab hold of the drunk.

Since the other man did not appear to be drunk, I told him to stop interfering and let us do our job. I gave him the chance to walk away but he stuck his finger in my face and said, "I'm going to kick your ass". At that point, I said, "Turn around and put your hands behind your back. You are under arrest". He was a very large man and he said, "You ain't big enough to arrest me, Motherf----r". As it turned out, he was partially correct – I wasn't big enough. However, I was mean enough.

So, I stooped down, grabbed him by the knees and jerked forward and upward. He went down on his back quite heavily. I rolled him over, put my knee between his shoulder blades, pulled his arms behind his back and handcuffed him. We got him to his feet and took both of them to the base. We were assisted in this effort by Gy/Sgt Johnson's team because now both men were squirming around a lot and continually trying to break away. All the way, the drunk kept looking at me and shouting things like, "Hey, ass----, I'm not your dog" and "Hey, ass----, I'm not your boy". At no point during the confrontation had I ever called him a dog or a boy. I had consistently addressed him as either "Marine" or "Young Man".

We finally got them to the Guard Shack, where we took their ID cards and started the process of getting them confined pending trial. The drunk was L/Cpl Ernest L. Black and the big one was L/Cpl Bobbie J. Nunn.

I decided not to release them to the Officer of the Day of their battalion because they had both been so violent. They needed to be behind bars. I also made arrangements for the big one to be checked over by a Corpsman because he had injured the back of his head when he fell backward.

L/Cpl Black was charged with public drunkenness, disturbing the peace, resisting arrest, attempted escape, five counts of disrespect to a Noncommissioned Officer for his words and actions toward my Sergeants and Corporals, five counts of disrespect to an officer for his words and actions toward me, five counts of disobedience of an order because he repeatedly refused to hand over his ID card, and conduct unbecoming to a Marine.

L/Cpl Nunn was charged with disturbing the peace, resisting arrest, assault on an officer (only because I was forced to physically subdue him), attempted escape, interfering with an officer in the performance of his duty because he tried to get L/Cpl Black away from us, seven counts of assault on a Noncommissioned Officer because he repeatedly pushed my Sergeants and Corporals aside while trying to get his hands on L/Cpl Black, four counts of disobedience because he repeatedly refused to hand over his ID card, nine counts of disrespect to an officer for his repeated actions and words toward me, nine counts of communicating a threat to an officer for the times he told me he was going to "kick my ass", and conduct unbecoming to a Marine.

Disaster Strikes

At 11:56 am, on Friday, 29 August 1980, my daughter, Brandie Lynn, died. She had lived on this earth for only 3 months and 1 day. She choked on her formula and died while in the care of our babysitter. It wasn't the sitter's fault. She had three children of her own, so she was very experienced. It just happened. It's difficult for anybody to get their breath back after choking and it was impossible for a baby.

We took Brandie to Winchendon, Massachusetts for the funeral and buried her on 6 September 1980. After 3 weeks, my military duties required me to return to Okinawa. Cindy stayed with her parents. As I traveled back to Okinawa, I prepared to throw myself into my work. I knew that I would need to focus specifically on the tasks at hand. (Reader, please note I am not dismissing my daughter in favor of my military life. She is discussed in detail in my first book, *Thicker than Water*).

Carrying On

In my absence, it had been necessary to replace me at the Consolidated Issue Point at Camp Hansen so when I arrived back on Okinawa and got checked in, I had transfer orders from 3rd Force Service Support Group to Marine Corps Base.

I took over as Officer in Charge, Base Motor Transport Operations Section. Within a few days, I also took over as Officer in Charge, Base Motor Transport Maintenance Section. I was uniquely qualified in both areas by the experience I had from years ago, working in the Readiness Office, controlling the distribution and maintenance of motor transport equipment on a world-wide basis.

And this time, doing two separate jobs simultaneously was not difficult for me because THIS time, my immediate supervisor was not a backstabbing jerk, like CWO Stricklin had been. The Base Motor Transport Officer was Captain D. R. Bennett, a really good guy.

As the Operations Officer, I supervised the distribution and operation of about 1,000 motor vehicles (including material handling equipment, such as forklifts and warehouse tractors) to provide transportation and operational support to all Marine units on Okinawa.

As the Maintenance Officer, I supervised all echelons of maintenance and repairs for those vehicles and pieces of equipment. I also supervised all supply functions necessary to obtain replacement parts, tools and equipment.

Overall, I supervised 60 Japanese civilians, WG-3 through GS-9, and 52 enlisted Marines, Private (E-1) through Master Gunnery Sergeant (E-9), all of whom worked as vehicle operators and mechanics - or supervisors thereof.

And as usual, I also served as the Platoon Commander for the enlisted Marines assigned at Base Motor Transport Section.

Very early during my assignment at the Base Motor Transport Section, a couple of young Lance Corporals (named Ruddell and Proper) committed an infraction of Marine regulations, which I discovered in my position as both their Section Supervisor and Platoon Commander. Rather than place charges against them, which might have resulted in reduction of rank or payment of fines, I offered them the option of spending some of their free time doing a little painting around the motor pool, an alternative which they gratefully accepted.

Since I had not been specific regarding what kind of painting they were supposed to do, they painted a semi tractor on the side of the Operations Building. It was extremely good artwork. They both turned out to be very talented artists. The truck looked great and the theme could not have been better chosen. I was somewhat amused by their rather free interpretation of my basic instructions to 'do some painting' around the motor pool when I saw their artwork in its very early stages, so I allowed them to continue because the quality of their work was so good. On learning that I approved of their efforts, they elaborated on their theme, adding a road, mountains in the background and terrain features around the diesel semi truck. The mural covered the entire side of the Operations building.

True, these two Marine artists were tractor-trailer operators, so it might seem only natural that their artwork would depict a diesel tractor but the message that was communicated to me was that this painting represented the artists' appreciation to me for being allowed to avoid alternative official punishment and for being allowed to accomplish their assigned mission in their own particular way.

I was touched - and very pleased - because this incident occurred quite early during my assignment at the Base Motor Transport Section and it established a good working relationship between us. This incident gave us a common bond.

Additionally, these two young Marines/drivers/artists did a separate painting near the front of my office. It was a picture of Mount Fuji, Japan. They did this in order to commemorate a trip I had recently made to Japan on temporary additional duty to hold an inspection/instruction visit to a unit that was having some procedural problems. A Sergeant who had been assigned to Camp Fuji while I was there had told some of the enlisted Marines that I had jogged up Mount Fuji on an off-day while I was in Japan. That helped to establish my 'bona fides' as a hard-charger.

Platoon Commander Philosophy

My performance as a Platoon Commander at the Base Motor Transport Section was exactly the same as it had been every other time when I have served in that capacity. It was my opinion that each Marine in the entire Marine Corps should have at least some justification in believing that HIS platoon commander was the best in the Corps.

I always believed that it was my responsibility to provide my troops with an example, a standard against which they could measure themselves. Whenever one of my Marines fired the rifle or pistol for record, I wanted him or her to be trying to beat MY score. When they took the physical fitness test, I wanted them to be trying to beat MY time on the 3-mile run or to do more chin-ups or sit-ups than I had done.

Fortunately for me, it was ALMOST impossible for anybody to beat me so my macho image didn't have to suffer very often. I know that sounds like bragging but my abilities had been honed during the very early years of my life. When I was a pre-teen, I could already shoot the head off of a matchstick at thirty paces with a .22 rifle and I always qualified as high expert with both the rifle and the pistol, so by the time I became an officer, it was believed by some of my troops that I could practically 'will' my shots into the bulls-eye.

Physically, my abilities had been acquired during my early years, also. As a hay hauler, as a sawmill worker, as a shovel handler, as a country boy 'tough guy', I had very few equals. With the kind of 'training' I had endured as a child and teenager, running the Marine Corps physical fitness test was like taking a walk in the park.

Some of it was mental, too. I firmly believed that I had a sacred obligation to give the U. S. government the best I had to give - a healthy mind in a healthy body. I wanted my country to get its money's worth. Whether I was paid as a Private, Sergeant, Gunnery Sergeant or Warrant Officer, I wanted to feel that I had truly earned that pay. Granted, I was not always the best at EVERYTHING I tried to do in the Corps but I was SO good at so MANY things that no single person could ever beat me at more than one event.

It is important to point out that I had been extremely lucky. During my formative years, I was hardly ever sick. It's just the luck of the draw. I have had a great many injuries, wounds, breaks, cuts and 'boo-boos'. I have been afflicted with a form of dengue fever, my lungs are affected by exposure to Agent Orange and my feet have been afflicted from time to time with recurrences of 'jungle rot'. But these little problems hardly even slowed me down AT THE TIME. It is mostly during my older years, here lately, that the effects of these happenings have come back to haunt me. I hate old age! But I never smoked, drank or used drugs because I didn't want anything to impair my physical abilities or mental faculties. At my current age, I would be in a lot worse condition if I hadn't been so picky during my younger years.

Furthermore, as a Platoon Commander, I felt that it was my obligation to help my troops to be the best they could be. Sometimes I did this by LEADING them and sometimes I did this by PUSHING them. But I always tried to give them an example by which they could gauge themselves. I set the standards my Marines had to live up to.

My platoon members developed the habit of calling me 'Pappy'. The reason for this is because my leadership style was similar to that of a truly great Marine leader, Major Greg 'Pappy' Boyington, a fighter pilot and squadron commander during WWII. Don't worry if you never heard of him - he would be practically unknown outside Marine Corps circles, even though there was a television series many years ago called *Black Sheep Squadron*, which was based on his Marine Corps career.

If you have, by now, decided that I have a really colossal ego, consider the reasons for it. I earned the right to call myself a United States Marine. Being authorized to wear the Marine Corps Emblem - the Eagle, Globe and Anchor - is an honor and privilege that very few of my fellow Americans can understand. Then consider the fact that I was repeatedly awarded Superior Performance Pay as an enlisted Marine. Best of the Best! Then I was selected to advance from the enlisted ranks and become an officer.

And of course, the honor of being chosen to serve as a Platoon Commander is a privilege given to very few. As a junior officer, it is par for the course to be given a lot of collateral duties, such as Morale Officer, Recreation Officer, Voter Registration Officer, Club Inventory Officer or United Way Contribution Officer, for example. But Company

Commanders don't want to have just ANYBODY leading their platoons, so when a Commanding Officer chooses a Platoon Commander, that officer has to have already demonstrated his ability to truly BE a leader of Marines.

So, anyway, I said all that to say this: Those two young Marines, L/Cpl Ruddell and L/Cpl Proper, got caught at a couple of minor infractions but, instead of being punished without any consideration for their future potential and having a blight on their records, they were encouraged to show that they COULD put their best foot forward. Being allowed to render their painting on the side of a public military building gave the artists a lot of pride and personal satisfaction and they put their best effort into their work. As a Marine officer, I considered it an honor and a privilege to have had the opportunity to lead and to command such Marines.

During my time at the Base Motor Transport Section, I dealt with a few substandard Marines. Luckily, they were offset by some really outstanding Marines. For example, I arranged a Meritorious Mast for Corporal M. R. Perdue, for PFC T. D. Miller, for PFC Yvette Guy and for Gunnery Sergeant Carl J. Edwards. I recommended both PFC Miller and PFC Guy for meritorious promotions. I also recommended a Letter of Appreciation for one of the Japanese civilians, Mister Hoshu Hiyane, for his outstanding work at the Base Motor Transport Section.

A Wake-Up Call for Commanders

The following document is a communication from the Commandant of the Marine Corps (CMC) to the Commanding General, Fleet Marine Force Pacific, with information copies to the Commanding General, Marine Corps Base, Camp Butler and to the Commanding General, 3rd Force Service Support Group.

The subject of the message is a Congressional Interrogation regarding temporary additional duty at Camp Fuji in Japan. That is the unit I visited last April, along with Lt/Col Hitzelberger and Captain McTeague to figure out what their problems were. We did a pretty good job of that, I believe, and we pointed out every problem we discovered, not only to the people in charge at Camp Fuji, but also to the parent commands back on Okinawa.

We turned in our reports. We told our senior officers exactly what was wrong at Camp Fuji. We told our senior officers exactly what corrective action needed to be taken to fix the problems at Camp Fuji. We gave our findings, our opinions and our recommendations to our senior officers. That was all we could do. We were not in a position to say, "Okay, General, here's what is wrong. Now FIX it".

This message from the Commandant is proof positive that nobody listened to us. The officers at Camp Fuji knew they would be rotating out soon so they didn't bother to make the changes and improvements we recommended. And the senior officers back on Okinawa (the Colonels and the Generals) were too remote from the problems to fully grasp the fact that some changes NEEDED to be made. Or they were too lazy to take action. Or perhaps they simply didn't care about those problems… after all, those problems only affected a very few junior officers and a bunch of enlisted men, people who they considered to be not really worth worrying about.

So what finally happened was that one of those insignificant young Marines on temporary additional duty at Camp Fuji wrote to his Congressman and complained about the conditions there. Then that Congressman went to the Commandant and asked a few pointed questions. That is referred to as a Congressional Interrogative. Generally speaking, Commandants usually hate to hear about internal Marine Corps problems from someone OUTSIDE the Marine Corps.

So, he lit a fire under the Generals on Okinawa. How embarrassing, especially since they could have fixed these problems a year ago if they had listened to us. Those Generals and other senior officers on Okinawa had forgotten the two main basic guidelines every officer must follow: (1) Accomplish the mission; and (2) Ensure the welfare of the troops. They were very obviously not accomplishing the mission because vehicle maintenance was sloppy or nonexistent and supply support was poor. And they were obviously not ensuring the welfare of the troops because the food was still poor and living conditions were still deplorable.

The incorrect spelling and terrible grammar in the Commandant's message are presumably present because the young Marine's letter was supposedly quoted verbatim, although I simply can't imagine that a Lance Corporal in the Marine Corps would ever refer to himself as a soldier instead of as a Marine. However, he DID manage to get his point across. And he also managed to get some very high-ranking officers extremely excited. I sure would hate to be one of those people who were named specifically in that message. Being the subject of a Congressional Interrogative is an instant career killer.

Anyway, here is a reproduction of the message exactly as it was received on Okinawa:

P 071428Z Jan 81
Fm CMC WASHINGTON DC
To RUHQHQA/CG FMFPAC
INFO RUADANA/CG MCB CAMP BUTLER JA
RUADBEJ/CG THIRD FSSG
BT
UNCLAS //N05730//
SUBJ: CONGRINT RE TAD AT CAMP FUJI, JA: CASE OF LCPL ALBERT S. N. GOGUE
REP GEORGE C. EUSTAQUIO HAS CORRESPONDED WITH THIS HQ ON SNM'S BEHALF RE SUBJ MATTER. SNM'S LTR QUOTED AS FOLLOWS:

"I am a Lance Corporal in the United States Marine Corps who has decided to write to you out of frustration and despair over what is going on at my present unit.

This unit is displayed as maintenance and motor transport organization stationed at training Camp Mt. Fuji, Japan in which is presently designated as C.S.S.D.-31.

This letter is written not as a 'spur of the moment' idea but only a little much 'soul searching' and personal anxiety over any consequences that may come to bear. The most basic problem we have now is our food.

Chow hall
    a. not enough given out to each individual
    b. inadequate eating utensils
    c. not enough variety of meals such as food not being prepared properly

Activities
    a. club system unsanitary
    b. movies being shown unable to hear
    c. liberty calls secured on week days
    d. lack of special services

Motor Transport Operations
    a. safety deadline. Vehicles going out of motor pool on Japanese roads. Such as a tractor trailer and troop cargo trucks
    b. using official government vehicles for personnel use which to include staff noncommissioned officers and officers
    c. at this time no safety inspection for vehicles departing to go on the road
    d. majority of vehicles not painted in regulation manner

Maintenance
    a. vehicles leave maintenance shop with incomplete work due to lack of supply support
    b. supply department giving inadequate support
    c. maintenance mechanics missing special tools to do basic maintenance repairs
    d. maintenance reportedly unable to account for thousands of dollars worth of gear

Leadership
  Warrant Officer Hobbs
    authorize unsafe vehicles for road use
    authorizes illegal modifications or questionable modifications
  Staff Sergeant O'Leary
    does not know his job and legally not qualified as a motor transport maintenance chief
  Staff Sergeant Mingle
    has been in the Marine Corps for 19 years as a typewriter mechanic in which also not
    qualified in his job as maintenance chief and order men of specific military optional skills
    to work on their work area
No temporary additional duty pay for highly cost living area. Infantry men on this operation get them but soldiers attached to C.S.S.D.-31 don't.
Towards my conclusion, I personally feel that though we are in a field operation, much of this news could be more shaped up and well pleased for in which too include that we are soldiers protecting our country and in return all we ask for is a little sympathy and reality while legally participating with this operation on Mt. Fuji's training camp, Japan".

Request all allegations be investigated and report sent to CMC (Code LA-2) by 19 Jan 1981.
BT
NNNN
IN   00061/08 JAN   /ACK

Note: Remember, the message is reproduced here exactly as it was received on Okinawa, with all grammatical and spelling errors left uncorrected. Even so, enough details were provided by L/Cpl Grogue that his Representative would have been absolutely COMPELLED to direct some very pointed questions to the Commandant of the Marine Corps. I absolutely believe that the officers and staff NCOs named in the letter should have most definitely be sent before a performance review board, but I also think the Generals on Okinawa should have faced charges of conduct unbecoming to a Marine Officer, at the very LEAST. All of the problems highlighted in this Congressional Interrogative already had been brought to the attention of those Generals a year earlier when Lt/Col Hitzelberger, Captain McTeague and I had turned in our reports on what we had found at Camp Fuji. There would have been no mercy shown on those Generals if a Board of Inquiry had been convened and staffed with officers who thought the same way I did because dereliction of duty would have been one of the charges filed against them.

Presumed Innocent

5 Feb 1981-I got a call from the legal section at Camp Pendleton. Cpl Laver, a legal clerk there, asked me if I remembered a Marine named Corporal Neftali Rivera. I did. He had worked for me in the Subsistence Section of Base Food Service when I was assigned as the Subsistence Officer. The problem was that Rivera, currently assigned at Camp Pendleton, had been charged with armed robbery and assault and had requested my presence as a character witness. This was not a unique situation, as the Marine Corps will spare no expense when it comes to allowing an accused Marine the opportunity to properly and completely defend himself against charges.

9 Feb 1981-I received orders to go to Camp Pendleton, in a temporary additional duty (TAD) status, to testify in the trial of Cpl Rivera. I packed a few things, got a ride to Kadena Air Base, boarded a plane at 1715 and we took off at 1800. I was very pleasantly surprised to discover that Master Sergeant Jose Mora was on the flight with me. He was the Subsistence Operations Chief and worked for me when I was in Subsistence. In fact, he was still working there. He's a really great guy. And he remembered Rivera, too.

Although we left Okinawa at 1800 on 9 Feb 1981 on a flight that lasted many, many hours, we still arrived at Camp Pendleton at 2100 on 9 Feb 1981, three hours later, even though we had a two-hour stop in Alaska, another one-hour stop somewhere in northern California and waited an hour at Los Angeles International Airport for the military vehicle to pick us up and take us to Camp Pendleton. We had crossed the international date line, which made all the difference. Our flight number from Okinawa was F 256. If you add those digits, you get 13. When we got to Camp Pendleton, we were billeted in Area 13. They put me in the Bachelor Officers' Quarters (BOQ) in building 1342. My assigned room number was 148 - those digits total 13. M/Sgt Mora was billeted in building 16146 in room number 427 - those digits also total 13.

11 Feb 1981-M/Sgt Mora and I met with Lieutenant Rogers, who was brought from Quantico, Virginia to Camp Pendleton to defend Rivera,

at Rivera's request. We told him everything we could remember about Rivera. I also told him that Rivera had received a Letter of Appreciation from the Battalion Commander for his work while he was assigned to Subsistence. I had written the rough draft of the Letter, myself. Lt Rogers said he appreciated the information and insight.

13 Feb 1981-The trial was a very quick affair early this morning. The 'victim' and his witnesses (his buddies) were quickly proven to be liars when other witnesses came forward and testified that the entire altercation had been initiated by the 'victim' and that, in fact, there had been no robbery at all. It was true that Cpl Rivera beat up the guy pretty badly but it was only in self-defense after he was provoked by the 'victim' and his buddies. The guy was quite embarrassed that Rivera had won the fight because Rivera was considerably smaller, so the 'victim' tried to get revenge by lying. As a result, that man and his buddies faced charges of perjury. M/Sgt Mora and I were allowed to testify for the record about Rivera's character (and I made reference to the award Rivera had won), even though Rivera had already been proven innocent, at that point. M/Sgt Mora and I treated Corporal Rivera to lunch and visited with him for a couple of hours. It was a really great day. Oh, and by the way, it was Friday the Thirteenth.

Fitness Report for 1 October 1980 through 28 February 1981

Section C: Performance of Duty:
Regular duties   Outstanding
Administrative duties   Outstanding
Handling enlisted personnel Outstanding
Training personnel   Excellent

To what degree has he exhibited the following:
Personal appearance   Outstanding
Military presence   Outstanding
Attention to duty   Outstanding
Cooperation   Outstanding
Initiative   Outstanding
Judgment   Outstanding
Force   Excellent
Leadership   Outstanding
Loyalty   Outstanding
Personal relations   Outstanding
Economy of management   Excellent
Growth potential   Outstanding

Your estimate of this Marine's general value to the service:
Outstanding

Considering the requirements of service in war, indicate your attitude toward having this Marine under your command:
Particularly desire to have

Narrative comments:
    CWO Morris is a highly efficient and professional Marine Officer. He performs, in an outstanding manner, all duties required of him. For this reporting period, CWO Morris has been the Operations Officer for Base Motor Transport. This billet is for a Captain. However, CWO Morris has displayed outstanding resourcefulness, initiative and dedication to duty in maintaining an efficient and economical operational section. Due to the size of the GME motor transport fleet, approximately 800 vehicles,

CWO Morris' duties have been very difficult and demanding. Without hesitation, CWO Morris has accepted all assigned tasks and additional responsibilities with enthusiasm. CWO Morris is a dedicated, mature Marine Officer. He reflects concern for the well-being of all Marines in his section, and he dedicates many extra hours in assisting Marines with personal or military problems. CWO Morris is always available to advise or assist Marines who need consultation. CWO Morris maintains an outstanding personal and military appearance at all times. He passes the PFT consistently with a high first class rating. CWO Morris sets high standards and expectations for himself and for all Marines. He has been very instrumental in influencing many Marines in this section to achieve higher standards in appearance and conduct. Although CWO Morris' MOS is 3050 (Warehousing Officer), he is quickly becoming technically proficient in the motor transport field. This is a tribute to his professionalism, dedication to duty, willingness to learn and positive attitude. He is a valuable asset to this section and the Marine Corps and he has outstanding potential as a Marine Officer.

    Reporting Officer
    D. R. Bennett
    Captain USMC
    Motor Transport Officer
    Base Motor Transport Section
    Marine Corps Base
    Camp Smedley D. Butler

UNITED STATES MARINE CORPS
Headquarters and Service Battalion
Marine Corps Base
Camp Smedley D. Butler
FPO Seattle, Washington 98773

RLM/st
13 Mar 1981

From: Operations/Maintenance Officer, Base Motor Transport Section
To: Commanding Officer, Headquarters and Service Battalion, Marine Corps Base
Via: Motor Transport Officer, Base Motor Transport Section
Info: (1) Officer In Charge, Direct Support Stock Control Branch (DSSC)
(2) Officer In Charge, Stores Accounting and Supply System Management Unit (SASSY Management Unit)

Subj: Supply Procedures

On many occasions, the Base Motor Transport Section has submitted new item requests to DSSC for locally manufactured/locally available repair parts applicable to Japanese vehicles in the Base Motor Transport Commercial Fleet with somewhat less than satisfactory results. Too often, we have not received any return information regarding the assignment of local stock numbers to these repair parts. Upon review, I discovered that we had 89 new item requests which had not been responded to by DSSC. In some instances, these parts may have had a stock number assigned, had been procured and had been stocked at Issue Point 61 long ago. However, without having knowledge of the stock number assignment, the Base Motor Transport Section cannot acquire the part through IP 61. Therefore, we have continued to use Blanket Purchase Agreements (BPA) to purchase the items from local vendors while the items were sitting idle at the Issue Point.

In the past, before I was assigned to Base Motors, the Base Motor Transport Section often purchased repair parts through BPAs without processing a new item request. Now, to ensure that the usage data gets recorded on DSSC records, I talked with the NCOIC of Stock Control and the NCOIC of Customer Service and determined that the following procedures should be followed: All BPA documents will be routed through the Customer Service Section of DSSC. If a stock number has been previously assigned for the part, the stock number will be annotated on the document before the document is returned to the Base Motor Transport Section. This gives us the opportunity to obtain the part through regular supply procedures (through IP 61) if it is in stock. Even if the repair part does not have a stock number assigned, or if it is not in stock, the usage data (the requirement) for the item is still registered on DSSC records because they have the capability to record "hits" against part numbers as well as against stock numbers. And if a part number gets three "hits" in six months, it is automatically assigned a local stock number and becomes eligible to be stocked, thus becoming readily available through regular supply channels.

I talked again with the NCOIC of Stock Control, who has taken appropriate steps to ensure that the Base Motor Transport Section will receive all information regarding stock number assignments for new item requests. Additionally, he researched the 89 new item requests for which the Base Motor Transport Section had no response. He determined that approximately 70% of them had stock numbers assigned. He provided me with the appropriate data to update our records. The new item requests which have no record at DSSC will be resubmitted.

I also talked with Lieutenant Snow, the Officer in Charge of I and O Control Section. I asked him to provide me with a mark IV program which would extract the following items of information from DSSC computer records: part number, manufacturer's name, stock number, unit of issue and nomenclature. At first, he was reluctant to fill my request and pointed out that a listing of that type was already available. I was familiar with the listing to which he referred, so I pointed out to him the one defect in that listing: the part number is listed in FL 1 (field # 1) of the listing. However, whenever the part number has too many characters to fit into FL 1, the remainder of the part number is continued in FL 5 (field 5) of a completely separate listing, which is not readily available. Therefore, a great many of the part numbers are unrecognizable because the last few digits are not printed, rendering the listing to which he referred useless for our purposes. Lieutenant

Snow agreed that this listing would not suffice and said that he would be willing to build a mark IV program in accordance with my specifications and that it would be printed in part number sequence.

Lieutenant Snow indicated that this program would be run on a one-time basis, only. I did not argue the point at that time because I knew that he had seen the logic of my ideas and that, once I had my foot in the door, I would be able to convince the appropriate people of the need for a continually updated listing of this nature. I asked if the output from this program could also be provided in card format. This would give us the capability to frequently update our information whenever a new stock number is assigned to a new item request, or when our research revealed that a stock number has been assigned for any other reason, simply by adding a keypunched card to the existing deck. Lieutenant Snow said that it would probably not be possible to get the output in card format but that IBM cards could be keypunched later, using the listing as a source document. This does not constitute a problem for me, as I have keypunch experience and I know a few people who would be willing to take keypunch training from me and to help keypunch IBM cards whenever necessary.

I must point out that, too many times in the past, the maintenance crews at the Base Motor Transport Section have been their own worst enemies. Over the course of time, as I have become more knowledgeable of motor transport maintenance procedures and also as I have increased my understanding of the Japanese language, I have been able to communicate more and more freely with the 60 Japanese civilians who are employed as drivers, mechanics and technicians at Base Motors. Here is an example of what has happened frequently: there may be a requirement for a part, say for example, a carburetor rebuild kit for a common vehicle. The part was bought from a local civilian source through a Blanket Purchase Agreement (BPA). At the time of the purchase, the Maintenance Chief said thought, "Why should I buy just one? I have the paperwork available. I might as well buy half a dozen." So he installs the one he needed and puts the remaining five in a wall locker in the maintenance shop. As time goes by, whenever he needs a carburetor rebuild kit, he gets one out of the locker and installs it. This is all well and good but he has unwittingly left out a few steps in the process. He's a maintenance expert in motor transport, highly skilled at what he does, but he is not trained in the supply field. He doesn't register the purchase of these six repair parts with the supply section, which is outside his area of expertise. The supply system doesn't know that a requirement ever existed for any of those six repair parts, so no usage data gets recorded. Therefore, there's no need for the supply system to respond to the fact that this particular repair part was ever needed. Without usage data, this item will not be stocked through routine supply procedures. When those six carburetor repair kits are depleted, they may no longer be readily available on the local Japanese civilian market and the supply system can't respond in a timely manner to a demand for this item because there is no knowledge of the item, in the first place. Through casual inspection of the maintenance area, I have discovered a great many repair parts in wall lockers and drawers all over the section. The mechanics know where to find gaskets, oil filters, wiring harnesses, spark plugs, distributor caps and literally hundreds of other repair parts. When they need something, they go and get it out of the wall lockers, install it in the vehicle and it's a "done deal". Having these parts on hand is not necessarily a bad thing, but if the usage data from the repair parts in all of those wall lockers doesn't get transmitted to DSSC, the supply system can't provide proper support in the future because the system of supply and demand is usurped. They can't supply an item unless they know that a demand exists for that item. On so many occasions, when the supply system failed to do its job, it's because it didn't even know there was a job to be done, in the first place so the supply system is often unfairly maligned for a failing that is not its fault. Simply put, the Motor Transport Maintenance Section suffers from a self-inflicted "wound".

There are two other sources of repair parts which should be addressed here: (1) Scrounging from another unit; (2) Cannibalization and/or Selective Interchange.

The art of scrounging: Borrowing a repair part from another repair facility is an acceptable method of obtaining a much-needed part. However, the usage data must still be presented to DSSC so that a record of the usage will be made. If the supply system gets valid updates regarding the use of a part, any part, then the supply system will be better able to support a requirement for that part in the future.

Cannibalization and/or Selective Interchange: Example – if a jeep gets involved in a wreck and is "totaled", even if the engine is destroyed, the transmission or the transfer case may still be serviceable, or the axles, or the electrical components, or a thousand other parts. Using these parts to avoid having to dead line another vehicle is acceptable, even preferable. But the usage data simply must be recorded.

I told you so

On 30 March 1981, I had an interesting conversation with S/Sgt Cleveland. He's the Noncommissioned Officer in Charge (NCOIC) of Material Handling Equipment for 3rd Force Service Support Group. He told me he has had two different bosses just since he started.

That means there have been at least three different Officers in Charge of MHE since I was relieved of that duty. I know what MY problem was - I was assigned simultaneously as Officer in Charge of Material Handling Equipment and as Officer in Charge of Bulk Storage Section and I worked for a backstabbing jerk named Chief Warrant Officer Stricklin who absolutely would not allow me to initiate the actions necessary to fix the problems I had inherited, simply because he had previously assured the 3rd FSSG staff officers that no significant MHE problems existed and he didn't want to be exposed as an idiot.

First Lieutenant Anderson, the officer who took over MHE after I was fired had no other assignments, only MHE. He and the 3rd Supply Battalion Executive Officer both very smugly and very confidently assured the 3rd FSSG staff officers that MHE would be at least 95% operational within 60 days. They were so eager to make me look stupid and incompetent by showing how easy it would be to properly manage MHE. They were apparently mistaken. I had tried to tell them how many different factors were involved in simply getting one single forklift repaired and removed from dead line status but nobody wanted to listen. They had to learn the hard way, I guess.

But at least, Lt Anderson had it easier than I did because he didn't have to try to work around CWO Stricklin. MHE responsibility was removed from Storage Operations and was placed directly under the authority of the 3rd Supply Battalion S-3 section, so Lt Anderson was able to go directly to the Battalion Commander, Lt/Col Caputa, with any problems he might be having in accomplishing his mission. And yet, even with all that horsepower behind him and with all of that manpower under him, he apparently still could not accomplish the mission

S/Sgt Cleveland also told me he had ten people working for him in the MHE section. That was interesting because when I had responsibility for MHE, there were only three people in the MHE section and that INCLUDED the NCOIC.

I could have gone to the Commanding Officer of 3rd Supply Battalion and said, "I told you so", but he would have probably just got mad.

Commanding General's Inspection

A Commanding General's Inspection is the second most important inspection that can be conducted for a Marine unit of any size. The results of a CG Inspection go directly to the Commandant of the Marine Corps, after personal perusal of the Commanding General, himself. The CG may make an appearance in any area of the command to observe any particular episode of the inspection but he usually doesn't actually conduct the inspection, although he may walk through the ranks of a platoon which is taking part in the drill and personnel inspection portion of the overall inspection.

There is a large group of officers and senior staff NCOs who actually conduct the detailed segments of the inspection. As odd as it may seem, they are referred to as the detail inspectors. They delve into absolutely every aspect of a unit's business. Administrative procedures and records, logistical and supply procedures, maintenance, training, personnel inspections, drill and tactical maneuvers, safety protocols, judicial procedures and every other area of interest that might impact on a unit's readiness for action are all closely scrutinized.

14 April 1981 (Tuesday)-I was informed that I had been RANDOMLY selected to be the Platoon Commander of the platoon which had been assembled to participate in the platoon drill and personnel inspection portion of the upcoming CG Inspection. This was not MY platoon. This was a hodgepodge collection of people from various units thrown together temporarily simply in order to form a platoon-sized unit for inspection purposes, only. The platoon had formed about a month before and had been practicing drill for one hour three mornings each week. I don't know who the original platoon commander had been but, for some reason, he had been taken out of the assignment and I had been thrown into it. The platoon drill and the enlisted personnel inspection portion of the CG inspection was scheduled for the next Tuesday, 21 April, so I would have one hour each on Wednesday, Friday and Monday to conduct drill practice with my new platoon.

15 April 1981 (Wednesday)-I was out on the parade ground with my new platoon to conduct platoon drill practice. If the original platoon commander was fired, I could see why. And if the original platoon commander had asked to be relieved of the assignment, I could still see why. It was for the same reason in both cases. Those people had forgotten just about everything they had learned in boot camp about platoon drill and he had apparently been unable to re-teach them.

16 April 1981 (Thursday)-I had previously been assigned as the Pit Verification Officer for the rifle range detail at Camp Schwab. I didn't have to be there for the practice shooting during the first few days of firing but I had to be there for pre-qualification day and qualification day. My job on that firing detail was to stay downrange in the 'pits' to observe the performance of the relay groups who would be running the targets up and down while the other relays fired and to verify that there was no hole in the target if the pit crew registered a complete miss by the shooter. The morning was very cold and it rained heavily for the first two hours so we all got thoroughly soaked and almost froze to death. However, by the end of the day, we were all hot and miserable.

17 April 1981 (Friday)-I didn't get to go out and work on drill practice with my newly-inherited platoon because I had to go to the rifle range again as the Pit Verification Officer. I couldn't do both so I was going to have to hope that the senior Sergeant would run them through some drills. I had already told him what I wanted them to work on.

18 April 1981 (Saturday)-As of 0800 that morning, I was on duty as Officer of the Day for Marine Corps Base at Camp Butler. That was better than being Officer of the Day at Camp Hansen because I didn't have to go out to check guard posts. Mostly, I just had to sit in the office of the secretary of the CG and monitor the message traffic so that I could spread the word in case the Chinese Communists or the Russians tried something sneaky. I also observed the raising and lowering of the flag, morning and evening, to ensure that the proper procedures were followed. And I would have to sign the confinement orders in case the military police brought in somebody who needed to be locked up. Mostly, I just had to maintain communications with the various Battalion

Officers of the Day and generally ensure that the neighborhood didn't 'go to hell in a hand basket' while everyone else was off duty.

However, at 1000, I had to take a break from my duties as Base Officer of the Day and go participate in another part of the CG inspection. I had previously been RANDOMLY selected to take part in the Officers' Full Dress Uniform Inspection portion of the CG Inspection. I had to march into the inspector's office in full dress uniform so he could inspect the serviceability and tailoring of my uniform and, of course, at that time, I was quizzed on various subjects that officers should know. Naturally, I passed the inspection with an 'outstanding' rating. Then I went back to my duties as Base Officer of the Day.

19 April 1981 (Sunday)-When I got off duty at 0800, I proceeded to the enlisted barracks area to check on some of the people who were in my 'inspection platoon'. When I had first seen my 'inherited' platoon on Wednesday, just a few days ago, I had been unhappy with the appearance of some of my platoon members. With the platoon drill and personnel inspection only two days away, I was giving them the opportunity to show me the uniforms they would be wearing for the inspection so I could check the uniforms for serviceability. They weren't going to have to be wearing the uniforms, although they might have to try on a few articles if I wanted to check out the fit of the item (that is why I was willing to meet them at their barracks). But I was going to be held responsible for their appearance and I didn't want any surprises.

Regarding the Women Marines who were members of my 'inspection platoon', I wanted to assure myself that none of them could charge me with any sort of incorrect behavior while I was in their rooms so I had asked a Woman Marine Staff Sergeant friend of mine to accompany me while I was in the WM barracks. I would later repay her for her time by buying supper for her and her friend at the Club. One of the young Women Marines in the platoon had given me cause for considerable concern when I had first seen her at my original meeting with the platoon because she was wearing her hair in such a huge afro that her cap would not fit properly on her head. That simply would not do. I told her if she did not show considerable improvement, then she was going to be kicked out of the platoon and would be facing charges. Of course, she knew she was in violation of the uniform regulations but she had not realized that I would be quite so familiar with the clothing regulations regarding Women Marines. However, when I saw her on Sunday, she had her hair braided and wound tightly around her head and it looked very nice, and was in compliance with regulations. I thanked her courteously and told her that, if she presented that nice of an appearance on the day of the inspection, then we would get along very well.

During the next week, I made a point to have a little chat with the Staff Sergeant who was her immediate supervisor and told him that I would charge him with dereliction of duty if I ever saw his subordinate anywhere on base wearing her uniform improperly - any part of her uniform.

20 April 1981 (Monday)-At 0600, I was at the chin-up bars next to the obstacle course by the parade ground. I had previously been RANDOMLY selected to be one of the officers to take the physical fitness test portion of the CG Inspection. On the PFT, I always score in the high Class V rating. That means I always get a high first class rating. Over the years, the Marine Corps has had several different types of physical fitness tests but at that time, we did chin-ups, sit-ups, and a timed 3-mile run.

I had arranged for my inherited platoon to do their practice platoon drill at 0800 that morning because I knew I would be finished with the PFT by then. However, I could not leave the PFT area until after the administrators, inspectors, scorers and timekeepers had finished running everybody through the various events, so I had to attend the platoon drill practice in my sweat suit. The platoon members knew the reason why I would not be in uniform for the practice.

21 April 1981 (Tuesday)-Today was the platoon drill and enlisted personnel inspection portion of the CG Inspection. My inherited platoon had passed. Oh, they weren't outstanding or even excellent but they passed. I'd only had two sessions of practice with them but I had tried to turn the collection of individuals into a cohesive unit. While conducting drill, if the instructor gives the preparatory command and the command of execution at the proper moment, in a loud and clear voice, the platoon can respond to those commands in an orderly fashion. A good drill instructor can help a platoon perform better…and I was a very good drill instructor.

Regarding being randomly selected to participate in the CG Inspection: Commanding officers can SAY that they randomly select the people who serve as a platoon commander, or who take the physical fitness test, or who get inspected in full dress uniform but the reality is that a unit commander is not going to draw names out of a hat because he might draw somebody who will embarrass the command by looking less than perfect in uniform or perform poorly on the PFT, or especially somebody who doesn't know how to conduct platoon drill. My CO knew I would not let him (or the Command) down. That's why I was RANDOMLY selected for every event.

BASE MOTOR TRANSPORT

The Commanding General's Inspection of Base Motor Transport was conducted on 5, 6 and 7 May 1981 and was comprised of the following:

AREA	GRADE
Standing Operating Procedures (SOP)	Outstanding
Publications Control	Outstanding
Records Control	Outstanding
Tool Control	Outstanding
Calibration Control	Outstanding
Training	Outstanding
Supply Procedures	Excellent
Maintenance Resources Utilization	Outstanding

There were no major discrepancies or trends noted during the Commanding General's Inspection within Base Motor Transport Section.

Marines considered worthy of recognition for exceptional performance are:

Captain Bennett	-Expertise, Knowledge and Leadership
Master Gunnery Sergeant Johnson	-Publications and Training
Gunnery Sergeant Draper	-Material Handling Equipment Shop NCOIC

Gunnery Sergeant Kindig	-Camp Kinser Sub Pool
Gunnery Sergeant Towery	-Truck Master
Gunnery Sergeant Cogar	-Responsible Officer
Gunnery Sergeant Edwards	-Operations NCOIC
Staff Sergeant Fowler	-Road Master
Sergeant Sanchez	-Tool Room and Calibration

Civilians considered worthy of recognition for exceptional performance of work:

Mister Arakaki	-Camp Kinser Sub Pool
Mister Heshike	-Material Handling Equipment Shop
Mister Arashiro	-Records Clerk
Mister Tamamoto	-Fiscal Manager

The Supply Procedures as such are not Outstanding because of administrative problems not necessarily the fault of the Motor Transport personnel. However, the established procedures are working well and with more emphasis on follow-up procedures, then the Supply Procedures could be Outstanding.

It is the opinion of the Inspection Team that the Base Motor Transport Section has become the exemplary section in Maintenance Management within the Marine Corps Base, Camp Smedley D. Butler.

R. A. McMahon
1st Lt   USMC
Senior Member
Motor T Team

Excluded for Spite

The preceding report is an extract of the overall Inspection Team's report which was presented to the Commanding General, subsequently to be sent to Headquarters Marine Corps for the Commandant's attention. This portion pertained to Motor Transport. You might notice that my name was conspicuously absent from the list of Marines who were considered worthy of recognition for exceptional performance. In the original version of the report, my name and rank were listed directly under that of my boss, Captain Bennett. The original list of reasons for my being considered worthy of recognition (to the right of my name) took up five lines of type because of my various contributions in so many different areas within Base Motor Transport.

Incidentally, the original version of the OVERALL CG's Inspection report noted that I had participated in more 'special events' of the Commanding General's Inspection than any other officer on base. 1-I stood the Officer's Personal Inspection in Full Dress Uniform. 2-I took part in the Physical Fitness Test portion and attained a high first class rating, not only scoring higher than ALL of the other officers and Staff NCOs who participated but also beating almost all of the junior enlisted (younger) Marines who took the PFT. 3-I served as the Platoon Commander for the platoon involved in the drill and personnel inspection portion of the CG's Inspection. My name was seen and heard from every quarter. The chief inspector, a Colonel, thanked me for my efforts and for my contributions and told me that if the inspection team could name a MVP (Most Valuable Player), like they do in some football games, then I would definitely receive the award. All things considered, that had turned out to be a pretty good day.

But my name was left off the list and I didn't get even an honorable mention in the final report because of Colonel Poland, the Assistant Chief of Staff (G-4) for Marine Corps Base. I will talk more about him, later.

Now, regarding the areas of Base Motor Transport that were inspected Standing Operating Procedures - I had written all of the Standing Operating Procedures (SOPs). What I would do was spend a day or two with each person in a key billet while he went about the performance of his duties. We would discuss every aspect of his job while I took notes. I would try to learn each person's job so well that I could have taken over in his absence, regardless of his assignment. Then I would go back to my office and write out a complete job description, detailing every possible contingency. Everybody agreed that I did this so well that most of the people could take over each other's job without any on-the-job training, as long as they knew how to read.

Publications Control - I took Master Gunnery Sergeant Johnson, the Maintenance Chief, with me to the Technical Research Library at Camp Foster (I had worked there when I was on Okinawa as a PFC many years ago). I showed him how to find every Marine Corps manual that dealt with 1st, 2nd, 3rd and 4th echelon maintenance on every vehicle and piece of equipment that was in our motor pool. More importantly, I put him in contact with the people who could assist him in obtaining multiple copies of those maintenance manuals for our own library at the Base Motor Transport Section. By the time I was done pointing the way, he could instantly put his hands on the correct book for any type of maintenance that was being performed on any of our vehicles. These books were complete, with diagrams and step-by-step instructions that our mechanics could use for diagnosis, maintenance and repairs.

Records Control - I went to see a Navy draftsman I knew at Camp Courtney and asked her if she could make a dozen 4-foot by 4-foot plywood panels, draw lines and spaces on them and then cover them with transparent acetate so we could use grease pencils on the acetate to list all of our vehicles, separated by type, in serial number sequence on the panels, with various bits of extra information in the spaces. Information such as where the vehicle was usually assigned, date and mileage of last maintenance, parts required for projected repairs, etc. The lines and spaces on the panels would be permanent (behind the acetate) and we could make changes on the acetate, as required. I then had Mister Arashiro set up a folder on each vehicle and file those folders in serial number sequence, separated by type of vehicle. The folders would hold maintenance records, accident reports, copies of repair orders, etc.

Tool Control - There wasn't so much I could do here but I did manage to convince the Japanese mechanics that there were certain tools that should be kept put away in the tool room when not in use, such as some gauges and impact wrenches and certain precision diagnostic tools and equipment that required calibration. Each mechanic was given his own tool box, issued and stocked by the government and each mechanic could think of those tools as his own, but he was still responsible for the security and maintenance of those tools in neat, clean order.

Calibration Control - The only real impact I had in this area was the fact that I finally convinced the mechanics that they should return controlled and/or serialized tools and equipment to the tool room after they used them and that those tools should not be kept in individual wall lockers or tool boxes. That made it easier for Sergeant Sanchez to keep the tool room neat and orderly and to ensure that tools and equipment which required calibration got the necessary attention.

Training - What can I say about training except that I was all over it? This area of expertise included the training and testing that was done by our Road Masters, who taught and graded all of our Marines who wanted to upgrade their military licenses. For the vehicle training and upgrades, the Road Masters gave most of the road training and road tests but I drafted the written parts of the tests. However, when it came to training people to operate every type of material handling equipment (mostly forklifts), there was NOBODY who could do that as well as I could. I was the universally acknowledged MHE Master Instructor. I could teach every type and size of forklift. And it didn't matter if the student was a Staff NCO or the lowest private. If a person showed an interest in learning how to operate a forklift, I was eager to teach him or her as many 'tricks of the trade' as he or she was able to absorb. Over the course of time, it had become a preferred mark of distinction for a young Marine to be able to boast that he or she had been a personal student of 'Gunner' Morris. On their operators' licenses, my signature in the 'Testing Officer' block was regarded as a status symbol, indicating that the operator had been trained and tested by the best in the business.

Supply Procedures - With my extensive background in the supply and warehousing fields, I was really making considerable progress in that area of our business. I used my numerous contacts in the supply sections, from the Officer in Charge of the SASSY Management Unit, through the various members of the Direct Support Stock Control Branch, Customer Service, Technical Research, Keypunch and I and O Control, all the way down to the people who worked in the various supply issue points. I was able to speak their specialized supply languages, I knew the questions to ask and I knew the various solutions which might be available to solve our problems with obtaining repair parts and supplies. In fact, I had written a letter (for the record) discussing supply procedures back on 13 March 1981, a couple of months before, in which I detailed many of our supply problems and some of the solutions I was initiating to correct these problems. I just had not had enough time to get all of those solutions into working order before the CG's Inspection. Even so, the inspection report indicated that my established procedures were working well and that with more follow-up with the supply units, the Supply Procedures grade for the report would have been Outstanding rather than merely Excellent.

Maintenance Resources Utilization - This sounds like the most technical part of our operation but actually, it was the simplest. I utilized all available resources to our best advantage. For example, I made sure that the lubrication rack was never empty. I established a 'fast track' for vehicles that needed only the basic lube and oil change. I set aside a special area for vehicles that had electrical problems. I made sure that vehicles that needed major overhaul work didn't get in the way of vehicles that needed only tune-ups and minor repairs. I set aside a special area for tire and tube repair (actually, there was already an area for that but it was in an open bay that had nothing more than a roof as protection from the elements - I consolidated a couple of tool rooms and moved the tire and tube repair operation into one of them. Then I worked out a deal with the Facilities Engineers to install some very large, heavy duty fans so the workers had not only protection from wind and rain but they had good ventilation in the summertime. And in every work area, I stored all of the specialized tools that might be required for the tasks which would be performed in each given area.

Alright, there were 52 enlisted Marines (Private through Master Gunnery Sergeant) and 60 Japanese civilians assigned to the Marine Corps Base Motor Transport Section but there were only two officers assigned there - Captain Bennett and Chief Warrant Officer Morris. So I was not only the Motor Transport Operations Officer AND the Motor Transport Maintenance Officer, I also served as the Assistant Base Motor Transport Officer. And of course, I was also the Platoon Commander for the 52 enlisted Marines who worked in the Base Motor Transport Section. Now that you are aware of the extensive involvement I had in every aspect of the Motor Transport Section, you might very well wonder why my name was not listed on the final copy of the overall report that was given to the Commanding General of Marine Corps Base and would eventually be forwarded to the Commandant of the Marine Corps.

The basic answer is two words: Colonel Poland. Further enlightenment is provided as follows:

In the performance of my duties as Operations Officer of Marine Corps Base Motor Transport Section (my duties as Maintenance Officer did not pertain to this situation), I revoked the assignment of the sedan which was generally used to provide transportation for the Commanding General, First Marine Air Wing, Marine Corps Air Station (H), Futenma, Okinawa. I also revoked the assignment of the sedan which was generally used to provide transportation for Colonel Poland, the Assistant Chief of Staff (G-4) for Marine Corps Base. I revoked other assignments, too, but these two were the most significant.

Certain officers in key positions of command or authority are routinely assigned a military driver and a military vehicle for the purpose of conducting official business, such as providing transportation to and from units and sections under their command and control (for example, if they had a conference scheduled with some people at another base or if they had to greet and pick up a visiting dignitary at the airfield) they could ride and discuss business with members of their staff who might be with them without having to worry about watching traffic. However, the assignment of a military vehicle is intended for official use only.

The main problem with these vehicles was the fact that they were being misused by the people to whom they were assigned and I was therefore required by regulations to take actions to bring that misuse to a stop. To be more specific, the drivers assigned to those officers were using the vehicles to go to the bank, the post exchange, the laundry, the package sales liquor store and to carry the wives and families of these officers to various places on the island. The drivers of the vehicles were running errands and doing chores for the officers involved. The drivers were not assigned to the Base Motor Transport Section but the vehicles were. My Road Masters, S/Sgt L. Smith and S/Sgt J. Springer, had issued citations to those drivers on numerous occasions for being in areas where those vehicles were not supposed to be. Furthermore, every military vehicle is issued each day with a 'trip ticket', which is supposed to be filled out by the driver, listing each stop with the odometer mileage annotated at that stop. The visits to the unauthorized areas were never listed on the trip ticket, even though the Road Masters repeatedly caught the drivers there. Failure to properly fill out the trip ticket constitutes willful falsification of a government document, which is a separate violation of federal law. But every time I tried to process charges against those drivers, the charges always disappeared.

Also, on one occasion when Sgt Lopez came to the dispatcher's office to pick up the key to the Commanding General's vehicle, I was in the Operations Office. I saw that Sgt Lopez was wearing a summer service 'C' uniform with a civilian coat. The coat looked like a high school jacket. It had emblems and patches on the back and on one sleeve. I told him to step into my office. I confiscated the jacket and told him he would be charged with violating the uniform clothing regulations for mixing military and civilian attire. Although his language was at least reasonably respectful, he had such a disgusted, contemptuous sneer on his face while I was talking to him, I also charged him with disrespect toward an officer. Those charges also disappeared.

On another occasion, when I personally encountered Colonel Poland's driver in the post exchange parking lot, I had him taken, in handcuffs, to the Motor Transport Operations office by the military police and had the vehicle taken to the motor pool by a wrecker. Colonel Poland wanted to have me court-martialed for illegally having his driver arrested and for 'stealing' his vehicle.

When I was called before the Staff Judge Advocate, I explained that I had not arrested the driver but merely had him 'escorted' by military policemen to the Motor Transport Section and that the decision to have him handcuffed was the decision of the senior military policeman at the scene, based on the attitude, language and actions of the driver. I also told the SJA that the reason for the MP escort was because the driver had been ordered to report immediately to the Base Motor Transport Operations Office on many previous occasions by the Road Masters at other times when he had been caught in unauthorized areas and he had repeatedly ignored those orders. Furthermore, I explained that the driver had not been listing those unauthorized trips to restricted areas on his vehicle's 'trip' ticket, which constituted making a false statement on an official government document and that Colonel Poland was signing the trip ticket at the end of the work day, thus freely endorsing a false official statement. Then I showed the SJA copies of the federal regulations, orders and directives which explained that use of a government vehicle for personal convenience is a violation of the law. The SJA dismissed the charges against me.

Of course, Colonel Poland was furious. I did not have a 'death wish' so I had not set out to make an enemy of him but his callous disregard of the regulations did not set well with me.

It's true that, as Base Motor Transport Operations/Maintenance Officer, I was directly subordinate to Captain Bennett, who was the Base Motor Transport Officer, and he was directly subordinate to Colonel Poland, the Assistant Chief of Staff (G-4) but we were all supposed to answer to a higher authority - the citizens of the United States. And the citizens did not deserve to have their tax dollars squandered for the personal convenience of any officer, regardless of his rank or assignment.

Federal regulations forbade us from using public office for personal gain so when an officer sends his military driver in a military vehicle to the post exchange to make a purchase for him, or to the laundry to pick up his uniforms, or to the package store to pick up his alcohol, or to take his wife shopping at the commissary, that relieves the officer, or his wife, from having to use their personal vehicles (and their own gasoline) to perform those chores, then that constitutes using his office for personal gain.

Federal regulations forbade us from giving preferential treatment to any person or entity so when an officer uses his military driver and a military vehicle to run his errands for him, he is giving preferential treatment to himself because other Marines, whether they be officers or enlisted, who don't happen to have a military vehicle assigned to them have to make their own way around the base, using their own personal vehicles, or civilian taxis, or by walking.

Federal regulations forbade us from impeding government efficiency or economy so when an officer uses a military vehicle for personal convenience, he is adversely affecting government efficiency and economy because he is putting unnecessary wear and tear on that vehicle and is using gas and oil that was paid for by tax dollars.

Federal regulations forbade us from affecting adversely the confidence of the public in the integrity of the government and the average, law-abiding, tax-paying citizen would not think very highly of the integrity of an officer who would use a publicly funded military vehicle for personal convenience.

I had no personal animosity toward Colonel Poland but I was responsible for almost a thousand vehicles. It would be a violation of my oath of office to allow even one of those vehicles to be used to waste (actually, to steal) the taxpayers' money. It would be the same as allowing it to be used as a getaway vehicle in a bank robbery. I had a duty to at least try to stop it. And it wasn't as if I was trying to embarrass him for an occasional error in judgment - every person is going to make a mistake, once in a while. I do, too. But my Road Masters had caught his driver dozens of times. I didn't set out to make an enemy of Colonel Poland but that is what happened. And he couldn't court-martial me. However, he had other ways to 'put me in my place'. After all, he was the Assistant Chief of Staff to the Commanding General of Marine Corps Base and he had an incredible amount of power. So he used his power to have my name removed from the final copy of the Commanding General's Inspection Report.

What he stole from me was my moment of glory, my opportunity to have my star shine in front of the Commanding General and, subsequently, in front of the Commandant of the Marine Corps (CMC). I had EARNED the right to have my leadership abilities made known to CMC.

In my imagination, I had thought about what would happen when the Commandant would read that inspection report. I knew he would be impressed with the many ways in which I had participated (and excelled) in the various areas of the inspection process and the many ways in which I had contributed to the extremely high rating given to the Base Motor Transport Section. (Incidentally, it was the highest overall rating that had ever been given to any unit of any type).

Maybe he would have given me a promotion or something, maybe a medal. At the very least, I might have received a letter of commendation, personally signed by the Commandant. That would have been fabulous. But my chance to have my excellence recognized and officially acknowledged was stolen from me by the petty, childish actions of one of my senior officers.

P. S. Captain Bennett did not appreciate what Colonel Poland had done to me so, at the end of my tour on Okinawa, a month and a half later, when he wrote my fitness report, he made special mention of my efforts and contributions in both sections of Base Motor Transport (Operations and Maintenance) and he specifically pointed out the many improvements I had made in the Maintenance section. Furthermore, before he sent my fitness report up through the chain of command, he waited to process it until Colonel Poland had already been replaced as Assistant Chief of Staff (G-4) by Colonel Salter, so that Colonel Poland could not put a bad endorsement on my fitness report as the reviewing officer.

Fitness Report for 1 March 1981 through 16 June 1981

Section C: Performance of duty:
Regular duties	Outstanding
Administrative duties	Outstanding
Handling enlisted personnel	Outstanding
Training personnel	Outstanding

To what degree has he exhibited the following:
Personal appearance	Outstanding
Military presence	Outstanding
Attention to duty	Outstanding
Cooperation	Outstanding
Initiative	Outstanding
Judgment	Outstanding
Force	Outstanding
Leadership	Outstanding
Loyalty	Outstanding
Personal relations	Outstanding
Economy of management	Outstanding
Growth potential	Outstanding

Your estimate of this Marine's general value to the service:
Outstanding

Considering the requirements of service in war, indicate your attitude toward having this Marine under your command:
Particularly desire to have

Narrative comments:
 CWO Morris is a highly efficient and professional Marine officer. Extremely versatile and dedicated, CWO Morris performs, in an outstanding manner, all duties required of him. For this reporting period, CWO Morris, as the Operations/Maintenance Officer for Base Motor Transport, has displayed outstanding resourcefulness, initiative and leadership. Due to his efforts, the Maintenance Section of Base Motor Transport has become an efficient and economical operation with refined

supply and maintenance management procedures. Unselfishly, CWO Morris has dedicated many extra hours in applying his vast experience and technical knowledge of supply to improve the overall performance of this section. Responsible for the operation and maintenance of approximately 1,000 vehicles, CWO Morris has, without hesitation, accepted his demanding and difficult duties with enthusiasm.

CWO Morris has demonstrated the ability to perform the duties of a higher rank and of greater responsibility. CWO Morris is a mature Marine officer who reflects concern for the welfare of all Marines in this section. He dedicates many extra hours to assisting Marines in this section with personal or military problems. CWO Morris is always available, offering advice or assistance to Marines who need consultation.

CWO Morris maintains an outstanding appearance at all times and he passes the physical fitness test consistently with a high first class rating. Highly motivated, CWO Morris sets very demanding standards and expectations for himself and all Marines. He has been instrumental in influencing many Marines in this section to achieve higher standards in appearance and conduct.

CWO Morris has been a valuable asset to this section. His leadership, professionalism, technical experience and dedication to duty have enabled CWO Morris to contribute greatly to this section's mission.

    Reporting Officer
    D. R. Bennett
    Captain USMC
    Motor Transport Officer
    Base Motor Transport Section
    Marine Corps Base
    Camp Smedley D. Butler

    Reviewing Officer
    C. Salter
    Colonel USMC
    Assistant Chief of Staff (G-4)
    Marine Corps Base
    Camp Smedley D. Butler

For the Record

19 Jan 1981 - Gunnery Sergeant Edwards, Sergeant MacDowell, PFC Cohan and I went to see the Sergeant Major of Marine Wing Headquarters Squadron (MWHS-17). We took with us a Corporal who was the chief mess man at the Officers' Field Ration Dining Facility.

PFC Cohan had been on mess duty up there. Marines in the rank of Private, Private First Class and Lance Corporal get assigned to mess duty for two weeks each year. They are actually still attached to their parent command for administrative purposes but they work at the dining facilities. They clean tables, wash dishes and clean the dining facility. They are not in the same category as the cooks, who are assigned as permanent personnel at the dining facility.

PFC Cohan had been in a lot of trouble during his short time there. Even though he's 6'3" and about 240 pounds, he's sort of a gentle giant. He doesn't drink or smoke and he's a real-life body builder. But he had been in two fights up there. Racial conflict was terrible and some of the permanent personnel would come in late, drunk or stoned and the dining facility manager, Gunnery Sergeant Amituan, would do nothing to control any of those situations.

Early that morning, there had been a fight between a cook and a mess man. As long as the cook was winning, nobody did anything. When the cook started losing, the other cooks grabbed the mess man. Then the cook started hitting the mess man while he was being held. PFC Cohan jumped in and stopped the fight. Gy/Sgt Amituan, who had been watching the fight, started cursing at PFC Cohan.

PFC Cohan thought there was a lot of drug trafficking among the cooks and when somebody would get mad enough to write charges on somebody else, Gy/Sgt Amituan would keep the charge sheet and not send it up through the chain of command, especially if the charges were against one of his favorites.

When we talked with the Sergeant Major, we told him about the entire situation and I assured him that if action was not taken, then I would refuse to send any more of my Marines up there to serve on mess duty. That would require explanations that would get several people into trouble. The Sergeant Major promised that his CO would be advised of the situation and that he would investigate our charges. PFC Cohan was immediately taken off mess duty.

6 June 1981 - I couldn't believe it. There were STILL charges pending against PFC Cohan for fighting and drinking, after all that time. Our Battalion Commander, Colonel Monford, had bumped him up from Battalion non-judicial punishment to a Summary Court Martial. The possible punishments at a court martial are much more severe than any punishments that can be dealt out at non-judicial punishment.

I suspected that Colonel Monford had done this because PFC Cohan worked for me - and I was not very popular with the Colonel because my Road Masters kept catching the Colonel's driver using the Colonel's government vehicle to run errands for the Colonel in restricted areas, which constitutes improper use of an official vehicle for personal convenience. At one time, I'd had the vehicle confiscated, which embarrassed the Colonel because he had to go through official channels to request that the vehicle be reassigned to him.

Anyway, there was nothing the Colonel could do to me, so he was presumably taking it out on PFC Cohan by trying to have him court-martialed. A couple of witnesses had been temporarily assigned to Japan, so the trial had been delayed until they could return. A court officer, Major Michel, had been appointed and a court date had been set for Friday, 5 June 1981. However, on Thursday, 4 June, I got a call from the Marine Corps Base Chaplain, of all people, to tell me that the court martial had been cancelled and that PFC Cohan had been bumped back down to face Battalion non-judicial punishment. I called the admin section at battalion to confirm it. It was true but I thought I knew why it had happened. From a conversation I'd had with Major Michel, I believed he was going to rule in favor of PFC Cohan and drop all charges against him. I suspected that Colonel Monford found out the court was going to be lenient and he wanted to punish PFC Cohan, himself, so he cancelled the court martial. My tour of duty on Okinawa was about over and I would be in a 'checking out' status by that time but I was going to be at that proceeding, no matter what.

11 June 1981 - What a day! We were all assembled in the office of the Battalion Commander. I will try to present the sequence of events as correctly as possible:

Col - PFC Cohan, you are charged with drinking and being drunk at work at the dining facility while you were on duty. How do you plead?

Cohan - Not guilty, Sir.

Col - When the military police came into the area, they found empty beer bottles in the trash.

Cohan - Sir, they must have been thrown there by somebody else because I don't drink at all, Sir.

Col - Does anybody else have any information on this charge?

I said - Sir, I have known PFC Cohan for almost a year and I can confirm that he does not drink at all, Sir.

Chaplain - I can second that information, Sir.

Col - Regarding the second charge, you are charged with striking PFC Bavers in the face with your fist while on mess duty. How do you plead?

Cohan - Not guilty, Sir.

Col - Okay, then you tell me what happened.

Cohan - Well, Sir, Bavers had been on my case the whole time I was on mess duty. He was always making remarks about honky white boys and what he was going to do to me when he got the chance. He was always coming in drunk and none of the NCOs could do anything about it because Gunnery Sergeant Amituan wouldn't let the charge sheets go through. Bavers wouldn't do any work and was always trying to mess up my work. I asked him several times to leave me alone but he just kept after me. Finally, he made a remark to one of his friends about using a knife on any white boy who got in his way. Then he raised his fists and swung at me. So I hit him and knocked him down. Then I grabbed him and held him down until some other people dragged me off of him. Then they took him to the hospital.

Col - Does anybody else have anything to say about this matter?

There was a Lance Corporal there who had been on mess duty with PFC Cohan. He spoke up and said - Sir, I was able to watch Bavers most of the day. I saw him trying to pick a fight with Cohan several times. And sometimes, I saw Bavers walking on the backs of Cohan's heels when Cohan tried to walk away.

Chaplain - Sir, PFC Cohan had come to me at least a couple of months before the incident and asked me to help him learn how to control his temper. He had been seeing me on a regular basis and I feel he had made good progress.
Col - Have you been going to church?
Cohan - Yes, Sir, I have, every week.
Col - Captain Bennett, have you anything to add?
Capt B - Yes, Sir. PFC Cohan has worked at Base Motor Transport for almost a year. Originally, he was a driver. He drove for a lot of VIPs and we got some good reports on him. He was also a bus driver and a military taxi driver. Currently, we have him working on the lubrication rack and that's about the dirtiest, toughest job in the motor pool. PFC Cohan has never complained about his assignments. He's a conscientious, hard working Marine.
Col - Well, Gunner, I have been led to believe that you might have some additional information about this case.
I replied - Yes, Sir. Back in January, PFC Cohan and a couple of the other mess men had come to me some time before this incident to inform me of some of the conditions at the dining facility. Many fights occurred, usually between the mess men and the permanent personnel (the cooks) but none of these altercations resulted in official punishment, at least not against the cooks, because of Gunnery Sergeant Amituan, the dining facility manager. Whenever charges were filed, he would not send the charge sheets up the chain of command, especially when the charges were against his cooks. Besides the fights, there was also racial conflict and suspected drug trafficking. None of the people in junior leadership billets were able to exercise their authority because those who tried were quickly cut short by Gunnery Sergeant Amituan. So Gunnery Sergeant Edwards, the Operations Chief at Base Motors, and I had a meeting with the Sergeant Major of MWHS-17, which had administrative control over the dining facility. We told him about the situation and he promised to investigate. Gunnery Sergeant Amituan was eventually 'relieved for cause' but not before this incident had occurred. When Bavers had continued to harass PFC Cohan, you can imagine, Sir, how Cohan probably realized that it would be useless to approach Gunny Amituan to try to complain so he had to solve the problem on his own. After the incident, PFC Cohan came to me and told me about it. He was

man enough to do that and didn't want me to hear about it from anyone else. I talked with Sergeant Dupont, who was in charge of the mess men. He told me that he knew that Bavers had come to work drunk that day. I also talked with the doctor at Kuwae Hospital who attended Bavers. He told me that Bavers refused to take a sobriety test when he was treated for the injuries he had received during the incident. And Sir, if I had been in PFC Cohan's situation, I have to say that I would have hit Bavers, myself, and I certainly would not have waited as long as Cohan did. And Sir, we have worked for several months without hearing anything about this situation and we all thought the charges had been dropped.
Col - Well, do you have anything further to add, Gunner?
I said - No Sir, except that I want to thank you for your indulgence and for your patience while I explained this situation. PFC Cohan is a good man and he deserved to have this information entered into the record.
The Colonel sat for a minute, while he looked around at all of us. Then he closed PFC Cohan's service record and said, "The charges are dismissed. The reporting of the charges will be purged from PFC Cohan's record and, if PFC Cohan has been eligible for promotion while he has been awaiting the results of these charges, he will be promoted immediately, with an appropriately backdated promotion warrant. I declare this hearing to be closed. Gunner Morris, will you stay back for just a minute?"

I was so happy that I could have shed tears of joy. After the others had gone, I thanked Colonel Monford again and told him that attending this hearing had been my last official act on Okinawa and that I was, in fact, already checked out of the command and awaiting my flight assignment. He actually shook my hand and thanked me for all that I had done. Then he told me he had heard many good things about me and wished me good luck back in the States. True, we had been at odds with each other on several occasions but he proved to me that he was a better man than Colonel Poland was by the fact that he wanted us to part as friends rather than as enemies. He need not have worried about that. His final treatment of PFC Cohan had already proved that he was trying to make things right. It was a good day.

Starting Over…..Again

When I returned to the States, I journeyed to Winchendon, Massachusetts, to pick up my wife, Cindy. She was my second wife and the mother of my daughter, Brandie, who had died at the age of 3 months and 1 day. Cindy had changed drastically since her return home about nine months before. She had gotten reacquainted with her childhood friends, had a job and had apparently settled back into some of the habits she had acquired as a teenager. She did not want to be reminded of the life we had started together and she especially did not want to be reminded of our daughter. In fact, she became quite emotional and got hysterical. Her father asked me to leave. I had no choice but to walk away. I hitchhiked to the nearest town and caught a bus to Camp Lejeune, North Carolina, my next duty station. Cindy quickly divorced me.

At Camp Lejeune, I was assigned as the Officer in Charge of the Bins Storage Section, Storage Operations, Stores Accounting and Supply System (SASSY) Management Unit, 2nd Supply Battalion, 2nd Force Service Support Group (FSSG), Fleet Marine Force, Atlantic, Camp Lejeune, North Carolina.

The last time I was a part of a Storage Operations unit was on Okinawa, where I had been assigned simultaneously as both the Officer in Charge of Bulk Storage and Officer in Charge of Material Handling Equipment, working for a backstabbing jerk named CWO Stricklin. He was not assigned at Camp Lejeune. I checked. Maybe he had died. That would have been nice.

It took the Company Commander only a few days to decide that he wanted me to take over as one of his Platoon Commanders. I had always enjoyed having that job as one of my collateral duties at all of my other bases.

After working as OIC of Bins Section for just a few weeks, I knew I had a lot of good Marines working for me so, as usual, I set about trying to get official recognition for some of the more exceptional ones. On 28 August 1981, I wrote a letter of commendation for PFC Y. H.

Kallenberger. Even grouped among the best of the best, she was a real standout.

On 18 September 1981, I recommended the following Lance Corporals for promotion to Corporal: 1-M. J. Alford; 2-J. L. Edwards; and 3-W. A. Moreland. However, there were two Marines who were technically eligible for promotion to Corporal but I did not recommend them because of recent serious non-judicial punishments: 1-B. E. Keys; and 2-A. Hubert.

On 8 October 1981, I recommended both L/Cpl R. L. Skaggs and L/Cpl J. M. Lucas for Meritorious Promotion to Corporal. In the case of L/Cpl Lucas, I also recommended her for Marine of the Month.

On 13 October 1981, I was moved up the chain of command to take over as Officer in Charge of Storage Operations. The former OIC was being transferred and, at Camp Lejeune, I was the senior officer present who was qualified to assume that post. So I would have Warrant Officer R. J. Cristman in charge of Bins Section, Warrant Officer J. T. Pollard in charge of Bulk Storage and Warrant Officer W. C. Parrill in charge of Issue and Receiving Section. The job I was taking over was a Captain's billet but I had served in Captain's billets several times before so I did not consider it to be much of a challenge. I was taking over the same type of job that CWO Stricklin had on Okinawa when I had served simultaneously as OIC of Bulk Storage and OIC of Material Handling Equipment. I would have bet any amount of money that I could be a better Storage Operations Officer than he had been. But of course, that would not have been difficult because he had been a really terrible Storage Operations Officer. He had survived for a long time in that capacity because he had been taking advantage of the intelligence and performance of his subordinates.

13 October 1981-L/Cpl Lucas was one of the Marines to appear before the Company selection board for Marine of the Month. She won, easily. The CO told me that the Battalion Board would meet at 1500 on the 15th.

15 October 1981-At lunchtime, L/Cpl Lucas happened to meet Gunnery Sergeant Arnold, the Battalion Admin Chief, in the hallway and he told her the Board was going to meet at 1330 instead of 1500. L/Cpl Lucas had the presence of mind to call me, personally. I told her to go over to the battalion admin office and let the Sergeant Major know who

she was. I called the Sergeant Major but he told me they had no record of her being scheduled to go before the board. I asked him to hold the board after they finished with the other nominees until I could find out what was going on. He said he would hold them if he had to lock their door. He and I knew each other and had a lot of mutual respect for each other. I considered him to be a friend. He sent L/Cpl Lucas back to the company office, where I met her. Then I raised hell with the Company Admin Chief until I found my original letter of recommendation in a clerk's basket. An endorsement was typed immediately and I personally took it in and asked the CO to sign it. He was very embarrassed that the endorsement had not been typed as soon as she had passed the company board. Then, L/Cpl Lucas' training record wasn't where it was supposed to be in the files but we finally found it in a drawer of the training NCO's desk. I took L/Cpl Lucas back over to the battalion office and the Sergeant Major took her in to face the board. I was afraid she might not have much of a chance because I figured she might be a nervous wreck after what we had gone through. But she was better than even I thought she was. She beat out all of her competition and became the Battalion Marine of the Month. Hooray! I was extremely proud.

But she would not have been allowed to face the battalion board without my recommendation or without the endorsement of the Company CO. She just got lucky when she spoke to the Battalion Admin Chief in the hallway. And she had the confidence and the nerve to call me. And I was the type of leader who would do everything possible to ensure that my troops did not have to suffer because of the mistakes of others. And I had been with this unit just long enough that my people KNEW they could depend on me to fight for them when 'the system' failed them. Otherwise, she might not have had the nerve to call me, personally, and would have missed her chance to even be considered as a competitor for the honor of being recognized as the best in the Battalion.

To be known, by the troops, as that kind of a leader was always more important to me than any accolades I might receive from senior officers. It wasn't a question of wanting to be popular with the troops because they knew I would hammer them if they broke regulations. But they also knew I would fight 'the system' in their behalf when the chips were down.

Another Congressional Interrogative

On 29 October, 1981, a member of Congress wrote a letter to me, yes, a letter addressed to me, specifically, asking about a possible transfer for one of the people in my platoon. First of all, I decided that Congressman Guarini was an absolute idiot. He obviously had no idea what a Chief Warrant Officer was so he had no idea how to address me, except as 'Dear Officer Morris'. The punctuation and spelling in his letter were incorrect. He didn't know how to address a letter to a military organization. And he was apparently confused about the authority that a Platoon Commander has because I would not be the one to make the decision to arrange a transfer for the person involved. That decision could only be made at either the Company or the Battalion level, or even higher. The format of the Congressman's letter showed such a total lack of writing skills, I had severe doubts about the intelligence level of the citizens who had elected him. Congressman Guarini was not only stupid, he had apparently surrounded himself with staff members who were just as stupid as he was, if not more so. One of them could have helped him draft the letter in such a way that he might sound at least a bit more intelligent. One of them could have looked up the correct address of our military unit. One of them could have corrected the spelling and grammar in his letter. None of them did any of that.

The following document is a precise replica of the Congressman's letter exactly as it was when I had received it, with the incorrect spelling and grammar included, unless my editor or publisher automatically corrects it for inclusion in my book:

Frank J. Guarini
14th District
New Jersey

Congress of the United States
House of Representatives
Washington, D. C. 20515

October 29, 1981

WO Officer Morris
Supply Company & Supply Battalion
Camp Le Jeune, North Carolina 28542

Re: Michael Weiner
Supply Company & Supply Battalion
Camp Le Jeune, North Carolina 28542

Dear Officer Morris:

I have been requested by my constituent, whose name appears above, to assist him regarding his request to be transfered.

After you have the opportunity to review and consider his request, I would appreciate being furnished with a report.

Thanking you for the courtesy of a prompt response, I remain,

Sincerely,

FRANK J. GUARINI
Member of Congress

On 13 November 1981, General Moss, the Commanding General of 2nd Force Service Support Group signed a first endorsement on Congressman Guarini's letter and forwarded it to me for action through the Commanding Officer of 2nd Supply Battalion, and subsequently through the Commanding Officer of Supply Company, who gave it to me. I don't know why that process took two weeks. Because of the stupid way the letter was addressed, it may have taken the post office a while to figure out where the letter was actually supposed to go.

But first of all, I couldn't believe that General Moss had this letter sent all the way down the chain of command to me, a mere Platoon Commander. I also couldn't believe that nobody at Battalion or Company level realized that the solution to Private Wiener's problem would not be solved at the platoon level.

It seemed obvious to me that General Moss had panicked over the thought of a Congressional Interrogative. He thought he had a 'hot potato' in his hands and he wanted to get rid of it before he got burned so he passed it on down the chain of command all the way to me.

It also seemed obvious that the people on General Moss' staff were either too stupid or too afraid to point out to the General that HE was the ONE person who could most readily solve this problem, but only if he was willing to get off his butt and take the necessary action.

I took action by replying to Congressman Guarini's letter, telling him exactly what I had done for his constituent and by informing him that the final decision regarding a transfer would have to be made at a higher level, based on recommendations and information I had previously given to my senior officers. A copy of my letter follows.

UNITED STATES MARINE CORPS
SASSY Management Unit
2nd Supply Battalion
2nd Force Service Support Group
Fleet Marine Force, Atlantic
Camp Lejeune, North Carolina

From: Chief Warrant Officer Roy L. Morris
To: Congressman Frank J. Guarini
Via: (1) Officer in Charge, SASSY Management Unit
(2) Commanding Officer, Supply Company, 2nd Supply Battalion
(3) Commanding Officer, 2nd Supply Battalion, 2nd Force Service Support Group
(4) Commanding General, 2nd Force Service Support Group

Subj: Congressional Interrogative; case of Private Michael Wiener

Ref: (a) Congressman Guarini's ltr of 29 October 1981

As directed by the Commanding General's endorsement to reference (a), the following information is provided.

Private Wiener came to me on 13 October 1981 to request that I assist him in obtaining a humanitarian transfer to a base or unit closer to his home in New Jersey. He told me that his mother has epilepsy, his father is currently unemployed, his older brother is living elsewhere (exact location unknown), his younger six-year-old brother is living at home. Private Wiener told me that he is the sole source of support for his family.

I told him exactly what he had to do to get a humanitarian transfer approved. Since he had no verification of his statements regarding his family, I told him he could get that backup data from the American Red Cross. I assured him that he would not have to call the ARC in New Jersey, that he could obtain the data confirmation through our local ARC located right here on the base. I even gave him their phone number. I advised him that the ARC here would contact the ARC in New Jersey, who would visit the family at home, verify their situation and send the information to our local ARC here on base.

After receiving the backup data confirmation from the ARC, his next stop would be the Supply Company admin office, where he would fill out an Administrative Action Request (AA Form 5216). This form would list his request for transfer, with his reasons. Along with the backup data confirmation from ARC, the request would then go to 2nd Supply Battalion, for consideration. If the request were granted at that level, appropriate orders would be issued and it was quite possible that he could be gone within a very few days.

Not only did I discuss all of these things, at length, with Private Wiener, I even wrote out instructions regarding what he was supposed to do. It did not occur to me that I might need to personally take him by the hand and walk him through the entire process but he seemed to be an adult who was mature enough to want to take care of his family, so I perhaps mistakenly assumed that he would be able to follow simple written instructions.

I had, however, assured him that he would have absolutely no difficulty in contacting me, either by phone or in person, if he had any difficulties at any point in the process. Any member of my command will confirm that I am probably the most 'approachable' officer in the unit, whenever a Marine has a problem.

I also assured him that there were plenty of military bases close to his area and that there would surely be no difficulty in determining whether or not there might be a local need for his military occupational specialty, so that his request would probably not be contrary to the needs of the Marine Corps.

Private Wiener has not attempted to contact me since our meeting, so I was able to assume that reasonable progress was being made regarding his request. But I have 218 Marines, either in Storage Operations or in my platoon, who look to me for leadership, guidance, counsel and control, so I cannot always follow their individual progress through the various administrative procedures which I guide them into, especially after I have been so thorough in my instructions as I was with Private Wiener. There should have been no need for extensive follow-up.

I respectfully submit, Sir, that if Private Wiener had told me of any difficulty, then he might not have felt the need to waste the time of a member of Congress over something as mundane as a routine request for transfer but if a young Marine does not let me know that he has encountered an obstacle, I can't help him over or around it. To put it more simply, "I can't fix it if I don't know it's broken".

Today is the 14th of November 1981. I had no idea this was a problem until yesterday, when I received your letter, with the Commanding General's endorsement. Your letter was given to me for my response. This letter constitutes the only response I can make. If there is a problem with Private Wiener's request, that problem does not exist at this level because I took all the actions I could logically take when I gave my instructions to Private Wiener and got him started on his path through the administrative processes.

I do not have the authority to control the approval or disapproval of his request. Therefore, any additional information which might shed more light on the status of his request must be obtained at some point further up the chain of command.

Sir, I apologize if this part of your response is not couched in official language more appropriate to your station in life but I felt that I should state plainly what I have done for your constituent and I hope that the follow-up responses from my senior officers might provide more enlightenment on the current status of his request.

Roy L. Morris
Chief Warrant Officer
USMC

Meanwhile, it was business as usual in the Storage Section. We were able to get a lot of work done and we completed a lot of special projects involving the warehousing functions, in spite of interference from Lt/Col Elsworth, the Officer in Charge of the SASSY Management Unit, my boss.

In fact, one of my special project teams had performed so well, I recommended a Meritorious Mast for them. They were Cpl James G. Jackson, Cpl George L. Murdock, Cpl Ronald B. Swope, Cpl Franklin L. Johnson, PFC Stephen Bones and PFC Arnold A. Kelly.

I was approached by several Women Marines who were curious about the possibility of having an organized sports program in which they might be eligible to compete. They also asked about the chance of having at least one of the weight/exercise areas declared off-limits to males at least one day/night per week. They wanted to be able to use the equipment and facilities at least occasionally without having a bunch of males trying to flirt with them or ogling them while they tried to exercise.

Only three of those Women Marines were actually in my platoon but they had convinced the others that I was one of the 'good' officers and that I would try to help in any way possible because I honestly believed in ensuring the welfare of the troops - and these Women Marines were undoubtedly 'troops' in the same sense that the male Marines were. I was pleased to help their cause in any way that I could.

Also during February 1982, I was pleased to be able to recommend Corporal Earnest R. Van Cooney for meritorious promotion to the rank of Sergeant.

See who catches hell

I'm not allowed to drive the train
The whistle I can't blow
I'm not allowed to decide
How fast the train will go
I don't say how many cars
From engine to caboose
And if the load's too heavy
Which ones will be cut loose
I'm not allowed to debate
Just where the train will stop
Or when consolidating routes
Which ones we'll have to drop
I don't get to holler, 'Board'
Or do conductor-type things
I don't get to punch the tickets
The lantern I can't swing
I'm not allowed to hold the oil can
Or ring the little bell
But let the damn thing
Jump the tracks
And see who catches hell

January 1982

This was inspired by a four-line poem that I saw in the office of the Company Executive Officer of Headquarters and Service Company, Supply Battalion at the Marine Corps Base, Camp Lejeune, North Carolina where I served as a Platoon Commander and as a Warehousing Officer. In the military chain of command, a company executive officer is second-in-command to the company commander. In this particular case, both the CO and the XO were really good people and both had a great sense of humor. I don't know who wrote the original few lines of the poem or how many versions may be in existence out there somewhere. But from those four lines I saw, the above poem is my version.

Original anonymous version
I'm not allowed to drive the train
Or ring the little bell
But let the damn thing jump the tracks
And see who catches hell

Commanding General's Inspection
25 February 1982

There were two platoons scheduled for the personnel inspection and drill competition part of the CG's Inspection. The first platoon was made up of people RAMDOMLY selected from Headquarters and Service Company. The second platoon was made up of people RANDOMLY selected from Supply Company. I had been RANDOMLY selected to serve as the Platoon Commander of the second platoon.

We had been ordered to form up at 0500. The troops drew their weapons. I had my dress uniform with my officer's sword. It was to be the classic Marine Corps white gloves inspection. We got into platoon formation. We waited. And we waited. And we waited. It was very cold and windy. The temperature was 30 degrees. According to the radio, the wind chill factor was 22 degrees.

We were in the parade ground area just across the street from the barracks. About every ten minutes, I would send one squad at a time to the barracks so they could get warmed up in the recreation room. The very young Lieutenant who was serving as the Platoon Commander of the other platoon followed my lead in that regard. He had previously called me aside and asked me for guidance and I had reminded him that he had only two main responsibilities as a Marine Officer: (1) Accomplish the mission; (2) Ensure the welfare of the troops. I assured him that his mission would not suffer if he did the same thing I was doing - and he earned the respect and admiration of his troops by following my example.

We were out there for 2 ½ hours. In all that time, our Company Commander had come out only twice. He wouldn't let me send all of the troops inside at the same time, although it would not have made any difference to the CG. In fact, he would probably have enjoyed watching the troops assembling into a platoon formation upon his arrival. These people are really sharp and they have been working hard. (I never saw the Commanding Officer of Headquarters and Service Company at any time during that morning).

At 0730, General Moss finally arrived with his detail inspectors. When he got out of his heated automobile, he put on his military overcoat. Our people had not been allowed to wear their own overcoats for the inspection because the detail inspectors had to be able to check our ribbons and badges and the fit and serviceability of our uniforms. Surprisingly, the General actually did his part by walking up and down between the ranks of the first platoon. He even stopped a couple of times to ask a question or two. But it was obvious he was freezing and we all quickly realized that he could not handle the cold.

After he finished with the first platoon, he came over to me. I called the platoon to the position of attention and rendered the sword salute to the Commanding General. He returned my salute and talked with me for a couple of minutes. Then, he looked over my shoulder at the troops and said, "Well, Gunner, if your Marines are as 'squared away' as you are, then I would certify them as being first class. I want you to get them in out of this cold weather. This inspection is over and you've passed with high marks". I was terribly disappointed. I didn't really know what to say except, "Aye, aye, Sir. Thank you, Sir". Then he got back into his car and was driven away.

The troops were disappointed, too. But more than that, they were really mad. They felt cheated. They had endured the cold and wind for 2 ½ hours waiting for the Commanding General, but they didn't even get the opportunity to look him in the face because he was too much of a wimp to stay out there long enough to walk up and down through our ranks.

By the time the detail inspectors finished with everybody, it was about 0830. They had really speeded up their inspection process as soon as the General had departed, so they just barely looked at my people in the second platoon.

Unfortunately, all of our Marines had missed breakfast. Nobody ever admitted it but I think there was a mix-up regarding the scheduling of the personnel inspection. We had all felt quite ridiculous assembling in the dark under the floodlights of the parade ground area but we were faithfully following the orders that we had been given. And the company admin people didn't even think about the fact that we might have to wait so long for the inspecting party that we might not get to go to the dining facility. It was closed by the time we were able to turn our people loose.

So, everybody had to just change into their work uniforms and go to their various work sections. If I could have afforded it, I would have taken the entire platoon over to the post exchange café and treated them all to breakfast.

It would be a long, long time before General Moss would be able to earn back the respect those people used to have for him, if ever.

At 1230, I reported back to the same parade ground area. I had been RANDOMLY selected to participate in the PFT (physical fitness test) portion of the CG's inspection, along with various other selected officers and senior Staff NCOs. It was supposed to start at 1300 but I had learned my lesson earlier that day. I wore shorts, sneakers and a short-sleeved pullover shirt for the actual test but over that, I wore a sweat suit and a hooded jacket for the waiting period which I knew would be inevitable. And I did short jogs and wind sprints around the parade ground area so the cold would not cause my muscles to tighten up.

It was after 1400 before the detail inspectors arrived. I was glad to see them for more reasons than one. First of all, I was glad to get the whole thing started. Secondly, I was afraid the other officers and Staff NCOs were going to attack me and draw lots for my sweat suit and jacket. It was after 1600 before we all finished the PFT and, of course, none of us were allowed to leave the area until the last man finished the last event. I was the first to finish, naturally, but I had my sweat suit and jacket available, so I didn't freeze to death while waiting around. Also, of course, I out-performed every other officer and every Staff NCO in the group. It wasn't easy being me back in those days but I had a great deal of personal pride in being the best that I could be at my chosen profession.

A General's Letter

The following document is an exact reproduction of a letter that was written by Brigadier General Moss, the Commanding General of 2nd Force Service Support Group. The letter was written in response to a letter of complaint he had received from PFC John Glover's wife. I was given a copy of the General's letter because Glover was one of my people and because I would be required to take certain actions to deal with the situation. However, I never received a copy of Mrs. Glover's original letter of complaint. It must have been really something!

PFC Glover had been a member of Storage Operations (and Supply Company) long before I arrived and took over. He had been in the Corps quite long enough to have been a Sergeant if he had stayed out of trouble. When I had first reviewed his service record (upon my arrival), I asked First Sergeant Johns why Glover hadn't already been kicked out of the Corps. Glover had already had four office hours (non-judicial punishment from the Company Commander), so the Special Court Martial should have kicked him out of the Corps. In fact, I could not comprehend how Glover was still a Private First Class instead of a Private. First Sergeant Johns was unable to give me an answer.

Glover was never anything but trouble. He was a non-performer and a malcontent. He was disrespectful and disobedient. It didn't matter what he was ordered to do or who gave him the order. He always questioned not only the order, but also the authority of whoever gave him the order.

When the Company Commander arranged for a bunch of officers and Staff NCOs to inspect the barracks, I was the one who found a marijuana pipe in Glover's desk (a health and comfort inspection is actually a 'shake down' inspection, ordered by the CO, to look for contraband and drugs). If I had not had Gy/Sgt Sullivan with me at the time, as a witness, Glover would probably have tried to say that I had 'planted' the evidence against him. Glover hated all officers but he especially hated me because he actually used to get away with a lot of bad behavior before I arrived.

So anyway, I will get back to the General's letter to Mrs. Glover. It had several grammatical, punctuation and spacing errors and those were bad enough, considering that it was signed by a General. But I shall point out three errors, in particular. In the fourth paragraph, General Moss said, in part, "….he would not have gone into an unauthorized absence, thereby subjecting his family to the depravations caused by restriction and forfeitures". The use of the word, DEPRAVATIONS, is incorrect. He was trying to say DEPRIVATIONS, which means that Glover was actually DEPRIVING his family by getting into trouble which would DEPRIVE his family of much-needed money because of forfeiture of pay. (The act of subjecting his family to DEPRAVATIONS would be an entirely different matter). Also, the General used incorrect grammar when he said, in part, "I truly believe the First Sergeant was acting in you and your husband's best interest…. He should have said, "I truly believe the First Sergeant was acting in both YOUR and your husband's best interest". The last sentence of the General's letter has a grammatical error. The General was speaking about the efforts that would be made to hasten Glover's discharge, the pending charges and the necessary paperwork when he said, "I assure you that they will receive my personal attention and are completed as expeditiously as possible". Perhaps he could have said, "I assure you that they will receive my personal attention and they will be completed as expeditiously as possible". Or maybe he could have said, "I assure you that they will receive my personal attention to guarantee that they are completed as expeditiously as possible". See what I mean? There are other grammatical errors but these are the most obvious, not to mention the most ridiculous.

If somebody else actually drafted this letter for the Commanding General, then the CG should have proofread it before he signed it. If the CG actually drafted the letter, then the Chief of Staff should have proofread it. Or perhaps, at least the FSSG Admin Officer or Admin Chief should have proofread it. And even then, the typist could have inserted the proper punctuation marks and maybe even corrected the spelling and grammar. I mean, after all, if you're the typist for a General, you really need to be just about the best and smartest typist on the whole base. Wouldn't you think so? I know that if I was a General, I would want to have the best assistants available.

So the bottom line is this: Either (1) the Commanding General was an idiot and the people around him were afraid to correct him; Or (2) the CG had voluntarily surrounded himself with idiots and didn't mind the fact that they were idiots; Or (3) the CG had unwittingly surrounded himself with idiots and was too much of an idiot, himself, to realize it.

Anyway, I will reproduce General Moss' letter exactly as he signed it. And if my editor or my publisher doesn't automatically correct all the errors, you, the reader, will have to agree with me that the General should not be allowed to draft his own correspondence because that allows his lack of intelligence to show.

24 February 1982

Dear Mrs. Glover,

I received your letter of 14 February 1982 and I am hastening to respond. I will key my response to your questions which you raised in your letter.

Your husband, Private First Class John Glover has a total of eight office hours in addition to a conviction by a Special Court-Martial. It should be noted that four of his office hours have occurred since joining the Second Supply Battalion in January of 1980. You are correct in your assertion that "he qualifies for some kind of discharge," specifically a misconduct discharge based on his frequent involvement with military authorities. This discharge when awarded will probably be under other than honorable conditions and will severely prejudice him in terms of veteran's benefits, employment opportunities, etc. for the rest of his life.

As you know, your husband was in an unauthorized absence status for four and one-half days during December. Currently, he is only being charged with that four and one-half days of unauthorized absence since he called in concerning his inability to assume the Assistant Duty Noncommissioned Officer Watch. Since he was living at Midway Park with you at the time the fact that his car would not start is an unacceptable excuse for this four and one-half days period of unauthorized absence. It appears that he made no effort to obtain transportation to work or notify his work section that he was nearby in Midway Park lacking transportation. In essence, at this time he is only being charged with the unauthorized absence and not for missing his assignment as Assistant Duty Noncommissioned Officer.

Prior to his office hours for the unauthorized absence, First Sergeant Johns did tell your husband that he would recommend the maximum punishment in view of his lackluster record of performance. However at office hours your husband was awarded 45 days restriction and a forfeiture of $300.00 per month for two months. Following office hours, First Sergeant Johns suggested to your husband that he take you home and offered him a 96 hour pass as well as leave in order to accomplish this if he agreed. First Sergeant Johns also recommended that your husband check with a doctor to insure that it was safe for you to travel. Your husband later reported that he had checked with a doctor and that he intended to fly you back to Florida since he had the funds for an airplane ticket. It seems to me that if your husband was concerned over your welfare he would not have gone into an unauthorized absence thereby subjecting his family to the depravations caused by restriction and forfeitures. I truly believe the First Sergeant was acting in you and your husband's best interest, also I am certain his recommendation to send you home was distasteful to both you and your husband.

I feel that I should also inform you that on 20 January 1982 during the time your husband was on restriction a health and comfort inspection was conducted in every room of his Bachelor Enlisted Quarters. During this inspection a homemade smoking device was found in his secretary which revealed positive marijuana residue. The day the laboratory report of this residue arrived (7 February 1982) your husband began another period of unauthorized absence. Furthermore, on 6 February 1982, Private First Class Glover was apprehended for driving under the influence of alcohol. I think you will agree with me that in view of his past record and current pending charges his performance as a Marine has certainly been poor.

I am concerned over your medical condition and agree that it would be in your best interest if your husband was there with you at this time. I cannot agree however, that the Marine Corps has treated your husband unjustly. I strongly suggest that you urge him to return to his unit as soon as possible in order that we may commence processing him for a discharge. It will be necessary for us first to resolve the pending charges against him and process the necessary paperwork. I feel confident that we can accomplish all of this within three to four weeks after his arrival back at Camp Lejeune. Accordingly, I strongly urge you to encourage his early return so that we may initiate these efforts as soon as possible. I assure you that they will receive my personal attention and are completed as expeditiously as possible.

Sincerely

R. E. Moss
Brigadier General, U. S. Marine Corps
Commanding General

I didn't have any respect for General Moss. That's a simple fact. My respect isn't just blindly and mindlessly given. My respect has to be earned by a display of professionalism, initiative and intelligence. General Moss didn't have any of those qualities.

For instance, he had previously written a rambling, absurd memorandum about drinking on duty. He said that the subject needed clarification since specific guidance was lacking. Perhaps he didn't know about Marine Corps Order 1700.1, signed by the Commandant of the Marine Corps, which covers the subject of drinking on duty.

Another example was when he received that Congressional Interrogative from Private Wiener's Congressman and passed it all the way down the chain of command to me when he was the one who should have taken corrective action on Wiener's problem, in the first place.

Yet another example was when he failed to demonstrate leadership by example when he wimped out and didn't perform his part in his own Commanding General's Inspection. He got back into his warm car and departed the area while leaving us - his Marines - out in the cold even though we had already been out there for 2 ½ hours awaiting his arrival.

And then there was the example of the error-filled letter he drafted, a copy of which is provided on the previous pages.

One thing the reader needs to be aware of is that these instances of General Moss' leadership failures and shortcomings were ONLY the incidents in which I was personally involved. There were hundreds of other officers at Camp Lejeune who were part of 2nd Force Service Support Group, which was headed by General Moss. If each one of those other officers presented his, or her, own personal examples of instances in which General Moss' leadership qualities left something to be desired, they might fill several volumes. But even if MY examples are the only ones that are ever brought to the attention of the world at large, one might easily wonder how he ever attained the rank of Brigadier General.

Fitness Report for 17 June 1981 through 28 February 1982

Section C: Performance of duty:
Regular duties	Excellent
Administrative duties	Excellent
Handling officers	Excellent
Handling enlisted personnel	Excellent
Training personnel	Excellent

To what degree has he exhibited the following:
Personal appearance	Outstanding
Military presence	Excellent
Attention to duty	Excellent
Cooperation	Outstanding
Initiative	Excellent
Judgment	Excellent
Force	Excellent
Leadership	Excellent
Loyalty	Outstanding
Personal relations	Excellent
Economy of management	Excellent
Growth potential	Excellent

Your estimate of this Marine's general value to the service:
Excellent to Outstanding

Considering the requirements of service in war, indicate your attitude toward having this Marine under your command:
Particularly desire to have

Narrative comments:
    This officer is an industrious, sincere and dedicated individual. He is tireless in his endeavors to do the best possible work. A strict military disciplinarian who demands the maximum from his subordinates and achieves those results necessary to maintain support for the units in II MAF. Provides that guidance necessary to sustain control over the numerous and complex functions of storage operations in the General

Account. This report submitted late due to the administrative oversight of the reporting senior.

Reporting Officer
Charles J. Barone
Major USMC
Officer in Charge
General Account
SASSY Management Unit

I continued to identify and give public recognition to the outstanding Marines under my control. On 2 March 1982 and on 8 March 1982, respectively, I recommended both Staff Sergeant DeWayne Allen Bentley and Sergeant Wendell Lee Pentecost for awards of the Navy Achievement Medal for their superb individual performance of duties in several different areas of our operation. On 15 March 1982, I recommended L/Cpl Y. H. Kallenberger for Marine of the Month. On 2 April 1982, I recommended Corporal G. L. Murdock for Meritorious Promotion to Sergeant. And on 28 May 1982, I recommended L/Cpl Billy D. Teetor for a Certificate of Commendation.

On 4 March 1982, the Commanding Officer of Supply Company had appointed me to an additional duty as the Company Remedial Physical Training Officer. Since I consistently scored much higher on the PFT (Physical Fitness Test) than all of the other officers and Staff NCOs in the company and considerably higher than 80 % of the troops (who were much younger than I by at least 15 years), he figured I knew a lot about getting into shape and staying in shape. And my platoon was generally recognized as the best platoon in the company, so he knew that I could achieve more success than any other officer in the company. I told him I would give my best effort and would try not to disappoint him.

The first group of Marines assigned to the program included people who failed or performed poorly on the PFT but it also included people who had actually managed to pass the PFT but who did not really present a neat and trim personal appearance or otherwise meet the traditional standards of appearance expected of military personnel. The roster of personnel assigned, as determined by the Company Commander, included members of the enlisted ranks from Private all the way up through Gunnery Sergeant. He did not assign any officers to the program because any officer who failed the PFT would not ordinarily be offered a chance to participate in a training program - that officer would simply have a severely shortened military career.

I designed a program of exercises, circuit training, obstacle course training, wind sprints and jogging. Over the course of time, I had an incredibly high success rate with the members of the program, probably for several reasons. First, I never treated any of them like 'losers', I never 'talked down' to them and I never berated them when they could not perform the exercises quite as well as I wanted them to. I tried to make each and every one of them feel that he (or she) and I had formed a partnership to accomplish the mission at hand - that mission being to perform well on the PFT or to drop a few inches from the waistline. And I brought such a high degree of self-assured optimism and enthusiasm to each training session that most of them could not help but respond in a positive way. I encouraged them in such a way that each small improvement would give them the initiative to reach for successively higher goals. I advised them that improvement would not be obvious at first and that they should not be disheartened by initial poor showings. And most of them took my words to heart. Being involved in this program was very gratifying. In most cases, I was able to reach inside them and find that person in there that wanted to be a good Marine…and to bring that person out.

Graduation Guest Speaker

Special Occasion: On 26 March 1982, I was invited to appear as the guest speaker at the graduation of Supply Administration Course 2-82. Staff Sergeant Herbert L. Hall, one of my Marines, was a graduate. He was second in the class with an average of 94.79 overall. He was only 0.12 points behind the first in the class. Wow! Staff Sergeant Hall was awarded the Marine Corps Association Certificate of Achievement in recognition of his superior academic effort. It was a singular honor to address the class, not only because of Staff Sergeant Hall, but because this was the same course I had attended eleven years earlier as a Sergeant. At that time, I had graduated in 9th place, although the only people who beat me were Staff Sergeants and Gunnery Sergeants. But my final grade point average was only 91.64. Staff Sergeant Hall beat my average by more than 3 full points. In fact, the # 1 student in my class had only a 93.55 final grade point average and Staff Sergeant Hall beat that by 1.24 points. If he had been in my class, he would have been the honor graduate. Wow, again!

These Marines, and so many others like them, made my existence as an Officer of Marines a really good life. And even the average Marines were a pleasure to deal with. They made the Storage Operations Section a really GOOD place to spend the workday. Just spending time with those regular Marines was enjoyable, and they definitely compensated for the times that I had to deal with substandard Marines, people who were slackers and non-performers and who taxed my patience with their stupidity and their insufferable attitudes.

The regular, everyday, average Marines provided me with a firm foundation from which I could determine the basic standards of performance and conduct that served as the criteria for my evaluations of all my subordinates. I didn't grade on a curve. Each Marine either measured up to the expected level or he did not.

In the course of my regular assignment as Storage Operations Officer, I used my contacts with the Environmental Health Section of the Naval Regional Medical Center and the Facilities Management

Section to have a lighting survey conducted in the Bins Storage Section of the warehousing area. The poor lighting was causing eye strain and improper stock management simply because the troops could not read the identifying data on the stock items or the location bins. Success! We got the new lighting. Many of the troops told me I was the best officer they had ever known. That is known as positive feedback. In my opinion, such praise from a junior Marine was better than a letter of commendation from a General.

So I'm a Neanderthal, So What?

31 March 1982: This was a momentous day but not really much of a surprise. There had been many times when I 'butted heads' with officers who were significantly senior to me. I never disagreed with a senior officer when I knew he was right but I also never backed down from an argument with a senior officer when I knew I was the one who was right. When I disagreed with something, I had a habit of speaking out. When I disagreed with a senior officer, I tried to be as tactful as possible but I still got my point across. Well, some of those senior officers could accept a different point of view and some could not. I had never believed that a person should win an argument simply because he might be senior. He should also have to be right. So I hit the skyline again because I disagreed with my boss. Here's the story:

For the benefit of anybody who might not understand the system for promoting enlisted Marines, I will explain at least part of it. Commanding Officers, and ONLY Commanding Officers, have the authority to promote. For example, my boss was a Lieutenant Colonel but he couldn't promote one of our Marines, not even from Private to Private First Class because he was not the Commanding Officer. The Colonel could RECOMMEND one of our Marines for promotion but he had to send that recommendation to the Company Commander, even though the Company Commander was only a Captain. And if that Company Commander believed that Marine didn't deserve to be promoted, then he didn't have to promote him and the Colonel could not override the Company Commander's decision.

Furthermore, when the Colonel recommended one of our Marines for a promotion and sent that recommendation to the Commanding Officer, that Marine still could not get promoted without the endorsement of his Platoon Commander. Of course, the Platoon Commander would have to give a reason - to the Commanding Officer - if he declined to give his endorsement.

You see, there is a basic concept that governs the Marine Corps. Simply stated, it is this: EVERY MARINE IS A RIFLEMAN, FIRST.

That's the bottom line. That's our credo. At any given time, with no prior notice, ANY Marine can pick up a rifle and go fight, anytime, anywhere. The Marine Corps is a FORCE IN READINESS. That's why the United States needs us and that's our main reason for existence.

No matter what a Marine's job is, no matter what military occupational specialty is assigned, every Marine has to be able to function first and foremost as an infantryman. A Marine may spend his day keypunching data cards for computer updates, or running a typewriter, or repairing phone systems, or working as a mechanic, or whatever, but he still has to be able to pick up a rifle and go to war at a moment's notice. That's the 'Total Marine' concept and it has been valid for over 241 years.... actually, since 10 November 1775.

As the Officer in Charge of Storage Operations, I had over 200 Marines working for me but they weren't all in my platoon. Some of the people in my platoon were in the SASSY Management Unit, which was headed by Lt/Col Elsworth. Two of them worked directly for Lt/Col Elsworth as office clerks. Some worked in the Maintenance Float Section, or in the Direct Support Unit, or in keypunch operations or some of the other headquarters areas. There were 45 Marines in my platoon. So, I was the Platoon Commander for some people who didn't work directly for me as part of their regular daily duties

I'd had plenty of trouble with Lt/Col Elsworth ever since I arrived at Camp Lejeune, mostly because he kept trying to stick his nose into my warehousing business. He constantly tried to dictate policies and procedures affecting my business without consulting me. If he had ever bothered to ask, I would have been glad to give him a briefing which would explain why I would not (or could not) go along with his ideas. He was a supply officer but he was not a warehousing officer - I was. That's why I was Officer in Charge of Storage Operations. That was my area of expertise. If he had ever told me what he wanted to do, I could have told him whether or not it was feasible. Then he wouldn't have looked so stupid in front of the troops after he tried to start some project or other and I would have to cancel it or correct it. He was my boss. And he was senior to me. But that didn't mean he was always right.

Anyway, here's the problem that came up. He had two Marines who worked directly for him. Cpl Lahaie was his file clerk and Private Graese was his typist. Cpl Lahaie was meritoriously promoted to that rank just before I arrived and took over as his Platoon Commander. I could not imagine how he had earned that promotion. As his new Platoon Commander, I determined that most of his uniforms were not maintained in a serviceable condition, he still had Lance Corporal chevrons sewn on some of his shirts, he usually had to be told to get a decent haircut, he couldn't conduct platoon drill (or even squad drill, for that matter), he could not attain a first class rating on the physical fitness test and he could not qualify as an expert with a rifle. Granted, he DID manage to qualify but only as a marksman, nor even as a sharpshooter. But he was a Corporal.

Lt/Col Elsworth had recently recommended him for meritorious promotion to Sergeant. He wasn't allowed to go before the promotion board, however, because I would not endorse the recommendation. That's the way it's done in the Marine Corps. The rank of the officer who makes the recommendation is not a determining factor. Lt/Col Elsworth was a very high ranking officer but he was not the Commanding Officer. The CO was the man who would have to put his signature on that promotion warrant and he wasn't going to sign it unless he honestly believed the promotion was deserved. Furthermore, the CO was not going to promote a Marine unless the recommendation had the endorsement of the Platoon Commander.

Lt/Col Elsworth may have been able to force the FORMER Platoon Commander and the FORMER Company Commander to promote Lahaie but that wasn't going to happen while Major Tweed and I were around.

Lt/Col Elsworth also tried to get Private Graese promoted meritoriously to Private First Class but that didn't work, either. The Company Commander didn't even have to ask for my endorsement on Private Graese because she'd had a court martial for unauthorized absence less than three months before. The rule is that a Marine has to wait at LEAST six months after a court martial before even becoming ELIGIBLE for a promotion. And, even then, it certainly would not be a MERITORIOUS promotion. Since I was the one who had blocked Corporal Lahaie's promotion, Lt/Col Elsworth blamed me for the fact that Private Graese couldn't get promoted, either.

Lt/Col Elsworth tried to get me relieved from duty as Platoon Commander but that didn't work. He was not in charge of making that decision. The assignment to duty as a Platoon Commander was the responsibility of the Company Commander. There were plenty of officers available in the command, at any given time, who were ELIGIBLE for that collateral duty but the Company Commander was going to choose whoever he wanted to serve as his Platoon Commanders and he was most certainly going to choose ONLY those officers that he thought would do the best job. So, the CO would not relieve me, just because Lt/Col Elsworth wanted me fired. I appreciated the CO's vote of confidence but I knew that I had EARNED his vote of confidence because I did not (and would not) base my endorsement decisions on anything other than the performance of the Marine who was being recommended - and not on any personal considerations and certainly not based on the rank of the officer who made the recommendation.

At this point you, the reader, may be wondering why Lt/Col Elsworth allowed me to keep my job as Officer in Charge of Storage Operations. Well, I was the senior officer on the base who had a military occupational specialty in warehousing. He might eventually do what Chief Warrant Officer Stricklin had done back on Okinawa. CWO Stricklin found an officer who was senior to me and who was eligible for a warehousing assignment and had me 'reassigned'. He was afraid to have me 'relieved for cause' because I would have asked for a trial by military tribunal to fight the 'relief' and I had too much ammunition to use against CWO Stricklin in court. It would have been too easy for me to expose him as the backstabbing jerk that he was. That's why he simply had me 'replaced by a senior officer'.

It was basically the same situation with Lt/Col Elsworth. We had argued too many times - and I had won too many times. So, having me 'relieved for cause' was not one of his options. He would just continue to make things as rough as possible for me, in every way that he could.

So anyway, now we get to the part where Lt/Col Elsworth and I had our latest argument. That very morning, the Company Commander had announced that any Marine who got recommended for a meritorious promotion would have to be prepared for a complete clothing and personal inspection and would have to be able to properly conduct squad drill (for promotion to Private First Class or Lance Corporal) or platoon drill (for promotion to Corporal or Sergeant). Passing either of these inspections and performance checks would not guarantee that a Marine would pass the examination board but failing either of these checks would disqualify a Marine from even appearing before the board.

Lt/Col Elsworth really got fired up about that. He had a meeting of all officers in the SASSY Management Unit and he really started bad-mouthing the CO. I thought that was totally unprofessional of him. Here was a Lt/Col ranting and raving in front of us junior officers. He said the CO had a hell of a lot of nerve telling us who we could and could not recommend for promotion. That's the way he put it. He said, "I'm a Colonel and if I decide to put somebody up for a promotion, I don't need a lowly Company Commander second-guessing my decision". That was where I just couldn't keep quiet any longer so I said, "But Sir, he's not trying to tell us who we can or cannot RECOMMEND for promotion. It's just that he has to consider the 'Total Marine' concept. One of us might recommend somebody for promotion simply because he's a good office clerk or a good warehouseman but the CO can't promote just the part of that Marine who works in the office or in the warehouse. He has to promote the total Marine and if some part of that Marine has a deficiency, perhaps a failing that we don't recognize just because all we see is the part of that Marine who works in the office or in the warehouse, then the CO is responsible for discovering that failing".

That was where the meeting broke down completely. Lt/Col Elsworth actually turned purple in the face. If there hadn't been witnesses, he may have gone for my throat. No, I was not trying to argue with the Colonel. I was just trying to make sure that he understood the situation from the CO's perspective. At the same time, I was trying to point out to my own junior officers who were present that they also had a responsibility to consider the 'Total Marine' concept in the future when they would be sending recommendations for promotions or awards through me up the chain of command because some of them had occasionally been making recommendations while apparently wearing 'blinders' that kept them from seeing faults that existed in some of the people they had been recommending.

But the Colonel wanted to have the last word. After all, he was the boss. He told me that I had a Neanderthal mentality. He told me I was living in the past. He told me I was letting my collateral duties as a Platoon Commander go to my head. He told me that I apparently enjoyed looking for reasons to shoot down good people who deserved to be promoted. He told me I had a hell of a lot of nerve to deny a promotion to ANYBODY who had earned a recommendation from 'himself'. Then he went on to say that, in the era of such advanced weapons systems like the 'TOW' and the 'Dragon', and laser sighted anti-aircraft missiles, I was an idiot for expecting clerks and warehousemen and forklift drivers to be able to perform like infantrymen.

I HAD to respond to that, no matter what it was going to cost me in the future, so I said, "Sir, I don't expect our people to do any of those things, just as I don't expect them to jump out of airplanes, or drive a tank or even to field strip a machine gun. Not without proper training. However, I do most certainly expect EVERY Marine to properly maintain his uniforms, to be able to pass the physical fitness test, to be able to handle a rifle with at least a reasonable amount of skill, to know how to drill a squad and to understand at least the basics of individual and unit tactical maneuvers and personal protective measures. And as long as I'm a Platoon Commander, I will try to do my very best to TRAIN my people so they will have a grasp of those basics and they won't get recommended for promotion until they do".

The Colonel threw me out of the meeting. I went willingly. And I went straight to my office and wrote out a full set of notes on everything that had been said between us so that I could defend myself against any possible charges that he might file against me. From the looks on the faces of the other officers in that meeting, it was obvious they thought I had just committed professional suicide. In the long run, it turned out that their collective opinions, in that regard, were absolutely correct.

But you know, I didn't really care at that point. At no time had I been disrespectful. I had addressed him as 'Sir'. And I had not called him an idiot, although he deserved it. All I had said was what needed to be said, in defense of the Company Commander. If I had REALLY wanted to commit professional suicide, I would have reminded him that a Lt/Col should never lose his temper and start bad-mouthing another officer in front of junior officers. Granted, it would have been a different matter if he wanted to sit back with some of his fellow Lieutenant Colonels and talk about the CO in private but he was wrong to say the things he said in that meeting with Captains, Chief Warrant Officers, Lieutenants and Warrant Officers present.

After that, the rest of the day went really well.

Before you Jump

15 April 1982. I had an interesting encounter this morning. I met PFC Bradshaw, who was walking from the dining facility to the barracks. He looked like a warmed-over soup sandwich so I stopped him. He wasn't wearing any chevrons. His cap was worn and ragged. In fact, the bill of his cap was so ragged, the cardboard was sticking out. He had a sneering, contemptuous look on his face.

I took his cap away from him and told him to go away and report back to me at the Battalion admin office in less than 10 minutes. He arrived on time with PFC chevrons and another cap. I borrowed a pair of scissors from a clerk and cut the unserviceable cap into several pieces. I gave the pieces back to Bradshaw. Then I turned to the Battalion Admin Chief and told him to add some more charges to the record against Bradshaw. Three counts of Article 92 for not wearing chevrons, for wearing unserviceable uniform items and for needing a shave and one count of Article 91 for insubordinate conduct toward an officer. Bradshaw certainly was mad. He was a fat, obnoxious little puke who was already getting kicked out of the Corps with a Bad Conduct Discharge and now these extra charges against him were going to further delay his departure back to civilian life. The delay was what irritated him the most. What I couldn't understand was how he was still a PFC instead of a Private.

After I left, Bradshaw asked the Battalion Sergeant Major if he could file charges against me for cutting up his cap. Every clerk in the office started laughing out loud when they heard that. The Sergeant Major was laughing, too, when he said, "Bradshaw, this cap was already unserviceable. The Gunner just gave it a decent burial". Then Bradshaw said, "Well, after I get out, I'm going to find him and kick his ass". Everybody started laughing even louder. The Sergeant Major said, "Before you jump Gunner Morris, call me because we all want to watch".

Bradshaw brightened up and asked, "Why? Does everybody want to watch him get his ass kicked?" The Sergeant Major said, "You don't understand, boy. Gunner Morris is the Supply Company physical training officer and has a black belt in karate. We all just want to watch the demonstration when you make the mistake of jumping him". Then the Sergeant Major hooked his finger into a hole in Bradshaw's trouser leg and ripped apart his trouser leg from one side to the other.

Later that day, when one of the battalion admin clerks told me about Bradshaw, she was still laughing. It was another month before Bradshaw got discharged but in all that time, I never encountered him again. And he didn't try to find me after he got out, either. I wonder if he was avoiding me.

The Glover saga continues

26 April 1982. PFC Glover was back. He had been in an unauthorized absence status for more than two months, so his status had been changed to desertion. But he was back. He had reported in last night and, since he voluntarily came back, he wasn't automatically sent straight to the brig for confinement.

The Supply Company Gunnery Sergeant had simply brought him over to the warehouse and dropped him off. I was at the Monday morning staff meeting with Lt/Col Elsworth, so I was surprised to find Glover sitting in the Storage Operations office, drinking coffee and talking with my clerks. I was even more surprised that the Company Gunny had dropped him off in civilian clothes.

Glover was telling everybody that he had a letter from the Commanding General saying that he would let him out of the Corps. I cut Glover off by announcing to everybody that I had a copy of the letter and that it was nothing more than a response to a letter that Glover's wife had written...and the CG DID say that Glover would be getting out but it would be a Bad Conduct Discharge and that Glover would first have to face the penalties for the charges against him before his discharge took effect. I didn't want my admin people to be thinking that Glover had put one over on the Corps, so I put an end to his big talk by letting them all know the truth of the situation. And I didn't want them to be gossiping among themselves and the other troops, based ONLY on what Glover had been telling them.

I took him back over to the company office, ordered him into a chair and told the Admin Chief that if Glover even looked as if he was thinking of getting out of that chair, then the Admin Chief and every other male Marine present was ordered to tackle him and put him on the ground.

Then I asked for a private audience with the Company Gunny, the First Sergeant and the Company Commander. In the CO's office, I reminded all of them that there was a prescribed procedure for processing personnel returning from deserter status and, if they didn't know what it was, I would be glad to show them the Marine Corps Orders that pertained to the situation. Both the CO and the First Sergeant were jogging buddies (and friends) of mine, so I was sorry to embarrass them that way but I did it in private and not in front of the admin clerks.

The CO told the Company Gunny to find out if we still had Glover's uniforms in storage. (When a Marine deserts, his property is inventoried and stored). The First Sergeant was ordered to contact the Battalion admin people to find out what status Glover was supposed to be in. Then the CO apologized to me for dumping Glover in my area. I told the CO that I didn't want Glover in my operational area, bad-mouthing the Corps and stirring up trouble with my people and that I would officially request pre-trial confinement while Glover was waiting for his court martial and his discharge because I figured, sure as anything, the disbursing people would probably do something stupid, like giving Glover back pay for the time he was gone - then he would be gone again with his pockets full. The CO agreed with everything I said and assured me that Glover would not be my problem at all, from that moment on. When I went out through the admin office, Glover was still in that chair while the Admin Chief and his male clerks looked like they really wanted him to stir just once so they could tackle him. I admired their display of enthusiasm but it was obvious that Glover didn't.

I went back to work but I didn't think I'd heard the last of Glover because one of my MANY collateral duties is that of Correctional Facility Visitation Officer for members of our battalion who are confined to the brig.

I was correct in that assumption. During my visit to the correctional facility in May 1982 one of the prisoners I visited was J. A. Glover who registered the following complaints: (1) He was not being advised in a timely manner regarding the charges against him; (2) His wife was not receiving her government allotment; (3) The Navy Relief and the Red Cross were not providing assistance to his wife; (4) He was not receiving treatment for his alcoholism.

I provided the following responses to Detainee Glover: (1) His service record and charges were at the office of the Staff Judge Advocate and he would have to wait for his turn in court behind others who had entered the judicial system ahead of him; (2) His assigned defense attorney was Captain Wuest and the visitation register at the correctional facility indicated that the Captain had conferred with him on a schedule that was prescribed by regulations; (3) All government allotments to his spouse had stopped when he had first entered into an unauthorized absence status and he would have to restart her allotment if or when he might ever reenter a pay status after completion of his confinement period and after all fines and forfeitures were final; (4) I advised him that Navy Relief and Red Cross funds were reserved for emergency, one-time situations, but not for continued support for dependents of confined military personnel who were awaiting judicial processing. Support for his spouse might or might not be available through a local county or state agency in Florida but his spouse would have to apply, in person, to one of those agencies; (5) I informed him that, if he had an alcohol dependency problem, it might be handled through the Correctional Facility Counseling Section but I reminded him that it would basically be considered to be a self-inflicted problem and that the Marine Corps was under no obligation to either support or cure his alcoholism, although he might be involuntarily 'cured' if his incarceration covered an extended period of time.

Fit for Duty

When Gunnery Sergeant William J. Polk finished a sea deployment and came back to work at the Direct Support Unit (DSU) within the SASSY Management Unit, he came to the attention of Major Tweed, the Supply Company Commander, because he was so fat. He was actually only about 180 pounds but he was very short. He was terribly out of shape and he had been getting away with it for almost two years because, sometime in July of 1980, he got a doctor at the Naval Hospital to excuse him FOREVER from having to run the physical fitness test.

At that time, he should have been processed out of the Marine Corps. But he kissed up to some of the officers and got them to let him stay in, in spite of regulations that would have caused just about anybody else to get discharged. You see, Marine Corps Regulations and Orders are only as good as the senior officers who are willing to abide by and enforce them.

Gunny Polk got away with being out of shape and not having to be a REAL Marine Corps Gunnery Sergeant for almost two years, until Major Tweed caught him. In March of 1982, Major Tweed started up the Remedial Physical Fitness Training Program and assigned me to run it (as one of my many collateral duties) and he tried to get Gunny Polk into the program. But as soon as Major Tweed assigned him to the program, Gunny Polk got another medical evaluation (on 16 March 1982) to reconfirm that he couldn't do physical exercise.

Imagine that - a Gunnery Sergeant in the Marine Corps who couldn't be forced to do physical training. Well, with his renewed confirmation from the doctor that he didn't have to worry about his physical fitness, he apparently figured he had 'dodged the bullet' so he relaxed again. Rather, he relaxed until the 20th of April 1982, when he encountered me at a Staff Luncheon. The thing that brought him to my attention, besides his obvious weight problem, was the fact that he had a very large set of keys hanging on a chain suspended from a hook device attached to one of his belt loops.

I approached him and asked to see his identification card. When he asked what the problem was, I told him there were two things about him that bothered me - his weight and the fact that he was in violation of the uniform/clothing regulation for having that large chain hanging off of his belt loop. He said, "Well, Sir, I'm temporarily unable to exercise because of a medical problem but I'll find another way to carry my keys".

At the time, I was willing to let it go. He appeared contrite and wasn't obnoxious, like some junior Marines get sometimes when I correct their appearance and he seemed to be willing to accept the fact that I was pointing out a failure on his part and he seemed to be ready to correct it when he put the keys in his pocket.

The very next day I went to the Direct Support Unit to take some paperwork to Captain Motes, the Officer in Charge of the DSU. On my way out, I met Gunny Polk in the hallway. He looked absolutely sick when he recognized me because he had that same set of keys hanging on his belt loop by that same long chain. I said, "Well, Gunny, here we are. Let me make a list for you so you'll know what the charge sheet is going to say when I go see the CO. First, there's a violation of the clothing regulation for Marines, which specifies that you can't have that huge hook and long chain hanging from your uniform. Second, there is disobedience of a direct order because, when I told you to take off that hook and chain, that didn't mean you could put it right back on as soon as I was out of sight. Third, there's disrespect toward an officer because it was a willful act of disrespect when you decided that you were going to do exactly as you pleased, even though I told you, just yesterday, to stop wearing that hook and chain. Fourth, there is another charge of disrespect because you are not standing at the position of attention while I'm here talking to you. Fifth, while I'm on my way to the company office, I will probably decide to add a charge for conduct unbecoming to a Marine Staff NCO because you have obviously been setting a bad example for your junior Marines with your appearance for quite a long time". Then I took the chain and the hook device, handed the keys back to him and walked out of the building.

Gunnery Sergeant Polk decided that he did not want to risk facing Major Tweed for office hours (non-judicial punishment). He knew the CO already didn't like him because of the way he skated out of the physical fitness program. He also knew that I would find out he had told me a lie at the luncheon when he said he had a TEMPORARY medical condition that excused him from physical training because he was actually permanently excused. That lie would cause his non-judicial punishment to be bumped up to a special court martial because I would add a charge of making a false official statement.

Gunny Polk decided to cut his losses and try to retire while he could still go out as a Gunnery Sergeant so he talked with his boss, Captain Motes, while I was talking to Major Tweed, the Company Commander. When Major Tweed called Captain Motes, the Captain told him they would send a letter requesting retirement for Gunny Polk. (Informed sources later told me that Gunny Polk had often bragged that he was going to stay in for thirty years and never have to run any farther than the distance from his office door to his car and then only if it was raining).

I regret that I don't have a copy of Captain Motes' letter requesting retirement for Gunnery Sergeant Polk. It was a work of art. However, I do have copies of the three endorsements.

Lt/Col Ellsworth had to write the first endorsement because he is the Officer in Charge of the SMU, of which the Direct Support Unit is a subordinate section. He was really upset because he had to send his endorsement to the Company Commander, a mere Major (Major Tweed).

When Lt/Col Elsworth learned about my two confrontations with Gunny Polk, he 'went public' with his past criticisms about me, saying that I had 'a Neanderthal mentality' and that I was 'back on that crap about the Total Marine concept, with no consideration for Gunnery Sergeant Polk's worth as a supply administration man'. When he wrote his endorsement to Captain Motes' letter, he stressed that Gy/Sgt Polk's performance of duty in his technical field was not impaired in any way by his physical condition and he stressed that Gunny Polk had served at sea with no adverse effects on his performance. Lt/Col Elsworth was wrong. He was still trying to separate the many functions of a Marine and that just can't be done. Being a Marine means that you can not only perform your assigned tasks but you can also pick up a rifle and go to battle at a moment's notice. That's the Total Marine concept. Furthermore, physical fitness sits at the very core of everything that is involved with being a Marine, in the first place.

The second endorsement, which was from the Company Commander (Major Tweed), disagreed with Lt/Col Elsworth's assessment of the situation. Major Tweed gave the opinion that Gunny Polk's physical condition DID adversely affect his overall performance as a Staff NCO. Major Tweed quoted a Marine Corps Order (MCO 6100.3H), which stated, in part, "It is essential to the day-to-day effectiveness and combat readiness of the Marine Corps that every Marine be physically fit, regardless of duty assignment. Physical fitness is an indispensable aspect of leadership. Marines who are not physically fit are a detriment to the readiness and combat efficiency of their unit and detract from the performance of the Marine Corps". That Marine Corps Order was signed by the Commandant of the Marine Corps and I really doubt that Lt/Col Elsworth would have referred to the Commandant as a Neanderthal mentality. Not publicly, anyway.

The third endorsement was by Lt/Col J. D. Stewart, the Commanding Officer of 2nd Supply Battalion. He also disagreed with Lt/Col Elsworth's statements. In fact, the last paragraph of his endorsement regarding Gunny Polk stated, "Inasmuch as he is not able to participate in the physical fitness test, I do not believe he is capable of satisfactory performance as a Staff Noncommissioned Officer".

So the Company Commander and the Battalion Commander both agreed with me in regard to the fact that a Marine's performance of duty includes his responsibility to remain physically fit.

Maybe I wasn't the only Marine officer who had a 'Neanderthal mentality'.

Gy/Sgt Polk probably still curses the day he ran into me. That hook and chain cost him a lot of money, even though he's going to be allowed to retire at twenty years. He really wanted to hang around for a full thirty years, skating through life, probably even getting another promotion along the way, somehow, so he could have retired at FULL pay as a Master Sergeant instead of retiring at HALF pay as a Gunnery Sergeant. But he had the bad luck to run into me.

But Gunny Polk still got away with one thing that was strictly against another Marine Corps Regulations. They let him take 80 days of terminal leave. There was no way he could possibly have 80 days to take. Regulations state that a Marine cannot accumulate more than 60 days of leave time. Any leave time accumulated over 60 days is automatically wiped off the books. It's a 'use it or lose it' policy, so Gunny Polk still got to screw the system because there was no way he could accumulate 80 days of leave time.

Even more so, he was apparently not going to have to face punishment for the charges I filed against him because the Commanding General, our own General Moss, was going to allow him to retire without going to trial.

Training Reservists

During June 1982, the Marine Reservist Detachment from Jacksonville, North Carolina reported to Camp Lejeune for their yearly assignment to temporary active duty for training purposes. The reservists who were assigned in the warehousing field were further detailed to my Storage Section for training.

Upon their arrival, I gave a brief conversational lecture on overall Storage Operations procedures. I explained and/or described such functions as processing issues to the customers, control procedures for the accurate processing of both receipts and issues, location verification procedures and working from computer updates.

I gave them an orientation briefing regarding safety features, safety regulations, general operation and operator maintenance of the 4,000 lb warehouse forklift. Then, at some point during their assignment to the Medium/Bulk Storage Section, each Reservist was allowed to operate a warehouse forklift in the process of routine warehouse operations, after completing a written test and after successfully negotiating a demanding and exacting obstacle course which I designed with the very capable and imaginative assistance of my Storage Operations Chief, Gunnery Sergeant Truman Sullivan. We provided forklift certification and licensing documents to the Reservists who were involved in the warehousing portion of the yearly training.

Lt/Col Brewster, the Officer in Charge of the Reservist Detachment, had attended my initial in-briefing, my warehouse training sessions, my forklift operation seminars and my forklift obstacle course certification sessions and I could tell that the Reservists appreciated his interest in their training.

However, I was very surprised (and quite pleased) to hear about all the nice things he and his senior advisors had to say about the clean and orderly setup of my warehousing areas, about the efficiency and professionalism of the personnel in my Storage Section and especially about me during their after-action out-briefing.

But I was NOT surprised that I did not hear about their nice comments from Lt/Col Elsworth. He would never repeat any comment that was ever made about me unless it was derogatory. No, their praise was passed on to me by other officers who had been present at the out-briefing.

Thanks for Trying

Major Tweed was getting ready to leave Camp Lejeune and proceed to his next assignment but before his departure, he wanted to let me know that his regard for me was high, although I already knew he had a high opinion of my professional abilities because otherwise, I would not have been chosen as a Platoon Commander in his Company, plus I had never disappointed him with my performance at any of the many other collateral duties that had been assigned to me.

But since HIS involvement in the physical training program was ending, he wanted to give particular emphasis to my assignment as the Remedial Physical Training Officer, so he presented me with the following Letter of Appreciation.

UNITED STATES MARINE CORPS
Supply Company
2nd Supply Battalion
2nd Force Service Support Group (Rein)
Fleet Marine Force, Atlantic
Camp Lejeune, North Carolina 28542

WAT/amj
1650
28 June 1982

From: Commanding Officer
To: Chief Warrant Officer Roy L. Morris

Subj: Letter of Appreciation

From March to June 1982, you were assigned the difficult task of organizing, implementing and supervising the Supply Company Remedial PT Program conducted at 0540 each workday. Your tireless efforts and unusual dedication to duty have set you apart as a superior leader worthy of high praise and special recognition. You singlehandedly designed a strenuous, comprehensive program that would help overweight Marines lose weight while enabling those who have failed the PFT to improve their physical fitness to an acceptable level. In addition, you took extra time to counsel them in a manner that led to a change in attitudes and an improvement in self-esteem which caused assigned personnel to want to achieve.

I wish to take this opportunity to personally express my appreciation and admiration for your unique abilities. You are truly an outstanding leader of Marines.

W. A. TWEED

Memorandum for the record dated 30 June 1982

Sergeant Raymond R. Williams

    On the 6th of May, Sergeant Williams was given to me by the Supply Company Commander, with the approval of every single officer in every command position between myself and the Commandant of the Marine Corps, including my immediate supervisor, Lt/Col Elsworth, the Officer in Charge of the SASSY Management Unit. The Commandant wanted an evaluation of Sergeant Williams' performance to determine if he had a viable future in the Marine Corps. It was decided, by all concerned, that I was the best man for the job of providing this evaluation. It was common knowledge that I was very firm but also very fair. That was the true reason why Major Tweed, the Supply Company Commander, and every officer in the chain of command above him wanted me to have the assignment of evaluating Sergeant Williams.

    Now, the true reason why Lt/Col Elsworth wanted me to have the job of evaluating Sergeant Williams was simply because he wanted me to have just one more extra collateral duty, one more administrative detail to worry about, one more source of aggravation.

    He tried to send as many extra duties my way as he could. He even pulled strings to get me assigned to stand duty as Battalion Officer of the Day on weekends because standing weekend duty was more of a hassle than standing duty during the week. He just enjoyed trying to irritate me. He was such a spiteful person. He couldn't win arguments with me because he was always wrong and I was always right, so he tried to get even by being underhanded and devious. (Note: I would never argue with a senior officer when I knew he was right because there would be no reason to argue).

    Lt/Col Elsworth always made the mistake of assuming that he could say the sky was green and the grass was blue and nobody would argue with him because he was a Lt/Col. I didn't play that game.

    But Lt/Col Elsworth didn't have any personal connections with Sergeant Williams, so he didn't care whether my final evaluation would be favorable or unfavorable. He just wanted me to have the inconvenience and aggravation of having to go through the motion of actually doing the evaluation.

By the end of June 1982, my evaluation was completed. I had kept Sergeant Williams at my side, practically like a second shadow for over 7 weeks. His future in the Corps depended on my opinion and I wanted to give him every opportunity, in every type of situation, to either prove or disprove his right to be a Marine.

I had not informed anybody of his true status or the reason for his assignment as my assistant, although I had asked Gunnery Sergeant Truman Sullivan, the Storage Operations Chief, to give me his opinions and evaluations regarding Sergeant Williams.

The results of my evaluation were presented in the following letter, which I drafted to the Commandant of the Marine Corps.

UNITED STATES MARINE CORPS
SASSY Management Unit
Supply Company
2nd Supply Battalion
2nd Force Service Support Group
Fleet Marine Force, Atlantic
Camp Lejeune, North Carolina

RLM/eja
4400.5
30 June 1982

From: Officer in Charge, Storage Operations
To: Commandant of the Marine Corps (Code MMEA-6)
Via: (1) Officer in Charge, SASSY Management Unit
    (2) Commanding Officer, Supply Company, 2nd Supply Battalion
    (3) Commanding Officer, 2nd Supply Battalion, 2nd Force Service Support Group
    (4) Commanding General, 2nd Force Service Support Group

Subj: Standards of Professional Performance; case of Sergeant Raymond R. Williams

Ref: (a) CMC letter MMEA-6/jr 1600 dated 5 April 1982

    As directed by reference (a), with endorsements, the following evaluation is submitted.
    During recent months, Sergeant Williams has shown some slight improvements in the area of job performance. He has demonstrated a desire to expand his proficiency by seeking and accepting more responsibility. However, he has a tendency to get involved in more than he can effectively handle, resulting in decreased quality of efficiency and production.
    Sergeant Williams has consistently maintained an excellent personal appearance and generally has a good military bearing but he does not receive the level of respect from his junior Marines that would normally be freely extended to a Marine Noncommissioned Officer. This is

partially due to his inability to tactfully communicate with subordinates. He is often overbearing when issuing instructions, providing guidance or supervising a project.

I have tried several different methods of evaluating (and effecting changes) in his abilities, his professional aptitudes and his conduct:

I gave him a project and described the end result I wanted him to achieve, then asked him to write out and describe the steps he would take to accomplish the assigned task.

I have lectured him about the leadership traits and principles.

I have had him accompany me while I toured the various subsections under my control, so that he could observe how I interact with the personnel in the Storage Section, ranging in rank from Master Sergeant all the way down to Private, adjusting my style according to the situation and the individual involved.

I have engaged him in casual, one-on-one conversations regarding various warehouse projects in the Storage Section.

I have allowed him to sit in (as a note taker) at meetings with various section heads while we discussed various projects, priorities and upcoming events.

I have informed nobody regarding his status, although I have asked my Storage Operations Chief, Gy/Sgt Sullivan, to give me feedback regarding his own impressions of Sergeant Williams.

It is my considered opinion that Sergeant Williams is simply not Staff NCO material, although he may eventually learn to function as a Sergeant. Of course, I know that a person would not be allowed to pursue a full career in the Marine Corps without being able to rise above the rank of Sergeant.

It is obvious that Sergeant Williams is not an original thinker. I don't know what his IQ is, but I can readily perceive that he simply is not exceptionally bright. This is not intended to say that he is really stupid, either, because he isn't. It's just that he doesn't have that special 'spark' that I have always come to expect from Staff NCOs, so he just doesn't have what it takes to become one - not in the foreseeable future. If I were still a Gunnery Sergeant, this is simply not a Marine with whom I would care to share Staff NCO status.

Finally, I would have to say that although Sergeant Williams has been making some admirable efforts at improving his professional performance during his assignment with Storage Operations, I would hasten to add that it is significant that he had to be TOLD (by Headquarters Marine Corps, no less) that he needed to make that effort. Any Marine who wants to stay in the Corps - and to advance up through the ranks - should ALREADY have that internal drive, that competitive spirit, that 'Gung Ho' attitude that is the hallmark of true Marine Corps leaders.

Roy L. Morris
CWO USMC

Thanks for Trying...Again

After Major Tweed completed his tour of duty at Camp Lejeune, First Lieutenant (Captain Selectee) J. V. Hinds replaced him as Commanding Officer of Supply Company. Lt Hinds had no idea of the scope and complexity of the training program established for the personnel in the Remedial Fitness Program, as requested by Major Tweed and as designed by me until he chose to attend one of the training sessions one morning during the first month of his assignment as CO of Supply Company. At that time, he was clearly amazed at the progress that had been made by the people I was training.

He apparently did not know that Major Tweed had awarded me a Letter of Appreciation only about a month before so he drafted his own Letter of Appreciation. When I received it, I did not want to embarrass him by telling him about the other one, although the time frame covered was different. However, since the time frame WAS different, both were considered valid.

A reproduction of the second letter is provided, as follows:

UNITED STATES MARINE CORPS
Supply Company
2nd Supply Battalion
2nd Force Service Support Group (Rein)
Camp Lejeune, North Carolina 28542

JVH/blb
20 July 1982

From: Commanding Officer
To: Chief Warrant Officer Roy L. Morris
Via: Officer in Charge, SASSY Management Unit

Subj: Letter of Appreciation

While assigned as the Remedial Physical Training Officer for this unit, you singlehandedly developed a demanding Physical Fitness Program. As a result of your superb leadership and outstanding example, many of the Marines of this Company were able to meet the Marine Corps weight and physical fitness standards. Your attention to duty, high standards and superior leadership ability sets a sterling example for all to follow. Few officers could have achieved such excellent results in such a short period of time.

I wish to take this opportunity to express my sincere appreciation for a job 'WELL DONE' and to wish you success in all your future endeavors.

J. V. HINDS

The end is near

All things considered, I was almost perfect. I had come incredibly close to being 'the best of the best'. I really did have powers and abilities far beyond those of normal men. I was at the peak of physical fitness. My qualification scores with rifle and pistol were amazingly high. My abilities as a drill instructor for my platoon garnered top marks in any competition. My ability to handle combat units in tactical situations was second to none. My talents as both a Supply Officer and Warehousing Officer were textbook perfect. Marines from other platoons came to me for guidance and counseling rather than seeking the advice of their own platoon commanders. From various senior officers, I received letters of appreciation that applauded my superior leadership abilities.

But there was something wrong. I had a fault…a flaw. There was a chink in my armor. It was a shortcoming that would help to bring about the end of my military career. You see, my basic problem was the fact that I was, after all, a human being, susceptible to the same wants and needs that have always driven other humans. It didn't matter how intensely I had trained, or for how long. The one thing I couldn't train myself out of was my link to humanity.

There was a woman Marine Sergeant at Camp Lejeune who had known me on Okinawa. She knew that my daughter had died and that the mother of my daughter had divorced me. She knew how devastated I had been. She introduced me to a divorced Woman Marine Corporal named Linda Wolfe, who had a nine-year-old daughter named Carla. It turned out that Corporal Wolfe was in need of a babysitter for her daughter. Corporal Wolfe, who was an administrative clerk, was going to be spending a lot of time working evenings and weekends helping her admin section get ready for a Commanding General's Inspection.

I was obviously at loose ends. There I was, recently divorced, new to the area, with no social obligations, with no close acquaintances, and with no current girlfriend (and I didn't want one at the time because I was too bitter). Granted, I was an officer but Corporal Wolfe instinctively knew, without any hesitation or doubt, that I was also a gentleman and that I could be trusted to take proper care of her daughter. As incongruous as it may sound, I was a perfect babysitter.

Carla and I did everything together…movies, miniature golf, swimming at the base pool, hiking, going to the beach, visiting local parks, canoeing on the inlets. That little girl brought me back to life and put a smile on my face, something that had been missing for a very long time.

Eventually, the inspection was over and Corporal Wolfe's work schedule returned to normal. In order to thank me for looking after Carla, she invited me to have supper with them. I should have declined but I didn't. That supper invitation turned out so well that future invitations were extended…and were accepted. Gradually, I stopped thinking of Corporal Wolfe as a Woman Marine and started thinking of her as the mother of a little girl who I had come to adore. We even started addressing each other by our given names, Linda and Roy, at least when we were together in private. I reached a point where I did not want to give up my association with either Carla OR Linda, so I asked Carla if she would give permission for me to propose to her Mom. Carla said 'Yes'. Linda said 'Yes', too.

But we had made the mistake of allowing the wrong people to see us together. Word got back to Lt/Col Elsworth. I was charged with conduct unbecoming to a Marine Officer for fraternizing with an enlisted Woman Marine. I was fined $1,000.00 and given a letter of reprimand, signed by General Moss. Yes, General Moss, the one man at Camp Lejeune for whom I had the LEAST respect was able to sit in judgment of me.

Shortly after that, General Moss was transferred to Headquarters, Marine Corps. Not very long after THAT, a message was received from Headquarters, Marine Corps ordering that I appear before a board of review to determine my right to continue my career as an officer of Marines. Justification was listed as 'unacceptable conduct'. How about that?

I was disgusted, but not with Lt/Col Elsworth or with General Moss or even with the Marine Corps. I was disgusted with myself. I had failed, not only as an officer but also as a Marine. It would cost me dearly but I felt I had no choice but to resign. Almost 17 years wasted.

Of course, Linda divorced me. But I didn't blame her. She had married an officer and a gentleman but had wound up with an unemployed bum. I lost my career. I lost my wife. I lost my step-daughter. I lost my self-respect.

It didn't have to end that way. I could have made other choices. I could have chosen not to argue with Lt/Col Elsworth. No, I take that back. I HAD to argue with Lt/Col Elsworth simply because he was wrong. I couldn't be his 'Yes' man when I disagreed with him. I couldn't roll over and play dead if I knew I was right and he was wrong. But I also did not have to accept the job of taking care of Carla, thereby allowing her into my heart. I didn't have to accept that very first invitation to supper or any of the invitations that followed. But there again, my humanity was in control. I will forever curse my link to humanity!

In the final analysis, Lt/Col Elsworth was not really responsible for the charge against me. He only took advantage of the opportunity I gave him. I gave him the ammunition with which to shoot me down. He didn't destroy my career. I did. How about that? I established a normal relationship with a real live actual female and we got married so I was getting kicked out of the Marine Corps for 'unacceptable conduct'.

In the past few years, there have been numerous concessions made for people who are not normal. It basically started with the policy of "Don't ask, Don't tell" regarding the sexual habits of members of the military but it rapidly got progressively worse. Before long, homosexuals were allowed to serve in the military even after publicly acknowledging their sexual orientation. And of course, it finally got totally out of control. For example, on 2 Nov 2013, the Arkansas Democrat Gazette reported that Larry Choate III, 27, of West Point Class of 2009, and Daniel Lennox, 28, Class of 2007, were set on that day to become the first men to marry each other at that military academy. At West Point!

What a couple of queer men do to each other is just too disgusting to even contemplate so why would the military establishment agree to such a course of action? Sodomy and oral sex between members of the same sex are still violations of the Uniform Code of Military Justice so what part of their situation could possibly be interpreted as acceptable conduct? Maybe the senior officers who were responsible for those two homos believed their sex life was going to consist of just shaking hands occasionally. Yeah, right! My normal, ordinary, regular marriage to a member of the OPPOSITE sex was labeled as unacceptable conduct by the military establishment simply because I outranked her but that same military establishment now sanctions and legalizes the marital union of two members of the SAME sex!

It sort of makes me glad that I am no longer a member of the military institution because it might appear that I would be giving tacit approval for the decisions of my military leaders who gave permission for a couple of pansies to get married. In the last 30 years, the United States has turned upside down.

There are probably a lot of people out there who will read this and be angry at me over the fact that I refer to gays as 'homos', 'queers', 'pansies' and 'fairies'. Maybe you think I am violating their constitutional rights to be gay, if that is the lifestyle they choose. Maybe you think I am offending their dignity. Well, what about MY constitutional rights? It offends MY dignity to be expected to address them as 'gay'. When did the terminology change? Who decided that the word 'gay' would be a logical and acceptable term to replace the word 'queer'? Back in my day, the word 'gay' used to mean happy. But how could anybody feel 'gay' about being 'queer'? What could possibly be happy about a man performing oral or anal sex on another man? I would think that the word 'sad' would be more appropriate than the word 'gay'. They refer to normal people as 'straight', so maybe they should be referred to as 'bent'. Why didn't they opt for a truly legitimate word, like 'homosexual', which more accurately describes their true state of existence? That covers the situation for both males and females because, according to the dictionary, it means a person who is sexually attracted to a member of the same sex, whether male or female. As a replacement word for either 'queer' or 'lesbian', it really makes more sense than the word 'gay'.

Actually, I probably know why they want to use the word 'gay'. As I said, they refer to normal people as 'straight' instead of normal. It's because they want to be considered normal, too, but just a different version of normal. They insist that it is a violation of their civil rights to classify them as being anything other than normal. So, in the final analysis, their deviant sexual behavior is considered acceptable conduct while my normal relationship with a member of the opposite sex was considered unacceptable conduct.

The really odd part of the whole thing is that, in civilian life, Linda had been a Licensed Practical Nurse (LPN). She could have joined the

Navy as an officer. By the time we met, SHE would have outranked ME. But she had grown tired of having to watch sick people get weak and die so she wanted to get away from the nursing profession. The most radical departure was to join the Marine Corps enlisted ranks as a Private. By the time we met, she was a Corporal just about to get promoted to the rank of Sergeant. That's just the way it goes sometimes. A turn not made, a path not followed, a decision altered by the merest of circumstance causes changes in the future that can only be properly interpreted through hindsight.

But there is nobody on earth who is immune to the basic wants and needs common to all of humanity. The highest ranking members of the military and/or political community are just exactly like all the rest of us. For example, General Douglas MacArthur kept a mistress (a Eurasian woman) in the Menzies Hotel in Australia while he was there, after leaving the Philippines, even though he had his wife and son with him. General Eisenhower had a mistress while he was stationed in England. She was the WAC Sergeant who served as his driver. The General even had her commissioned as a Captain so it would be easier to get her into and out of the officer billeting area. President Franklin Delano Roosevelt, even though he was in a wheelchair most of the time, had a mistress in Warm Springs, Georgia. In fact, he was with her when he died. President Thomas Jefferson had a black mistress 'bed warmer'. John and Bobby Kennedy were both having very active sex affairs with Marilyn Monroe at the same time. President Clinton is famous (or maybe infamous) for his sexual dalliances. There have been an incredibly large number of political figures who have had to give up their hopes and aspirations for higher office after their sex lives were made public.

And there were MANY mixed marriages between officer and enlisted during my era but they had not been subjected to the same public scrutiny that Linda and I endured. And regarding the 'relationships' between officers and enlisted, well, there were enlisted females ALL OVER the bachelor officer quarters every single night but they were very sneaky. I wasn't sneaky so Major Barone, my reporting senior, had no choice but to grade me as unsatisfactory in force and judgment but he also pointed out that my professionalism had not been affected by the setbacks in my personal life.

It's as simple as this: Some people can get away with everything and some other people can't get away with anything.

Fitness Report for 1 March 1982 through 12 September 1982

Section C: Performance of duty:
Regular duties	Excellent
Administrative duties	Excellent
Handling officers	Excellent
Handling enlisted personnel	Excellent
Training personnel	Excellent

To what degree has he exhibited the following:
Personal appearance	Outstanding
Military presence	Excellent
Attention to duty	Outstanding
Cooperation	Outstanding
Initiative	Excellent
Judgment	Unsatisfactory
Force	Unsatisfactory
Leadership	Below Average
Loyalty	Outstanding
Personal relations	Excellent
Economy of management	Excellent
Growth potential	Excellent

Your estimate of this Marine's general value to the service:
Excellent

Considering the requirements of service in war, indicate your attitude toward having this Marine under your command:
Particularly desire to have

Narrative comments:
    This officer is by far one of the most conscientious and loyal officers I have had the experience to work with. He is relentless in his attempts to do the best job possible. As is shown by the Letter of Appreciation he received, he completely dedicates himself to his assigned duty or task. During this period, as stated in the attached Letter of Reprimand, this Marine received Commanding General's office hours for

fraternization with an enlisted Woman Marine. This act is considered to show unsatisfactory judgment and force and impacts adversely on an otherwise excellent leadership ability. In an attempt to provide the fairest possible picture of this Marine's overall performance, it must be stated that he never swerved from his diligent efforts and maintained high performance throughout and subsequent to his indiscretion and office hours. Additionally, the morale and efficiency of his section were not diminished. Report submitted late due to administrative oversight and subject named Marine being on temporary additional duty with CSSD-21 at Fort Pickett, Virginia.
  Reporting Officer
  C. J. Barone
  Major USMC
  Officer in Charge
  General Account
  SASSY Management Unit

My letter of resignation was written and signed on 28 October 1982. The first endorsement was written by Lt/Col Dinkins, the 2nd Supply Battalion Commander, who knew me personally.

I was highly pleased by his comments. He was quite well aware of the difficulties I'd had with Lt/Col Elsworth, before he was transferred out of the SASSY Management Unit. He was also well aware of how highly I was regarded by Major Tweed, the CO of Supply Company, and by Major Tweed's replacement, 1st Lt Hinds. Furthermore, he knew of the respect that the senior Staff Noncommissioned Officers of the Battalion had for me.

The second endorsement was written by Colonel Winglass, who had taken over command of the 2nd Force Service Support Group after General Moss was transferred to Headquarters Marine Corps in Washington (where he was able to finish the destruction of my career). Col Winglass knew of the difficulties that General Moss had caused for my Marines and he was well aware of General Moss' many inadequacies and shortcomings as a leader. It was very gratifying to know that Col Winglass CONCURRED with the recommendations and comments Lt/Col Dinkins had made about me.

Their recommendations (about allowing me to finish out my career in the Reserves) were not accepted at Headquarters Marine Corps. That decision was probably spearheaded by General Moss. When he had me kicked out, he had me kicked all the way out.

Reproductions of the endorsements of Lt/Col Dinkins and Colonel Winglass are as follows:

UNITED STATES MARINE CORPS
2nd Supply Battalion
2nd Force Service Support Group
Fleet Marine Force, Atlantic
Camp Lejeune, North Carolina 28542

01/HHD/pal
1900
2 Nov 1982

FIRST ENDORSEMENT on CWO MORRIS' ltr RLM/st 1900 dtd 28 Oct 1982

From: Commanding Officer
To: Secretary of the Navy
Via: (1) Commanding Officer, 2nd Force Service Support Group
(2) Commandant of the Marine Corps (Code MMSR-3)

Subj: Resignation; request for

Subject request for resignation of commission is forwarded.

    Should this request be approved, a certificate of Honorable Discharge is recommended.

    CWO MORRIS has served this command with tireless persistent resourcefulness. He is an accomplished supply officer and has consistently produced accurate quality results. CWO MORRIS' unswerving attitude has made him a credit to the overall efforts of the Battalion.

    Should CWO MORRIS' resignation be accepted I would highly recommend him for a commission in the U. S. Marine Corps Reserve.

H. H. DINKINS

UNITED STATES MARINE CORPS
2nd Force Service Support Group (Rein)
Fleet Marine Force, Atlantic
Camp Lejeune, North Carolina 28542

7/JJY/WPC/ldc
1900
8 Nov 1982

SECOND ENDORSEMENT on CWO MORRIS' ltr RLM/st 1900 of 28 Oct 1982

From: Commanding Officer
To: Secretary of the Navy
Via: Commandant of the Marine Corps (Code MMSR-3)

Subj: Resignation; request for

    Forwarded concurring with the recommendations and comments of the battalion commander.

    The effective date of resignation of 30 January 1983 is concurred in due to the fact that Chief Warrant Officer MORRIS is currently deployed and not expected to return until mid-December.

                                          R. J. WINGLASS

Copy to:
CO 2nd Sup Bn

Final Assignment

My resignation would not become effective until after I completed a temporary additional duty assignment as Supply Officer of Combined Service Support Detachment-21. It would be my last official duty performed for the United States Marine Corps. And I was determined that it would be performed with the same intensity, thoroughness and dedication that I had brought to every other assignment I had ever been given.

Setting up the Combined Service Support Detachment was a logistical nightmare. If not for my personal intervention in several areas which were not normally presumed to be within my personal or professional area of expertise, then the Combined Arms Operation would have been a failure before it even got started. Because of my extensive knowledge, experience and expertise, more than ever before in my military existence, I was absolutely the right man in the right place at the right time.

The following entries are examples of the situations which would not have been resolved without my involvement, as confirmed by Captain P. G. Smith, the Commanding Officer of CSSD-21:

Problem: Identification cards and meal cards are a necessity for any deployment, yet these forms were not in the support block

Solution: The Headquarters and Service Battalion personnel officer was very helpful in providing these forms from her available stock after I explained the situation to her.

Recommendation: These forms should be automatically included in the administrative support block for future CSSD operations.

Problem: When I asked the Division G-4 (Ops) for a listing of the Job Order Numbers (JONs) to be used during the operation, I was given a copy of a modification (dated 3 Sep 1982) to an Inter-Service Support Agreement (dated 2 Sep 1981). There seemed to be considerable confusion among the supported subunits regarding the proper JONs to be used, as the JONs for Class IX repair parts was changed twice. Also, some documents for POL and batteries were forwarded to CSSD-21 without JONs listed, although these documents had been checked for completeness by the Comptroller's representative. Also, the JONs provided by Division G-4 (Ops) were not in agreement with the Division Logistics Plan. I had noted these discrepancies when I was first given the copy of the modification but when I tried to explain this problem to the Division Adjutant, I was told, rather bluntly and in no uncertain terms, that the problem existed only in my inability to grasp the finer details of the Division's accounting system. No apology was ever extended to me, even though my assessment of the situation proved to be correct, much to the chagrin of the Division G-4 (Ops).

Recommendation: That the Division Comptroller should begin reviewing the JONs assigned at least ninety (90) days prior to the start of the exercise.

Problem: Prior to departure from Camp Lejeune, CSSD-21 forwarded a letter (which I drafted) to Division G-4 (Ops) requesting that all subunits provide letters of authorization for personnel who would be signing requisitions and receipting for supplies. Two weeks later, only two units had responded with letters of authorization. In fact, most units did not respond at all until their unit representatives were turned away from the CSSD-21 supply section as unauthorized personnel.

Solution: Most of the supported units eventually utilized delegation of authority forms (MCBUL 5000/5) which I provided because I had acquired a supply of these forms prior to deploying from Camp Lejeune.

Recommendation: That all future subunit commanders be made more fully aware of their responsibilities relating to supply matters.

Problem: Many units did not have the blank forms necessary to requisition supplies and repair parts.

Solution: I provided requisition system documents (DD-1348) and general purpose transaction documents (NAVMC 10694) because I had the foresight to bring plenty of these blank forms from my available supplies at my regular permanent assignment as the OIC of Storage Operations within the SASSY Management Unit.

Recommendation: That subunit supply personnel review the availability of required forms and documents prior to being deployed.

Problem: The CSSD-21 supply block was 93 % complete upon transfer to Fort Pickett. However, this original supply block attained only a 10.15 % fill rate for requested parts and components in support of the operation.

Discussion: One of the reasons for this failing was the fact that I was not given the opportunity to review the listing of parts that would make up the Initial Support Package. I had extensive experience in the supply field. Also, I had been a key figure in establishing and maintaining combat readiness of weapons systems, tracked vehicles and motor transport for the entire Marine Corps when I was a Gunnery Sergeant. And I had a long and very successful assignment as a Motor Transport Operations/Maintenance Officer for the largest Motor Transport Section in the entire Marine Corps. I also had served as a member of a three-man Inspector/Instructor Team which evaluated the supply and maintenance capabilities of a support unit in Japan. I didn't know what criteria determined the makeup of the Initial Support Package but the total uselessness of the supply block could be demonstrated by the fact that we stocked such items as rearview side mirrors, tow ropes and highway warning devices in uncommonly large quantities, while there was only ONE spark plug on hand. I explained the following example to Captain Smith, the Commanding Officer of CSSD-21: If the mechanics ask for 40 fuel filters over a given period of time, but receive only 10 because the supply system at Camp Lejeune cannot supply the other 30, then the final usage data is going to reflect that only 10 fuel filters were used. This data turns a blind eye to the fact that the quantity NEEDED had no correlation to the quantity USED because the quantity used was inadequate. Future usage data should not be established ONLY for items which were actually issued during the operation but also for those items which were requested but were not provided. If I had been able to spend any time at all reviewing the supply block prior to deployment, I would have instantly recognized the shortcomings and potential problems in the Initial Support Package. We were unable to utilize any of my vast experience, knowledge and expertise prior to deployment simply because I was not given the opportunity to review the supply block. As long as the usage data reflects ONLY the repair parts that were actually ISSUED and ignores the other factors (such as the repair parts that were actually REQUESTED), then the decisions of the Plans and Analysis Staff will be erroneous because their entire premise will be based on flawed and inaccurate data. They need to be able and WILLING to seek the counsel of REAL experts.

Recommendation: That the use of the Initial Support Package be discontinued and that future operations be supported by a supply block built from past usage data compiled from similar operations, tempered by obvious differences in the density of the vehicles and weapons systems to be supported and that the usage data be based on the criteria discussed above.

Problem: The supply block was not automatically provided with such items as a Master Header Information File (MHIF), a Master Cross Reference List (MCRL), a Management Data List (MDL) or a Maintenance Float Catalog.

Solution: I acquired these items from various contacts within the SASSY Management Unit, just prior to deployment.

Recommendation: That these items be part of an automatic package to be provided, prior to deployment, to future CSSD supply officers, who may not have my intuition, knowledge or initiative.

Problem: The ammo technicians with the using units were not initially licensed to operate forklifts prior to their assignment to CSSD-21, so we were forced to use Army ASP civilians in the unloading and staging of ammo during the early stages of the operation, a service for which the Marine Corps will be billed. The ammo techs assigned to the supply section were also not licensed, which is why we could not use them during the first few days of the operation to perform those forklift duties.

Solution: I conducted an intensive training course for my assigned ammo techs and was able to certify several of them as being qualified to operate both the warehouse forklifts and the rough terrain forklifts so that they could replace the Army ASP civilians within three or four days. There is no estimate of the amount of money I saved the Marine Corps by being able to discontinue the use of the civilians. I might also point out that I had immediately begun forklift training for the ammo techs in my supply section, even before I was made aware of just how critical this training would turn out to be.

Recommendation: That the ammo technicians assigned to future CSSD's be more carefully screened and that possession of appropriate operator's licenses be a prerequisite for participation in the exercise.

The following document is the last fitness report I ever received in the Marine Corps. It was written by Captain P. G. Smith, the Commanding Officer of Combined Service Support Detachment-21. As did almost every other position I ever held as a Warrant Officer or Chief Warrant Officer, the billet I was filling as Supply Officer of CSSD-21 called for the assignment of a Captain. And as usual, I had absolutely no difficulty in grasping the complexities of the job.

Fitness Report for 13 September 1982 through 13 December 1982

Section C: Performance of duty:
Regular duties	Outstanding
Administrative duties	Outstanding
Handling officers	Outstanding
Handling enlisted personnel	Outstanding
Training personnel	Excellent

To what degree has he exhibited the following:
Personal appearance	Excellent
Military presence	Outstanding
Attention to duty	Outstanding
Cooperation	Outstanding
Initiative	Outstanding
Judgment	Outstanding
Force	Outstanding
Leadership	Outstanding
Loyalty	Outstanding
Personal relations	Outstanding
Economy of management	Excellent
Growth potential	Outstanding

Your estimate of this Marine's general value to the service:
Outstanding

Considering the requirements of service in war, indicate your attitude toward having this Marine under your command:
Particularly desire to have

Narrative Comments:
    CWO Morris is an energetic, conscientious and versatile officer. He is meticulously accurate as to his facts and thorough in his work. Highly intelligent with an alert, active mind, he quickly perceives and correctly evaluates the essential elements of any problem and arrives at a sound solution. Tactful and diplomatic, he has the ability to express

and strongly support his views. CWO Morris is a leader in every respect and is thoroughly well qualified to assume greater responsibilities.

Reporting Officer
P. G. Smith
Captain USMC
Commanding Officer
CSSD-21 (Fort Pickett, Virginia)
Camp Lejeune, North Carolina

Farewell to Arms

So, I got out of the Marine Corps. I was honorably discharged but the reason listed on my discharge certificate says 'unacceptable conduct'. That phrase could mean anything because it doesn't specify what that conduct actually was. It could mean something infinitely worse than simply being an officer married to an enlisted woman. That phrase will continue to haunt me until the day I die, as it has haunted me for the past 34 years.

But it can't change the fact that I was one of the best. In every instance when I was part of any given group of Marines, I was always the 'stand-out' member of that group, regardless of the criteria used to judge us. I was the most physically fit, the highest ranked rifle and pistol shooter, the best at drill and tactical maneuvers, the best close combat instructor, the best fire team leader, the best squad leader, the best Platoon Sergeant, the best Supply Officer, the best Warehousing Officer, and the best Platoon Commander.

My discharge certificate may tell part of the story but it doesn't tell the entire story. I had an amazing career in the Marines, even though it was not a full career. There were many things of which I can be justifiably proud in regard to my time spent in the Corps. First and foremost, I was a Marine…a Jarhead…a Leatherneck…a Devil Dog. And finally, as a Warrant Officer with former service as an enlisted man, I was a charter member of the most unique military group that ever existed. I was a Marine Corps Mustang.

Marines' Hymn

From the Halls of Montezuma
To the shores of Tripoli
We fight our country's battles
In the air, on land and sea
First to fight for right and freedom
And to keep our honor clean
We are proud to claim the title of
UNITED STATES MARINES

Our flag's unfurled to every breeze
From dawn to setting sun
We have fought in every clime and place
Where we could take a gun
In the snows of far off northern lands
And in sunny tropic scenes
You will find us always on the job
THE UNITED STATES MARINES

Here's health to you and to our Corps
Which we are proud to serve
In many a strife we've fought for life
And never lost our nerve
If the Army and the Navy
Ever gaze on Heaven's scenes
They will find the streets are guarded by
UNITED STATES MARINES

Anonymous

Code of Conduct

Article I: I am an American fighting in the forces which guard my country and our way of life. I am prepared to give my life in their defense.

Article II: I will never surrender of my own free will. If in command, I will never surrender the members of my command while they still have the means to resist.

Article III: If I am captured I will continue to resist by all means available. I will make every effort to escape and aid others to escape. I will accept neither parole nor special favors from the enemy.

Article IV: If I become a prisoner of war, I will keep faith with my fellow prisoners. I will give no information nor take part in any action which might be harmful to my comrades. If I am senior, I will take command. If not I will obey the lawful orders of those appointed over me and will back them up in every way.

Article V: When questioned, should I become a prisoner of war, I am required to give name, rank, service number and date of birth. I will evade answering further questions to the utmost of my ability. I will make no oral or written statements disloyal to my country and its allies or harmful to their cause.

Article VI: I will never forget that I am an American, fighting for freedom, responsible for my actions, and dedicated to the principles which make my country free. I will trust in my God and in the United States of America.

Oath of Acceptance

I do solemnly swear (or affirm)
In taking this oath, I make it a matter of conscience and, when combined with an invocation to the Deity, make it a covenant between myself and the Supreme Being in whom I believe. In my relationship with society, I understand this declaration may subject me to the penalties of perjury, if falsely made.

That I will support and defend the Constitution of the United States
The Constitution of the United States is the founding document of this nation. The original document, together with its amendments and the legal interpretations of its meaning and intent, form the basic charter under which our Government of Law operates. To preserve this nation as a Government of Law, I will uphold its provisions and will shield and protect it. I consider it my duty to act as its champion and advocate in the event of danger of attack through unlawful deeds or against any alien philosophies.

Against all enemies, foreign and domestic
I will do so in opposition to those who are hostile to its provisions and who seek to change it by threat, revolution or subversion, whether they be citizens of this country, residents who are not in accord with our system, or aliens from other lands seeking to impose a form of government or philosophy contrary to our laws and beliefs.

That I will bear true faith and allegiance to the same
In word and deed, I will continue to express my devotion and loyalty to our Constitution and the Government which operates under its charter. I have an obligation to uphold it and will say or do nothing which can be interpreted as expressing a lack of confidence or belief in it.

That I take this obligation freely, without any mental reservation or purpose of evasion
I commit myself to this course of action voluntarily and because it is my desire. I dedicate myself to its purposes completely and without limitation or exception. I do this because of my belief in its correctness and do not seek thereby to elude or circumvent any of my responsibilities to myself, to society or to my country. I have no commitments which would be contrary to this obligation or which would prevent its fulfillment.

That I will well and faithfully discharge the duties of the office on which I am about to enter

To the utmost of my ability and so far as I am able, I will endeavor to carry out with loyalty and devotion the tasks and responsibilities placed upon me. I understand all of the obligations of the office offered me and will do all in my power to fulfill those obligations. I will carry out the directives and orders given me and will take those actions which are necessary to carry out the purposes and achieve the objectives associated with them.

So help me, God

Through my belief in the Supreme Being, I hereby make this a covenant with that Being and invoke His assistance in carrying out this oath.

(On 26 October 2013, Lieutenant General Michelle Johnson, the superintendent of the Air Force Academy, said that out of respect for cadets' freedom of religion they no longer are required to say "so help me God" at the end of the Honor Oath) - Might as well not take the oath.

UNITED STATES MARINE CORPS
Leadership Traits

Bearing: Create a favorable impression in carriage, appearance and personal conduct at all times.

Courage: A mental quality that recognizes fear of danger or criticism but enables a person to proceed in the face of it with calmness and firmness.

Decisiveness: The ability to reach decisions promptly and to announce them in a clear, forceful manner.

Dependability: The certainty of the proper performance of duty.

Endurance: The mental and physical stamina measured by the ability to stand pain, fatigue, distress and hardship.

Enthusiasm: The display of sincere interest and exuberance in the performance of duty.

Initiative: The ability to see what has to be done and to commence on a course of action, even in the absence of orders.

Integrity: The uprightness of character and the soundness of moral fiber, truthfulness and honesty.

Judgment: The ability to properly weigh facts and circumstances in order to reach the best possible solution to problem situations.

Justice: The quality of being impartial and consistent in exercising control over subordinates.

Knowledge: Possessing and applying acquired knowledge, including professional knowledge and an understanding of your subordinates.

Loyalty: Faithfulness to Family, God, Country, seniors and subordinates.

Tact: The ability to deal effectively with others without creating personal or professional offense.

Unselfishness: The avoidance of providing for one's own comfort and personal advancement at the expense of others.

UNITED STATES MARINE CORPS
Leadership Principles

Become technically and tactically proficient.

Develop a sense of responsibility among your subordinates.

Employ your team in accordance with its capabilities.

Ensure that the task is understood, supervised and accomplished.

Keep your subordinates informed.

Know your subordinates and look out for their welfare.

Know yourself and seek self-improvement.

Make sound and timely decisions.

Seek responsibility and take responsibility for your actions.

Set the example.

Train your subordinates as a team.

www.ingramcontent.com/pod-product-compliance
Lightning Source LLC
Chambersburg PA
CBHW070527090426
42735CB00013B/2884